Data-Driven Law

Data Analytics Applications

Series Editor: Jay Liebowitz

Data-Driven Law
Data Analytics and the New Legal Services

Edited by
Ed Walters

CRC Press
Taylor & Francis Group
Boca Raton London New York

CRC Press is an imprint of the
Taylor & Francis Group, an **informa** business

AN AUERBACH BOOK

CRC Press
Taylor & Francis Group
6000 Broken Sound Parkway NW, Suite 300
Boca Raton, FL 33487-2742

First issued in paperback 2021

Printed on acid-free paper

ISBN-13: 978-1-4987-6665-4 (hbk)
ISBN-13: 978-1-03-209500-4 (pbk)

Visit the Taylor & Francis Web site at
http://www.taylorandfrancis.com

and the CRC Press Web site at
http://www.crcpress.com

Contents

Author

Ed Walters is the CEO of Fastcase, a legal publishing company based in Washington, D.C. He is an adjunct professor at the Georgetown University Law Center and at Cornell Tech, where he teaches The Law of Robots. Before founding Fastcase, he worked at Covington & Burling in Washington and Brussels, and in The White House from 1991 to 1993 in the Office of Media Affairs and the Office of Presidential Speechwriting.

Contributors

David Colarusso is the director of Suffolk University Law School's Legal Innovation and Technology Lab. An attorney and educator by training, he has worked as a public defender, data scientist, software engineer, and high school physics teacher. He is the author of a programming language for lawyers, QnA Markup, an award-winning legal hacker, an ABA Legal Rebel, and a Fastcase 50 honoree.

Gordon Cormack is a professor in the David R. Cheriton School of Computer Science at the University of Waterloo. He is a program committee member of the National Institute of Standards and Technology's Text Retrieval Conference and has served as coordinator of the TREC Spam, Legal, and Total Recall tracks. He is the coauthor of *Information Retrieval: Implementing and Evaluating Search Engines* (MIT Press, 2010, 2016) and more than 100 scholarly articles.

Rahul Dodhia trained as a cognitive scientist and statistician at Columbia University. After three years at NASA, he joined the tech industry and has worked as a data scientist at both startups and giants such as Amazon and Microsoft.

Aaron Crews serves as chief data analytics officer for Littler, where he manages the operations of Littler's data analytics practice. In the role, he leads the development of technology solutions that provide value to firm clients and uses data analytics tools to facilitate process efficiency. Aaron served as general counsel and vice president of strategy at artificial intelligence developer TextIQ, and as senior associate general counsel and global head of eDiscovery for Walmart.

Ken Grady is an adjunct professor at the Michigan State University College of Law focusing on increasing access to justice and improving application of the rule of law. He employs tools ranging from process improvement to artificial intelligence in new models for developing law and delivering legal services. He previously served as CEO of SeyfarthLean Consulting and as Lean Law Evangelist at Seyfarth Shaw LLP, where he worked with organizations around the world to provide innovative strategic support for General Counsel and in-house legal departments.

Maura R. Grossman, JD, PhD, is a research professor in the David R. Cheriton School of Computer Science at the University of Waterloo in Ontario and principal of Maura Grossman Law in New York. She also is an adjunct professor both at Osgoode Hall Law School and the Georgetown University Law Center. Previously, she was an of counsel at Wachtell, Lipton, Rosen and Katz. She is most well known for her influential work on technology-assisted review.

William D. Henderson is a professor at the IU Maurer School of Law, where he has served as the founding director of the Milt and Judi Stewart Center on the Global Legal Profession. He is a research associate with the Law School Survey of Student Engagement and a principal in Lawyer Metrics, a consulting firm that uses evidence-based methods to assist firms in identifying, selecting, and developing world-class lawyers.

Kumar Jayasuriya most recently served as a knowledge management attorney for the law firm of Baker, Donelson. After practicing law, he managed library and digital archival services for top-tier law schools, including the University of Texas and Georgetown Law. As an attorney, he manages data-analytic projects through the strategic deployment of technology.

Nika Kabiri is a consumer insights expert with 15 years of experience in social science and business-related research. She is currently a vice president at Radius Global Research. Previously, she worked as a director of Strategic Insights at Avvo. Before that she was a managing director of Ipsos Marketing. She received her PhD and master's in sociology at the University of Washington. She earned her BA in political science at Rice University. She also has a JD from the University of Texas School of Law.

Kingsley Martin has been at the forefront of technology innovation in the legal practice. He has 30 years of experience in the practice of law, software design and development, strategy and management, serving as the chief information officer of Kirkland & Ellis and as a senior director responsible for West KM at Thomson West (now Thomson Reuters). He has been recognized by the ABA as a legal rebel, as a member of the Fastcase 50; as an innovator by Law Technology News; and a National Law Journal Trailblazer and Pioneer.

Ed Sarausad has been building technology products and businesses across the United States, Asia, and Europe for the last 20+ years at GoDaddy, Avvo, Microsoft, IBM, and numerous startups. He is passionate about the transformative power of data and AI for independent business owners and consumers the world over. He holds an MBA in quantitative marketing and a BA in information systems and international business from the University of Washington. He is fluent in Japanese.

Stephen Wolfram is the creator of Mathematica, Wolfram|Alpha, and the Wolfram Language; the author of *A New Kind of Science*; and the founder and CEO of Wolfram Research. Over the course of nearly four decades, he has been a pioneer in the development and application of computational thinking—and has been responsible for many discoveries, inventions, and innovations in science, technology, and business.

Chapter 1

Introduction: Data Analytics for Law Firms

Using Data for Smarter Legal Services

Ed Walters

Contents

An essential part of legal services is to help clients understand and manage legal risk. However, when clients ask lawyers their most important questions, lawyers often answer with educated guesses based on limited experience. In law, this is often called professional judgment, but in other industries, these judgments would be called hunches—opinions formed without the benefit of data.

Clients ask their lawyers important questions—what are their chances of winning custody, how much legal exposure does their company have, how much they should offer to settle the litigation, what's the market for a particular provision, should they accept a plea deal, or whether a certain provision is standard in a contract. For clients, these can make or break families, business relationships, or whole companies.

The answers to these client questions are in data, and lawyers don't have that data.

Lawyers are not only answering these important questions with hunches—for the most part, lawyers aren't even giving clients the right kind of answer. The question, "How much is my case worth?" isn't answered with a number—the answer should be a distribution of outcomes in similar cases. "How much should we offer in settlement?" shouldn't be answered with a number—it should be a decision made probabilistically, with information about past settlements, costs to try the case, and likelihood of a successful outcome.

These are some of the most challenging questions facing families or businesses. Where possible, especially in business, clients answer these questions with data. Companies invest in identifying and tracking key performance indicators to hold managers accountable and to set budgets. Even individual clients track their fitness or set step goals with fitness trackers. For clients, data is a part of everyday life. Except when they have a legal question.

So for increasingly data-savvy clients, lawyers can no longer give "it depends" answers rooted in anecdata. Clients insist that their lawyers justify their reasoning, and with more than a limited set of war stories. The considered judgment of an experienced lawyer is unquestionably valuable. However, on balance, clients would rather have the considered judgment of an experienced lawyer *informed by the most relevant information required to answer their question.*

A data-driven approach to legal services may sound like a challenge for lawyers representing clients in the financial industry—large firms based in financial centers. But it's not. Lawyers in small firms handle more of these matters, and there is a lot at stake in matters handled by small law offices. According to the Legal Executive Institute, small law firms account for more revenue in the legal services market. Firms with more than 175 lawyers make $95 billion per year, a staggering number. But firms with fewer than 29 lawyers bring in $108 billion in annual revenue. There are opportunities to provide better legal services with data—in large firms and small ones.

Big Insights from Small Data

What keeps the manager of a small firm awake at night? From a solo practitioner to the managing partner of a boutique firm, the answer will not be legal tech or artificial intelligence, although both topics garner a lot of attention.

Law firm managers are more likely to be focused on day-to-day operational issues at their firms. According to the *2016 State of U.S. Small Law Firms Study* from Thomson Reuters, the top three concerns of small firms are (1) acquiring new clients and new business, (2) clients demanding more service for less money, and (3) wasting too much time on administrative tasks.

Although these issues challenge many firms, lawyers can start addressing them with small, relatively inexpensive systems. They do not need exabytes of billing data or a bank of servers running the IBM Watson Developer Cloud. Although more data is normally better, the challenges facing most law firms, such as finding new business, better service, and administrative efficiency, are small data problems.

Data-Driven Legal Marketing

Legal marketing—finding new business for your law firm—is one of the most vexing challenges that law firms face. In years past, lawyers might have found new clients from Yellow Pages advertising, informal networking, or community advertising. However, even at their best, these forms of advertisements require investments, and the returns from them are unreliable and virtually immeasurable.

Call centers, sponsored search, print or TV advertising, or social media marketing can be effective ways to find new clients, but without data, it is hard to know which methods are most effective. Legal marketing managers may sympathize with the old adage, "I know that half of the money I spend on advertising is wasted—I just don't know which half." New business tracking based on anecdotes will lead to wasteful investment (or worse, wasteful underinvestment).

Two related problems with ads are that they are overinclusive and underinclusive. Ads are overinclusive because advertising reaches many more people than it needs to in order to reach prospective clients. Ads are underinclusive because advertising often does not reach enough prospective clients. Advertising in any form is expensive and inefficient. Any one of these ad channels is expensive on its own, but without careful targeting and tracking, it is easy to spend a lot of money without knowing whether it's driving new business.

Data should tell law firms which advertisements work. Verification can be as simple as asking all new clients how they heard about the firm. On the other hand, law firms have begun taking cues from consumer marketing, using marketing automation tools, targeted discount codes, and customer relationship management ("CRM") tools.

Seth Price, the managing partner of Washington, D.C., firm Price Benowitz LLP, says that his firm uses Salesforce as its CRM system to keep track of potential clients, especially which lead source they came from, to maximize advertising where it's most effective. "We can run all sorts of reports which help us determine how to allocate resources," he said. CRM systems can help determine which ad campaigns were most effective in driving new business. They can measure return on investment for marketing expenses and even help determine which practices and clients are most profitable for the firm.

The challenge of finding new clients is not just about increasing revenues—it is also about identifying which clients are most profitable. Figuring out which clients create the most profitable business for the firm requires linking revenues and expenses for different clients, practice areas, and even lawyers at the firm in the firm's billing system. It's great to add revenues for the firm, as long as the added expenses aren't greater, and that the work isn't crowding out more profitable clients. But these are management challenges that can only be addressed with data.

Erik Mazzone is the senior director of Membership Experience for the North Carolina Bar Association, but before taking that role he consulted with lawyers as the association's practice management advisor. Mazzone recommends that phone calls and consultations are a good place to begin collecting data about the effectiveness of marketing. "Lawyers should know where the consultations come from—the firm's website, referrals from other lawyers or advertising. And they should track how many of those consultations result in an engagement letter."

Mazzone says that lawyers can track profits and revenues all the way back to lead sources, and they can do that without the benefit of software (although he advises lawyers that practice management software is the simplest way to do this kind of tracking).

Using Data to Provide Higher Quality Assistance

In addition to the pressures of finding new business, law firms also report that clients are expecting more work and better results for lower, more predictable fees. When corporate counsel are achieving more in house using technology, and starting to bring more work back from outside counsel, there is more pressure for firms to deliver results, understand their costs, and control prices.

Clients are not only looking for lower prices—they also want deeper understanding of their issues and better results. Clients, even individual ones, are making more decisions based on data. Businesses measure the return on investment down to the click, use A/B testing to measure the right messages, time of day, audiences, and images for advertising messages, and analyze data to make good business decisions. They use analytics to maximize their investments and purchasing power and to make hiring decisions. They manage inventory to reduce warehouse costs, and where possible, maintain just-in-time supply logistics. Businesses create personas for their customers, and when they hire employees, they use sophisticated data about the characteristics of their best performers.

For the most sophisticated clients, the only thing they do not purchase using data is legal services. Not because they don't want to, but because they can't.

Now clients have started to take matters into their own hands. BTI Consulting estimated that, in 2016, companies brought $4 billion worth of legal work back in house. Because they have tools that automate workflow, and in many cases, deep stores of their internal company information, corporate lawyers are choosing to do more work themselves, instead of employing outside counsel. When in-house lawyers can subscribe to the same research databases and e-discovery tools that their law firms use, they are finding that they can achieve comparable results with less uncertainty and risk. In short, it's time for law firms to handle legal matters with the same rigor that their clients do, or prepare for clients to handle the matters themselves.

It's no longer the case that data analysis is only for large firms with data scientists on staff, sophisticated knowledge management systems, marketing managers, and proposal writers. Firms may expect that only the most sophisticated clients want data-enabled decision making from their law firms. That may have been true in the past, but it isn't true any longer.

Even individual clients make decisions with data. Individuals, not companies, are responsible for the growth of services such as Mint, which consolidates diverse financial accounts such as checking, credit cards, mortgage, savings, investments, and bill payments into a single dashboard. Individuals track their fitness goals down to the step with fitness trackers such as Fitbit or Apple Watch. Small companies and individuals use data more than ever, and their expectation is that their law firms will as well.

In addition, consumer-focused legal services such as Avvo, LegalZoom, or even TurboTax are more accessible. These services are commoditizing many legal and tax services with document automation and expert systems, and because they are venture backed, they often have a scale and an advantage in consumer marketing. That means that commoditized legal services are in the reach of more clients every year.

For highly customized legal work, only law firms (and only certain law firms) will be capable of doing the work. But for the vast majority of legal services, clients may care very little about which firm provides the service. As Jordan Furlong has pointed out in his book of the same name, law is a buyer's market, and many types of legal work are becoming more commoditized. That means law firms won't present a unique advantage in providing the service, over each other, over peer professionals, or over software services. This commoditization will certainly lead to further erosion of the price of legal services, especially the billable hour.

Commodity pricing does not mean that the price of legal work must trend to zero, but it does mean that the most successful lawyers will have to find a way to differentiate their services. One easy way to do that is fixed-fee legal work—maybe not for all kinds of work, but at least for predictable, commoditized work. Fixed fees shift the risk in legal work from clients to law firms, and as the market becomes increasingly competitive, clients will more frequently insist on fixed-fee engagements. The law firms who insist on billing hourly in this environment will become less competitive.

One of the biggest challenges to offering fixed-fee work is that lawyers and law firms simply do not know what the costs are for their services. They don't know the distribution of costs, the mean or median, or what factors take costs outside of the norm. Law firms over the next 20 years will face the challenge of either winning less work (or lesser work) because they bill hourly, or losing money on mispriced legal services, because they do not have a financial understanding of their work for clients.

These problems of fixed-fee legal work are solved with data. Firms can collect and standardize the information about their time, expenses, and billables for different types of work. Even with limited data, firms will have a better understanding of the services they offer. More experienced lawyers and firms may be able to access some of the time and cost information from their practice management or billing software. New lawyers, or lawyers without practice management software, may have to find different means of collecting information from paper files or from other sources.

Artificial intelligence may open some data sources that previously have been out of reach. Firms that have been in business for many years may have extensive stores of digital and paper records—information that would be abundantly useful if it could be converted, standardized, and metadata collected from it. Today, that information isn't very useful, in paper files or unstructured billing information.

However, tools to extract metadata from unstructured data are better than ever, allowing firms to identify which documents are attached to certain matters, who the author of certain documents are, or when they were worked on. The IBM Watson Document Cloud Developer suite of application programming interfaces are more accessible than ever, and can be used to digitize and extract information from old paper or digital files, allowing late-adopting firms to extract insights from legacy data.

Practice management software and artificial intelligence tools can help lawyers better understand their business. The pricing pressures for fixed fees are greater in some regions of the country and in some practice areas more than others. Data can illuminate where the pressures are most intense. Each year, practice management software provider Clio compiles a Legal Trends Report that anonymizes and aggregates information about what firms bill, how they collect, and where the trend lines are heading.

The *2017 Legal Trends Report* from Clio aggregated anonymized data from more than 60,000 active users of its practice management software to identify national and regional trends. The report shows, for example, that bankruptcy lawyers and corporate lawyers on average have the highest billable rates, while criminal, personal injury, and insurance lawyers have the lowest billable averages.

The Clio survey also ranked metropolitan areas in which its users reported the highest and lowest billable hour averages, with New York City ($344), Los Angeles ($323), Chicago ($312), Miami ($310), and the District of Columbia ($304) at the top. Survey data such as the *Legal Trends Report* can help lawyers set a competitive hourly rate, including different rates for different practice areas in the same firm, in order to deliver services at a competitive price. Other data in the report, such as seasonality data for certain practice groups and information about the distribution of flat fees versus hourly billing for different practices, can help firms to budget more effectively and bill clients more competitively.

Clio's *Legal Trends Report* is a good example of external data that firms can use to better understand their practice. But lawyers can also collect "small data" inside the firm to better understand client costs and firm profitability. The best example of this is firm billing, personnel, and accounting information—these include a wealth of information about costs, timing, scope, and historical trends.

One recent idea that shows promise is uniform standards for legal tasks—a standardized vocabulary that lawyers, law firms, corporate legal departments, and clients can use to describe legal services performed. Using standard task IDs, Individual firms can compare how long it takes, for example, to draft a research memo, using a standard code. This would allow a firm to compare time and billing by different lawyers on different matters to complete the same task.

Because the task names would be harmonized across many different legal departments, it would be possible for the first time for corporate counsel to benchmark the average time and cost of common tasks across firms. Firms could use these common task standards to see where they outperform regional averages for the same work or where they need to become more competitive.

Especially for clients who employ many outside law firms (think insurance companies or large retailers), the ability to compare the work of law firms should establish well which firms are providing the best value. One additional benefit is that benchmark data from other firms will help law firms to better price fixed-fee legal work, with less risk that matters will require more than the estimated amount of work. In addition, published, anonymized information about the tasks and stages of different legal matters will help law firms better understand workflow and project management, and lead to industry best practices among law firms.

Standard legal task IDs are being developed by the Standards Advancement for the Legal Industry, a consortium of groups working on open matter standards. Adam Stock of the Standards Alliance for the Legal Industry (SALI) debuted the idea at Stanford CodeX's FutureLaw conference in April 2017. The idea promises to address one of the most vexing problems of value for legal services—comparing similar tasks across different firms, when each firm calls the service by a different name and groups the services differently. By giving the tasks open matter IDs, clients, firms, or researchers can compare levels of efforts on similar tasks, creating for the first time metrics across multiple firms and lawyers about the efficiency of legal services.

Ultimately, a uniform set of task codes could lead to more fixed-price engagements, better law firm management of legal projects, incentives for firms to work more efficiently, and better overall quality of legal work at lower prices. The lack of a common vocabulary and anonymized data are impediments to accomplishing these goals, and a standard language could well help to reach them.

Managing a Better Law Firm with Data

One of the most surprising findings of the *Legal Trends Report* was that the average collection rate for lawyers is 1.6 hour per day. For each 8-hour workday, the average firm does 2.3 hours of billable work. It invoices clients for only 1.9 hour, and collects only 1.6 hour worth of revenue. This is not the number of hours worked or billed, but instead, the number of billed hours for which the law firm collected. Remember, these are averages, so even though there are many firms that do better, there is a similar number of firms doing worse—billing fewer hours and collecting less.

The report calls out the culprits pretty clearly. The average firm spends 48% of its nonbillable time on administrative tasks, such as office administration (16%), generating and sending bills (15%), configuring technology (11%), and collections (6%). Firms spend almost as much nonbillable time on business development (33%), leaving a meager 2.3 hour a day for billable work. As the report pointed out, the fact that firms only collect 1.6 hour worth of time each day illustrates why, despite billing an average of $260 per billable hour, law firms nevertheless have a hard time running a profit.

These statistics will come as no surprise to many lawyers. These sentiments are echoed in the 2016 Thomson Reuters *State of U.S. Small Law Firms Study*, which ranked "wasting time on administrative tasks" as a top concern of small law firms. Even when firms can make time to do billable work, they often write off a great deal of time, and then don't collect all of what they actually bill. This disparity is why Mazzone advises lawyers to consider their billable hours, but to look more closely at revenue actually received when measuring the impact of marketing initiatives. The number of hours worked (utilization) is important, but so is the number of hours the firm can actually bill to the client (realization). Write-offs can be as destructive to firm profitability as idleness. Finally, no matter what tasks make it to the client's bill, ultimately it is how much the firm collects from its bills that affect the firm's success. Each of these presents a challenge for firms.

The crunch on collections has many different causes, but one is in plain sight: simply not enough work. The Clio *Legal Trends Report* shows that firms on average spend 33% of their nonbillable time on business development, as much time as they spend on billable work. Generating new business is an important challenge for most lawyers. According to the report, 54% of law firms actively advertise to acquire new clients, yet 91% of these firms can't calculate a return on their advertising investments, and 94% don't know how much it costs them to acquire a new client. Data-driven marketing and competitive, data-informed pricing may help to create new work.

Low collection rates also result when firms cannot allocate enough time to billable tasks. When the lawyer is the contract reviewer, Google AdWords administrator, webmaster, legal researcher, building supervisor, and HR manager, it's hard to make enough time for billable work. Added to that are the constant interruptions faced by lawyers, and it's hard to imagine when most lawyers get any work done at all. Data can help inform when it is time to outsource tasks to independent contractors or hire new staff, as well as what to pay them.

One way to increase the profitability of law firms is simply to work more efficiently—putting tools to use better and finishing more work faster, especially on fixed-fee work. This kind of smarter working likely requires investing training time and money in learning new tools, such as practice management software, smarter legal research tools, or even ways of more fully using standard tools such as Microsoft Word, Outlook, or Excel. Forty-nine state bar associations offer legal research free as a benefit of membership, allowing firms to recover thousands of dollars per year of unbillable subscription costs.

Law firms can be more competitive by investing in process improvements as well, such as collecting information about what legal documents the firm creates in a year. Forms that the firm creates frequently can be standardized for the benefit of all lawyers in the firm, or even for clients. Contract Standards, whose founder Kingsley Martin writes in Chapter 7 of this book, creates standard libraries of frequently used contract terms, which forms something akin to a Uniform Commercial Code for commercial contracts.

Contract Standards (discussed in Chapter 3) collects common contract terms, extracted from hundreds of thousands of public contracts, which form the basis of the company's term template for reuse. Imagine the value to clients if law firms don't have to argue over boilerplate contract language, but instead can agree on the deal terms and simply use standard contract terms in the deal documents. In addition, lawyers can use document automation tools to make these documents fillable and reusable (instead of finding and replacing party names and pronouns). If firms did little more than collect and count the number and type of documents produced by the firm, even that would be a novel data service the firm could use to better serve clients.

In addition, data can help law firms better manage their human resources. Well-managed firms can track which lawyers are billing the most, or who is doing the most successful or profitable work. Some firms have begun using consumer tools such as Net Promoter Scores to gauge how satisfied the clients are with the work of their lawyers. When a firm knows that it has lost money on an engagement, or that a client is not satisfied with his or her lawyers' work, firms can use that data to debrief and to learn from mistakes, or to direct more training for the lawyers involved.

Conversely, data that shows great efficiency, successful outcomes, happy clients, and profitable work can be used to promote, incentivize, and retain star performers. Small data of this sort can drive process improvements and better outcomes for clients at lower cost. Practice efficiency has many benefits. In addition to reducing the nonbillable administrative work of firms, these practices should help lawyers to serve more people more effectively. Kumar Jayasuriya discusses in Chapter 9 the ways to cull actionable data from existing employees and firm alumni.

Finally, data can help firms to invest more intelligently in their practice groups, identifying what lines of business show revenue growth, and more importantly, profitability growth. Firms might combine their own internal practice data with external data sources, such as the Clio *Legal Trends Report* and other studies of the legal market. For example, according to the Legal Executive Institute, the size of the market for legal services in the United States was $437 billion in 2015. But a 2014 study by the American Bar Foundation showed that approximately 80% of people who have legal problems do not address them through the legal system. Even if the latent market for legal services is not as lucrative as the traditional market, the total market for legal services may exceed $1 trillion dollars. So a more efficient, data-driven practice is not just a way to serve more people, it's also a way to tap into an enormous latent market for legal services.

Conclusion

Data analysis is often seen as the exclusive province of large firms or large corporate legal departments with troves of data from hundreds of lawyers, combed over by data scientists and knowledge management personnel. However, as this chapter shows, data has a place in a great many legal services, from firms of all sizes. Even small firms can improve their practices by using data that already exists in their firms today.

As Erik Mazzone suggests, firms can track a matter with data from beginning to end, from the marketing spend through to the type of matter, hours spent, billed, and collected, including metrics on profitability and success. Firms can organize and collect documents after a matter and even automate them for reuse. They can anonymize information about marketing and its connection through a matter to collected revenues for the firm can be an amazing source of insight about profitability, marketing, and which practice areas are most profitable for a firm.

Certainly software companies, computer scientists, and others will create amazing insights from analyzing big data. But the kind of data analysis explored in this chapter does not require the use of Exabyte data sets or in-house data scientists. In many cases, the use of practice management software will do some of the work natively. More than anything, using data in a law practice requires a different mindset about the value of this information in practice.

Data-driven decision making requires firms to think differently about their workflow. Most firms warehouse their files, never to be seen again after the matter closes. Running a data-driven firm requires lawyers and their teams to treat information *about* the work as part of the service, and to collect, standardize, and analyze matter data from cradle to grave. But it does not require vast data sets. Billings and collections are often seen as administrative tasks in small law firms, but they are a source of powerful insights into running a successful legal services business. And the insights from data analysis will help clients to make better legal decisions with data—just like they use data to make decisions in the rest of their business.

Chapter 2

Mining Legal Data: Collecting and Analyzing 21st Century Gold

Kenneth A. Grady[1]

Contents

---

[1] This chapter is based on an article of the same name, originally published in the Journal of Internet Law, volume 20, number 7 (January 2017).

A yawning data collection and analytics gap exists between savvy legal service providers and the rest of the pack, and an even wider gap exists between most legal service organizations and their clients.[2] As service providers outside the legal industry have learned, value resides not only in services but also in the unique data created while providing those services. Combining that data with data from other sources increases its value. Many well-known companies have learned this lesson, including Google and Amazon.

In this chapter, I contend that legal service organizations need to start collecting and analyzing legal data—data mining. Legal data includes (1) the structure and content of materials the legal service providers gather and create as part of providing services and (2) the processes they use to provide their services.

The chapter begins by exploring the increasing complexity of providing legal services and the relationship between that complexity and data growth. I then discuss the increasing competition among legal service providers, the decline in differentiation among legal service organizations, and how data mining could provide differentiation. Finally, I consider the risk to clients of advice based solely on experience versus advice based on data mining plus experience. I explain how data mining creates a basis for improving advice. In the second part of the chapter, I set out the challenge created by the growth of data. In the third part, I describe the need for and components of a data mining program. I also explain the importance and features of a data management plan (DMP) and why data mining should include text data and not just numerical data. In the fourth part, I talk about emerging data sources the legal service providers should consider. Finally, I summarize why legal service organizations should start now on data mining programs.

Complexity, Competition, and Experience

Legal service providers see data mining as something "in addition" to the delivery of legal services, creating a counterproductive split between the activities. Instead, they should integrate data mining with delivering legal services. I see three trends that justify this integration. First, legal service complexity has increased to a level where, without adding data to personal experience, legal service providers leave out much of what clients expect them to know. Second, legal service delivery also has become an intensely competitive field.

---

[2] The term "legal service provider" includes both lawyers and individuals without licenses to practice law who provide legal services to clients. This phrase avoids the pejorative term "non-lawyer" and the increasingly irrelevant task of parsing which services constitute the "unauthorized practice of law." The term "legal service organization" includes all entities functioning as part of the legal services supply chain. Someone with a law degree working at a bicycle repair shop is not a legal service provider and the shop is not a legal service organization. But, a project manager without a law degree working at an e-discovery services company is a legal service provider working at a legal services organization.

One legal service provider, or even many legal service providers, cannot compete effectively by relying on skills and personal experiences. Data provides a unique point of differentiation. Finally, legal service providers who rely on quick answers to client questions based on personal experience guide their clients using heuristics and cognitive biases and not data.

At best, this quick answer approach misses the experiences of other legal service providers. More typically, it misses the many variations of data that the collective experiences of all the legal service providers in an organization would show. In extreme cases, cognitive biases result in advice contrary to data-driven advice to the client's detriment. Clients should not bear the risk of advice limited to the experiences of a legal service provider or, worse yet, advice grounded in a provider's biases unsupported by data.

Legal Services Complexity

The complexity of legal services in the 21st century greatly exceeds the complexity of services in the late 19th century. A one- or two-page document in the late 19th century has grown to a 20 page or longer document.[3] Legal research that 20 years ago might yield 100 cases now can uncover two or three times as many cases.[4] To that complexity, we must add the expansions in breadth and depth of legal services. Topics covered by local, state, and federal regulations increase each year.[5] Cross-jurisdictional services, both within and among countries, have become common. The scope of statutory laws, volume of material interpreting statutory law, and the number of judicial decisions interpreting the law have all increased.

At one time, a legal service provider could say he or she was an employment lawyer and counsel clients on any questions arising under local, state, or federal employment law. That practitioner did not know all aspects of all employment laws in all states. However, the burden of gaining the knowledge needed to

---

[3] IBM Radically Simplifies Cloud Computing Contracts (December 18, 2014), available at https://www-03.ibm.com/press/us/en/pressrelease/45737.wss.

[4] Mary Whisner, reference librarian, Gallagher Law Library, University of Washington School of Law, did a preliminary research study on this question when I raised it on Twitter. The results of her study show that, in some cases, the number of documents retrieved with a search in 1996 had more than tripled by 2016 (e.g., 133–566). Whisner, Mary, "Comparing Case Law Retrievals, Mid-1990s and Today," (November 18, 2016), University of Washington School of Law Research Paper Forthcoming, available at SSRN: https://ssrn.com/abstract=2872394 or http://dx.doi.org/10.2139/ssrn.2872394.

[5] For example, the US Code now contains approximately 67,000 sections and over 92,000 in-text references, https://www.santafe.edu/events/computation-and-the-evolution-of-law. See also Katz, Daniel Martin and Bommarito, Michael James, "Measuring the Complexity of the Law: The United States Code," (August 1, 2013), 22 Artificial Intelligence and Law 337 (2014), available at SSRN: https://ssrn.com/abstract=2307352 or http://dx.doi.org/10.2139/ssrn.2307352.

answer a client's question was low, the cost to the client was manageable, and the client valued working consistently with one provider more than the transactional cost of shopping for a new provider each time a question came up in a different jurisdiction.

As law became more complex, the burden of staying current on the law in all jurisdictions grew and the cost of knowledge acquisition increased. Legal service organizations changed their practice architectures to cope with this increased complexity.[6] For example, providers narrowed the scope of their practices by focusing on part of a domain (e.g., Federal Labor Standards Act law) or one jurisdiction (e.g., Michigan). Organizations narrowed the scope of their practices in similar ways. Some kept their services broad by aggregating services across providers who each focused on part of a domain (e.g., providers who, collectively, knew about employment laws in all jurisdictions). These architecture changes mitigated, but did not eliminate, the growing complexity problem.

Legal services also became more isolated over the years, distanced from other disciplines that could help providers improve on what they do. Legal theorists reached out to psychologists, sociologists, economists, political scientists, anthropologists, mathematicians, and other fields for deeper insight into how laws and people interact. Practicing lawyers, however, ignored fields with significant experience using data such as strategy, marketing, operations, management, and supply chain management. Although legal service organizations have been described for many years as businesses, they operate without the sophistication of their business clients. This further reinforced the separation between law and client in many areas, including data collection and analysis. Clients, who today operate in data-intensive businesses, are confronted by legal service providers who operate without reference to data.

The legal industry responded to increasing complexity by adding labor. More labor—typically lawyers—allows legal service organizations to drive further specialization among legal service providers or to aggregate information across more providers. Organizations treat each provider as a data collection and analysis platform in his or her given field. However, complexity has outgrown this crude approach (if for no reason other than cost). The more sophisticated, scalable, and reliable approach uses data mining coupled with experience. Put another way, clients get the best services when legal service providers let computers and humans do what each does best. I call lawyers who use this approach "augmented lawyers." Computers do the data mining. They look for trends, gaps, and other patterns. Legal service providers then apply their skills—judgment, collaborative thinking, and empathy—to determine how to use what they learned from the data.

---

[6] Lawrence Lessig describes the four modalities of regulation in real space and cyberspace as law, norms, markets, and architecture. See Lessig, Lawrence, "The law of the horse: What cyberlaw might teach," 113(2) Harvard Law Review 501 (1999).

Legal Services Competition

Competition among legal service organizations intensified as clients focused on the increasing cost and declining quality of legal services.[7] Despite the rise in competition, legal service organizations have done very little to address competition by differentiating themselves. Clients perceive the services available to them as highly substitutable and, in the absence of some other differentiating factor, use price as the basis for their purchasing decision. Using the unique data stored in their systems, legal service organizations could differentiate themselves in ways other than price that clients will value.

For many decades, competition among legal service organizations was low. Clients compared organizations using easy to identify and measure factors. Those factors included geography, matter-relevant experience, provider pedigree,[8] market reputation, business conflicts (e.g., representation of a key competitor), and cost (hourly billing rates). Over time, most of those factors became unimportant or the differences from organization to organization became insignificant.[9]

For example, if in 1965, a client asked a North Carolina law firm a question about Texas law, the law firm probably had to contact a Texas lawyer to get an answer. The North Carolina firm did not have Texas cases in its library, online access to Texas law, or access to Texas court rules and customs. Fifty years later, assuming the North Carolina firm does not have a Texas office, it can access online the same information the Texas legal service provider can offer, including information about local court rules and customs. In 1965, geography, access to information, provider pedigree (Texas versus North Carolina law school), market reputation, and cost were important comparison factors. Today, cost could be the primary factor differentiating firms.[10]

In many ways, North Carolina law firms compete with Texas law firms. Law firms also compete with new organizations that have access to the same information and human skills as the law firms. Human resource consulting firms, alternative

---

[7] For a discussion of quality problems at large law firms, see Gulati and Scott, The three and a half minute transaction: Boilerplate and the limits of contract design (2012).

[8] Oddly, law school rankings are the only undergraduate or professional school rankings that seem to matter when it comes to job prospects. See, e.g., Taylor, "Why Law School Rankings Matter More Than Any Other Education Rankings," Forbes (August 14, 2004), available at http://www.forbes.com/sites/bentaylor/2014/08/14/why-law-school-rankings-matter-more-than-any-othereducation-rankings/#6f91493c7937. The higher paying ("better") jobs are with large law firms, who charge clients a premium partly because they provide access to these lawyers from higher-ranked schools.

[9] See, e.g., Wang and Dattu, "Why Law Firm Pedigree May Be a Thing of the Past," Harvard Business Review (October 11, 2013) and see Jessup, "Law Firms: How to Not Become a Commodity," Los Angeles Daily Journal (February 12, 2010), available at http://www.platformstrategy.com/news/FAME101_LADailyJournal.pdf.

[10] Id.

legal service providers (e.g., legal research services), and even foreign legal service providers claim a piece of the pie that once was devoured solely by law firms.[11]

The unique data set each legal service organization has and continues to generate offers a new differentiating factor. Even when two organizations have the same legal specialty—both defend clients in employment lawsuits—the organizations have unique data sets that include fact situations, client circumstances, and combinations of principals and agents in lawsuits different from their competitors. Data mining can give legal service organizations unique insights into ways to reduce client risk and improve efficiency, and give clients a unique way to differentiate organizations.

Experience as Incomplete Data

Legal service organizations have not used their data to improve the value of their legal services.[12] Put differently, legal service providers answer client questions with "based on my experience" rather than "based on the data" or "based on the data and my experience." Combining the skills and experiences of its legal service providers with its unique data collection, a legal service organization could deliver greater service and provide clients with data-driven insights. Data generated by dozens or hundreds of providers combined with the insights of even one provider creates a very powerful tool.[13]

Ask a legal service provider a question, such as "what are the chances we will win this motion," and you will get a response—almost immediately. But that quick response should worry you. Starting in 1960s, Daniel Kahneman and Amos Tversky published several papers tackling what in retrospect was a nagging problem for many of us when taught economics and law: People don't behave the way traditional economic theories tell us people should behave.[14] People behave

---

[11] I was contacted by an IT organization in Bulgaria that provides IT and legal services throughout Europe. It was considering entering the US legal service market. The organization already offered legal services in Europe, such as legal research, memorandum writing, and preparation of court documents including legal briefs.

[12] While this situation is changing, the number of legal services organizations—especially law firms—using their records as data sources is trivial compared with the total number of provider organizations. Drinker Biddle Reath, Littler Mendelson P.C., and Seyfarth Shaw LLP are examples of firms that have started using data they collect and create while providing legal services. See Strom, "Littler Mendelson Gambles on Data Mining as Competition Changes," Law.com (October 26, 2016), available at http://www.law.com/sites/almstaff/2016/10/26/littler-mendelson-gambles-on-data-mining-as-competition-changes/.

[13] Cummings, "Man versus Machine or Man + Machine?," IEEE Intelligent Systems (September/October 2014).

[14] Daniel Kahneman's recent book, Thinking, Fast and Slow, provides an excellent description of System 1, System 2, heuristics and biases. Kahneman, Thinking, Fast and Slow, (2011). For a complete list of Kahneman's articles and books, including the work he and Amos Tversky did starting in the early 1970s, see Daniel Kahenman's Publications, available at https://www.princeton.edu/~kahneman/publications.html.

irrationally, but in predictable ways. "In my experience" means an answer based on heuristics and cognitive biases, which likely cause that answer to deviate, perhaps substantially, from what data would show.

In the past 50 years, we have learned new reasons why data is superior to experience alone. Our brains operate using two systems: System 1 and System 2. System 1 works quickly, providing answers as soon as we query it. Think of any conversation. You say something, the other person immediately responds, you say something else, and the other person responds again. The conversation is like a tennis match, with a statement zipping across the net and the other party immediately volleying back. No delays.

System 1 uses heuristics (rules) and cognitive biases (rules gone wrong) to operate quickly. Researchers have investigated hundreds of potential heuristics and cognitive biases. The more rigorously tested and widely accepted ones include the availability heuristic, attribute substitution, endowment effect, hindsight bias, and observer-expectancy effect.[15] Ask a litigator about a judge and she will give you her opinion based on what she has heard, case decisions she has read, and her appearances before the judge. Seldom will you hear her ask to look at data before responding.

System 2 engages when we want to go deep and analyze data before responding. It considers data and prompts us to seek more if what it finds is not sufficient. As I write this chapter, my System 2 is working away synthesizing what I read and helping me formulate what I put on the page. System 1 would have splashed a few words on the page and moved on. Ask a litigator who relies on System 2 the same question about a judge and she will look at data before responding. The System 1 litigator may say the judge does not like large law firms. The System 2 litigator will use data to gauge whether that statement is correct.

Clients have exacerbated the already strong tendency among legal service providers to use System 1 by pushing for phone call answers over research. This client preference drove legal service organizations further into relying on providers who specialized. Legal service providers were specialized so they could keep up with the flow of substantive law in their domain and keep clients happy with System 1 response times. The employment lawyer became the Federal Labor Standards Act employment lawyer.

System 2 adds value by processing data to generate answers, but we pay a price—it is slower than System 1. It has other downsides. It cannot take on several tasks at the same time. If System 2 rather than System 1 handled most queries, we would have trouble interacting with the world. Imagine the line at Starbucks if

---

[15] See, e.g., Gilovich, Griffin and Kahneman, Heuristics and Biases: The Psychology of Intuitive Judgment (2002) (availability heuristic, attribute substitution); Kahneman, Knetsch, and Thaler, "Experimental Tests of the Endowment Effect and the Coase Theorem," 98(6) Journal of Political Economy 1325–1348 (1990), doi:10.1086/261737 (endowment effect); Hoffrage and Pohl, "Research on hindsight bias: A rich past, a productive present, and a challenging future," 11(4–5) Memory 329–335 (2003), doi:10.1080/09658210344000080 (hindsight bias); and Rosenthal, Experimenter Effects in Behavioral Research (1966) (observer-expectancy effect).

each customer relied on System 2 rather than System 1 to make his or her beverage choice. System 2 also requires data. Even if a legal service provider wanted to use System 2, in most organizations, he or she could not access the necessary data. How fast could you get data to tell a client the percentage of contracts your organization handled in the past year that included a certain clause? The keys are learning when to use System 2 and to have data ready when System 2 engages.

Legal service providers relying heavily on System 1 routinely provide advice based on small sample sizes—the personal experiences of a single services provider. Think of our litigator. If she tried one case a month, she would have tried 12 cases in the year or 240 cases over 20 years. Even in a smaller law firm, one provider's experience is a small fraction of the entire organization's experience (its data). In a large organization, a single provider's experience counts as a fraction of a percent of the organization's data. A provider has at best a small sample size—and most do not try anything remotely close to 12 cases per year.[16] Clients routinely make decisions on matters worth millions of dollars based on advice from providers who use almost no data to produce that advice. Collecting and analyzing data from an entire organization increases the sample size and improves the base for advice.

When data was difficult to collect and analyze, the System 1 approach to legal services delivery was accepted by clients and legal services providers. Today, when data is easier to collect and analyze, clients want legal service providers who use data in the decision-making process. Phone call answers should go beyond experience to include data. This paradigm shift only works for legal service providers if they data mine. Stated in behavioral economic terms, legal service providers need to access System 2 and supply it with data.

From Gold to Data

The data era has arrived and many claim that data is to the 21st century what gold was to the 19th century, and oil was to the 20th century.[17] But legal service clients today get 21st century substantive legal analysis coupled with data accumulated using late 19th century ideas about data. Compounding the problem, the Internet has given us new collections of data and easier and faster access to traditional sources of data. Legal service providers always could access "hard" copies of statutes, regulations, interpretive letters, and other primary substantive law sources,

---

[16] Although the number of cases a lawyer takes to trial varies considerably among lawyers, the trend is, and has been for many years, that fewer cases go to trial. See Gee, "As jury cases decline, so does art of trial lawyers," The Tennessean (February 5, 2011), available at http://usatoday30.usatoday.com/news/nation/2011-02-05-jury-trial-lawyers_N.htm.

[17] Vanian, "Why Data Is The New Oil," Fortune (July 11, 2016), available at http://fortune.com/2016/07/11/data-oil-brainstorm-tech/, Ed Walters, Data is the New Oil: Legal Management Lessons from John D. Rockefeller and Standard Oil, available at https://medium.com/@ejwalters/data-is-the-new-oil-refining-information-from-data-lessons-from-john-d-aa4b7b5ee1a3.

but manual access methods were inefficient and slow. Now, the Internet provides almost instantaneous access. While the size of this primary data set grows, its fundamental nature has not changed. Legal service providers' access to data about cases is limited to what is included in reported decisions. Online databases do not include granular details about public cases and most providers do not have access to the case files.

For example, case access typically includes only the court's reported decision. The electronic databases do not include the briefs filed by the parties, trial transcripts and exhibits, or any other materials giving details of the disputed matter. Some databases make part of this information available for appellate cases and other databases, such as the Public Access to Court Electronic Records system (PACER), make information available for federal cases, but accessing the data is difficult and costly. Legal service organizations have complete access to data about cases they handle.

Clients' problems include more than substantive law questions, and substantive law answers form only part of what clients need to solve their problems. Those problems also arise in business and political contexts, more complex than at any prior time. A regulatory question may involve accounting and finance issues, an advertising question may involve marketing issues, and an employment question may involve social media issues. The Internet offers a wealth of data on these related areas. When combined with data from an organization's files, the business and political data form a richer source for an answer than any provider could offer based on his experience.

Growth in complexity has led to increased legal service risks. We can place those risks in two broad categories: (1) risks of knowledge and (2) risks of ignorance. Knowledge risks arise when legal service providers use what they know or should know (e.g., from substantive law research) to provide legal services. The legal service provider gives faulty advice by misinterpreting what she knows or by assuming the data she used (her experience) reflects what analysis of more data would show. Ignorance risks arise from legal service providers failing to collect and use data that more accurately represents the real world. Clients always have faced both risks. But, the risks from a legal service provider's ignorance have increased rapidly over the past 30 years while knowledge risks have remained relatively stable.[18]

We can see the changes in the risks by considering a common legal advice situation. A client calls her legal service provider and asks whether she may terminate an employee, given a specific set of facts. The legal service provider has five years of experience practicing law. If we compared a fifth-year associate 10 years ago to a

---

[18] Although the costs to handle legal malpractice claims have increased and the cost of such claims measured in damages or settlements have increased, the number of such claims has remained relatively stable. See, e.g., Lawyer's Professional Liability Claims Trends: 2015, Ames & Gough (2015), available at http://www.law.uh.edu/faculty/adjunct/dstevenson/007a%20 Legal%20Malpractice%20Claims%20Survey%202015%20Final.pdf.

fifth-year associate today, we would find them comparable. That is, the skills of the two associates do not differ in any meaningful way. But, the organization employing the associate, the courts, and agencies at the state and federal level have seen many cases during those 10 years. The data set of cases (including relevant facts about those cases) increased. It is reasonable to believe that the fifth-year associate is familiar with a fraction of those cases—even ones handled by others in the associate's organization. Using the knowledge risk and ignorance risk classification scheme, we can say that the likelihood of the associate providing good or bad advice based on his knowledge was the same 10 years ago as it is today. But, we also can say the volume of data potentially relevant to answering the client's question (data about all the cases during those 10 years) has increased and risk to the client from the associate's ignorance has increased.[19] The growth in legal services complexity makes identifying risks, estimating probabilities, and providing legal services more difficult for many reasons, including the expanding number of possibilities in the solution set.

The gradual movement from public law to private law adds more weight to the complexity problem. In the 19th century and stretching far into the 20th century, society used courts to answer many questions of law. Clients could afford the transaction costs of litigation, the judicial system resolved lawsuits quickly, and the resolutions guided other legal service providers through public dissemination of information, such as case law. The law was public, even though difficult to access.[20]

In the latter part of the 20th century continuing through today, the percentage of private law has increased. For example, the high transaction cost of lawsuits coupled with, among many things, the risks and long time to resolution, encourage parties to resolve their differences without a judge or jury.[21] Parties resolve disputes through settlement negotiations, mediation, or arbitration. They do not publish the results. Commercial parties also have become more sophisticated in addressing risks through contracts. While downsides of that sophistication include growth in contract size and higher transaction costs for negotiating and documenting contracts, upsides include more contingencies covered in contracts. Parties can resolve a higher percentage of disputes without resorting to the courts.

---

[19] The following example gives you a simple way to think about the risk. Imagine you flip a coin and it lands with heads facing up. Heads represents the fact situation the client gave to the associate. The associate searches for a fact situation matching the facts given him by the client (another heads). For each case the associate reviews, the probability of finding a heads (match) is 50 percent (either it matches or it doesn't). But, as he looks at additional cases, the probability that he will find a string of cases that do not match decreases (that is, the probability of getting tails twice, three times, or four times in a row decreases, while the probability that a particular case will match remains 50 percent). As the number of cases the associate does not review increases, the probability that none of the cases matches the client's situation decreases, and the risk to the client increases.

[20] Even lawyers had difficulty accessing the law. See, e.g., Friedman, A History of American Law 356–358 (1973).

[21] Rakoff, "Why You Won't Get Your Day in Court," The New York Review of Books (November 24, 2016).

Privatizing law means that legal service providers have difficulty accessing data about disputes unless they handle them. The clients and legal service providers involved in the private matters bury the data in computers and files not open to the public. Legal service providers then face two challenging trends. The amount of data that would benefit their clients grows and the amount of public data about disputes declines. Both trends should cause organizations to focus on the data they can access—data from disputes they handled.

Legal Data Mining

To mine legal data, you must first define the data you seek. For a legal service organization, data relevant to providing legal services means anything in the files, whether analog or digital. It includes data found in email, voicemail, instant and text messages, databases, metadata, digital images and any other type of file, and extends to all types of storage devices.[22]

Although legal service providers could mine all this data, they have limited their efforts to a few, narrow data types. First, they collect financial data, which means everything from invoices to internal accounting data. Second, they collect simple descriptive data, such as the number and types of matters handled. Third, they collect billable hour data. This last area has received the most attention from legal data miners.

Noticeably absent is data from the documents they create every day for their internal files, clients, and third parties. That is, they omit the entire body of data generated by their services and focus almost exclusively on the financial side of transactions with clients.

Consider this common example. A corporate client asks a legal service provider to draft a contract covering the client's purchase of raw materials. The client sends documents to the legal service provider, who uses them in drafting the contract. The provider puts the documents, her handwritten notes from conversations with the client, and Web pages she downloaded about the company supplying the raw materials, in a file.

The legal service provider creates a draft of the contract. As the provider and client work through the contract, the provider saves multiple drafts of the contract on her computer. The number of drafts increases as the provider and her client negotiate with the supplying company and its legal service provider. When the contract is complete, the clients exchange signed copies. The provider puts the signed copies in the file with the other documents she gathered or created for the matter. The materials in the file and on the computer contain valuable data, but it was never mined.

Traditionally, the information in those tangible files and digital files falls outside any system a legal service organization uses to keep track of data. While in recent years, legal service providers have used knowledge management systems to

---

[22] See, e.g., Fed. R. Civ. Pro. 34.

track digital (and in some cases tangible) material, those systems have evolved to capture a very small percentage of the data types available.

In the contract example, uncaptured data includes the business terms of the contract (e.g., dates, amounts, locations, parties), the legal terms of the contract and any ancillary documents (e.g., specific performance, choice of dispute resolution mechanism), and the words and phrases used to "encode" the contract terms (e.g., the specific language used in the relevant documents). It also includes issues raised during negotiation (e.g., what the client requested and did not receive, what the client refused to offer the other party), and data about the instrument itself (e.g., number of words, complexity). Collectively, this data tells the story of the matter. Combined with other data (e.g., contract performance), it can give ways to improve future contracts and reduce risks to the client.

Some legal services organizations recognize the value of their data. One law firm says that it now collects around 500 data points for each lawsuit. It uses a team of data scientists to analyze and develop predictive models to benefit clients.

> At Littler [Mendelson], [Zev] Eigen has a broad mandate to apply data tools to clients' problems and develop products to address them. He said that much of his team's work—including [an] EEOC prediction model—would be difficult or impossible to build without the proprietary data the firm has gathered over six years from its CaseSmart software. For most firms, one of the biggest roadblocks to data analysis is simply that they haven't been collecting data from their own cases.[23]

Legal service providers at Google recognize the value stored in legal service materials and are finding ways to mine the data:

> "Law firms are sitting on millions and millions of documents that nobody has ever classified," said Julian Tsisin, who is attempting to wrangle other types of legal data as head of machine learning at Google's legal department. "Zev [Eigen] is in a very lucky position. Because he's in a firm that specializes in a particular type of case, and he's sitting on thousands and thousands of similar cases, and he has access to all that data."[24]

Over one year, a firm collecting data will build an impressively large data set different from the data set of any other legal service organization. To begin the process, it needs a plan.

---

[23] See Strom, supra n.11.
[24] Id.

Data Management Plans

Without a disciplined approach to data mining, an organization can quickly waste significant resources on efforts that yield slight value. A DMP is the first step toward creating that disciplined approach. It "is a written document that describes the data you expect to acquire or generate ..., how you will manage, describe, analyze, and store those data, and what mechanisms you will use ... to share and preserve your data."[25] Organizations that fund academic research often require a plan before they deliver the funding.[26] Legal service organizations manage data under standards set out in the applicable code governing the delivery of legal services. Those codes focus on protection from third-party disclosure, the ownership of materials, and retention requirements, but provide no guidance for those interested in the data value of the materials.

A DMP guides a legal service organization in three basic areas. First, it establishes procedures for ensuring the organization's data management program complies with relevant professional codes, a necessary part of data mining for any legal service organization today. Those codes often conflict across jurisdictions. Nevertheless, legal service organizations aggregate data from many jurisdictions without regard to specific jurisdictional requirements.

Complying with the global web of professional codes applicable to legal service data is beyond the scope of this chapter, though it is an area that is becoming more important as legal service providers deliver services around the globe. Second, a DMP lays the foundation for a successful data mining program. By establishing standards and processes, a DMP avoids the problem of each legal service provider doing things its way regardless of whether that way conflicts with the organization's goals.

Third, a DMP helps an organization create data that requires less processing prior to use. Data scientists estimate that up to 80 percent of their time is spent "data munging," the process of preparing data for analysis.[27] A DMP can reduce the data munging time. A DMP also simplifies data creation, by removing variability that increases waste, not value.

A DMP covers a broad range of issues and, while it may overlap with data protection plans and knowledge management plans, it includes many issues typically

---

[25] Stanford University Libraries, Data Management Plans, available at https://library.stanford.edu/research/data-management-services/data-management-plans. For a good description of what to include in a DMP, see C. Strasser, R. Cook, W. Michener, and A. Budden, Primer on Data Management: What you always wanted to know, DataONE (hereafter referred to as Primer), available at https://www.dataone.org/sites/all/documents/DataONE_BP_Primer_020212.pdf.

[26] Id.

[27] Although not all data scientists agree on the 80 percent figure, data scientists agree that a non-trivial portion of their time is spent preparing data for use rather than analyzing data. See Johnston, "Let Data Scientists be Data Mungers," ThoughtWorks (August 5, 2015), available at https://www.thoughtworks.com/insights/blog/let-data-scientists-be-data-mungers.

not addressed in data governance documents. For example, a DMP covers what Carly Strasser and her colleagues have described as the eight components of the data life cycle: (1) plan, (2) collect, (3) assure, (4) describe, (5) preserve, (6) discover, (7) integrate, and (8) analyze.[28]

Plan

A DMP should address client inputs, nonclient inputs, public inputs, created data, public outputs, nonclient outputs, and client outputs. Client inputs and client outputs contain data received from or delivered to a client. This material typically requires special attention in legal services because of confidentiality and privilege issues. Nonclient inputs and nonclient outputs include materials not subject to privilege claims, but which still may be confidential. Public inputs and public outputs contain data not subject to any confidentiality or privilege claims. Created data includes materials that (1) may be subject to work product claims, (2) may involve a mixture of inputs, and (3) may include things the legal service organization routinely uses across matters and clients (e.g., research memoranda).

Although legal service organizations always have relied on data from sources other than clients and opposing parties, the open data movement has accelerated the expansion of data sources available for even a solo practitioner. Service providers may combine publicly available content, not subject to use restrictions, with private data to yield rich insights about common practice areas.[29] The intermingling of data creates value and the need to establish procedures for handling the combined data.

For example, many entrepreneurs use contract information available from the US Securities and Exchange Commission's Electronic Data Gathering, Analysis and Retrieval (EDGAR) database to train text analysis software. They apply this software to draft documents and identify trends, opportunities, and risks. Other legal data scientists combine data from the Equal Employment Opportunity Commission (EEOC) with a legal services organization's records to develop predictive models for employment claims. A DMP should explain how a legal services organization will handle the public and client data before, during, and after it uses the data. Treating the several data streams the same on confidentiality, privilege, and trade secret dimensions could hamper an organization's data gathering and use program.

---

[28] Carly Strasser is a program officer at the Gordon & Betty Moore Foundation and former Leadership Team member at DataOne. See Primer at 3.

[29] A DMP should address the handling of data throughout its lifecycle. For example, a legal service provider receiving client inputs and combining them with public inputs should have a way to protect the intermingled data and proper restrictions on what may be done with the intermingled data.

Collect

Failure to properly collect data usually leads to the popular saying, "garbage in, garbage out." A DMP should include protocols for collecting data and identify not just what data to collect, but the ways providers should collect it. Providers could gather information from the Internet in the popular "portable document format" (pdf), through screen scraping into a spreadsheet, or in some other format such as a database file. A DMP can get quite detailed, covering conventions such as file naming, file type (e.g., .csv or .xls), and character encoding (e.g., UTF-8). Legal service providers should understand the differences between data format and presentation format. Confusing them can lead to large amounts of difficult to access data. A DMP should address these issues up front, so that providers collect data in ways that will make it most useful.

Assure

Legal service organizations know the custody requirements for materials relevant to litigation, such as those embedded in the US Federal Rules of Evidence. But, chain of custody is not the same as quality assurance. A corrupted file with a properly documented chain of custody is just as useless as an uncorrupted file without adequate chain of custody documentation. Assurance requires checking data to identify and tag quality issues, identify limits, and flag gaps. Poor quality data slows and may even prevent analytical work.

As data becomes increasingly important in legal services, taking appropriate steps to assure data quality becomes critical. Legal service providers know that a provider who relies on an overturned court decision will run into deep problems. Similarly, a provider who relies on erroneous data will put his client at risk. Bad data creates unreliable analytical results and distorts results in ways that could cause significant client injury. A client might give up the fight for certain legal terms in a contract if told only a small percentage of contracts have the terms, when correct data would have shown otherwise. Another client might agree to settle a lawsuit if given incorrect information about a judge's biases. These mistakes happen today when clients rely on the experience of their legal service provider and the provider's data (his or her experience) is flawed. Data assurance helps avoid the same mistakes when the legal services provider and client expand the data set beyond the provider's experience.

Describe

Legal service providers may include information describing litigation and due diligence data when preparing to meet chain of custody or other US Federal Rules of Evidence requirements. But, providers seldom prepare descriptions of data outside those specific uses. Proper data descriptions include file names, formats, and data fields. Additional descriptions include information to interpret the data, such as the meaning of codes and unique terms. Descriptions become more important as organizations combine data from different sources. Without adequate descriptions, a provider may combine data from two similar, but not identical, data fields creating a worthless data set.

Preserve

Legal service providers know the requirements for preserving data, such as mandates on retaining client information for certain periods. They also have backup systems for digital data, which simplifies the overall burden of preserving data. Still, many of them store and preserve files in tangible form, rather than digital. Storing boxes of material in offsite warehouses is not ideal when an organization could turn that material into digital data.[30] A DMP should address data preservation for analytical purposes and not just code compliance. It also should address software compatibility issues. Knowing how to retrieve data with older versions of software does not equal having ready access to data for analytical purposes.

Discover

Discovering the meaning of data starts the value chain that benefits legal service organizations and their clients. Discovery is the core of data mining, but many organizations treat data mining as the goal rather than the means to the goal. Legal service organizations should approach data mining with that cautionary note in mind. In the "discover" section of a DMP, an organization can define what it plans to do with the data—what it wants to uncover by collecting and analyzing the data. One organization may want to focus on process improvement and structure its data mining on data that will give it the granular information needed to improve processes. Another organization may want to discover negotiating patterns for critical contracts.

A third may attempt to discover whether certain employees agree to more lenient contract terms and, if so, the consequences of that behavior (do lenient credit managers lead to more defaults or more flexible lending arrangements that decrease default rates)? It can help organizations to define hypotheses and think of data mining as the way to evaluate those hypotheses, as much as researchers do when constructing their research programs and associated DMPs.

---

[30] Even case law, something which most legal service providers believe they can access online, is going through a digital revolution. Much, but not all, of case law is available through various online services. But recently, Harvard Law School and the startup legal research entity Ravel Law teamed up to scan and make available online for free in digital form Harvard's entire collection of US case law. See, e.g., "Harvard Law School launches 'Caselaw Access' project," Harvard Law Today (October 29, 2015), available at http://today.law.harvard.edu/harvard-law-schoollaunches-caselaw-access-project-ravel-law/. Harvard Law School is a legal service organization turning its unique and, to date, inaccessible data set into a data set other legal service organizations will be able to use in combination with their own proprietary data sets.

Integrate

A data set is like a pearl. One alone is valuable. String several together and their value becomes greater than the sum of the parts. Data collected by a legal service organization forms a unique data set. Even though two legal service organizations may provide only employment litigation services, they encounter different cases, clients, and situations giving each access to unique data.

The value of many data sets emerges when providers use them in combination, like pearls on a string. A legal service organization can combine its data with data from the client or any other source. In addition to the EDGAR and EEOC data sources, some startups use data sets covering patent litigation, judicial performance (e.g., time to decide motions), and trademarks. An organization's detailed data from employment lawsuits it handled combined with government data about employment lawsuits will yield a richer picture than what any litigator could supply from his or her experience. When added to the litigator's insights, the combined data set provides a basis for the client to make data-driven decisions and creates a differentiation point for the legal service organization.

Analyze

For many years, legal service organizations have had software that can do numeric data analysis. Most of the analytic work by legal service organizations has focused on time tracking and hour management. Software analytics available to legal service organizations today covers text and images and not just numeric data. Using their own data and data from others, organizations can expand their inquiries to service quality, process improvement, and trend analytics.

Natural language processing (NLP)—combining computer science, computational linguistics, and artificial intelligence—allows computers to "understand" text. Around since the 1950s, NLP progress was slow and intermittent until the 1980s when machine learning took off.[31] Modern machine learning employs techniques such as convolutional neural networks that can perform sophisticated and nuanced analyses of text from many sources, including the Internet. Today, employing NLP and machine learning an organization can analyze hundreds of thousands of documents in a few minutes using a laptop.

Google and other text analytics companies have made some of their text analytics software available to the public.[32] Anyone can use the software on text and

---

[31] We can date ideas relating to natural language processing back to much earlier times, but the modern era of NLP started with Alan Turing's article, "Computing Machinery and Intelligence" in which he proposed the idea of a test for human intelligence. Turing called the test "The Imitation Game," though today we know it as the "Turing Test." Turing, Computing Machinery and Intelligence, LIX Mind 433 (1950), doi:10.1093/mind/LIX.236.433.

[32] TensorFlow is an Open Source Software Library for Machine Intelligence, TensorFlow.org, and see Ingersoll, "5 open source tools for taming text," opensource.com (July 8, 2015), available at https://opensource.com/business/15/7/five-open-source-nlp-tools.

discover patterns hidden in the data. Although still struggling to deal with some unique aspects of legal texts, this software already has shown its power to review and analyze large quantities of data (more than what the largest legal services organization would have) and extract relevant concepts for use in litigation, transactions, contracts, and other legal service settings.

Data Portability

A DMP also should address Web 3.0 data portability. "In a decentralized environment, users own their data and choose with whom they share this data. Moreover, they retain control of it when they leave a given service provider (assuming the service even has the concept of service providers). This is important. If I want to move from General Motors to BMW today, why should I not be able to take my driving records with me? The same applies to chat platform history or health records."[33] When legal service providers move from one law firm (typically the only type of legal service organization where this issue comes up) to another, the law firm must grapple with which materials go with the legal services provider, which do not, and which may move at the clients' discretion.

Law firms that collect data from client materials and use that data as part of aggregated databases should consider and address at the outset of matters how the firm will handle the data if the client chooses to use a different legal service organization. For example, the law firm could ask the client to allow it to keep the data and use it as part of aggregated data sets, provided that the data is in an anonymized form. In any case, data collected should be stored with tags connecting the data to a client. Otherwise, the legal service organization risks having to delete entire databases when it cannot extract client records.

Value in Text Data

For most legal service providers, digital text files form the bulk of materials from which they can extract data. Prior to the personal computer, technology imposed constraints on the volume of documents a legal service organization could produce. Correcting anything more than a minor typographical error required retyping a document on a typewriter, a time-consuming and labor-intensive process. Once personal computers arrived and then became ubiquitous, modifying documents became easy and the practice of creating multiple drafts of a document proliferated.

A single contract could go through dozens of versions and each version was saved as a unique file. Organizations saved notes, emails, transcripts, and other materials in

---

[33] Hodgson, "A decentralized web would give power back to the people online," TechCrunch (October 9, 2016), available at https://techcrunch.com/2016/10/09/a-decentralized-web-would-give-power-back-to-the-people-online

digital form. The cost of computer memory began dropping and the cost of saving materials became negligible. Today, even a small legal service provider can generate in one day digitally stored text that, if printed, would fill hundreds or thousands of pages.

Legal documents do not have structure. By this, I mean that no one has assigned fields or tags to individual words or areas of text in the documents.[34] A human can apply structure when looking at an unstructured document, so the lack of structure does not stop a human from reading or using the document. For example, a human can identify the title of a contract, the introduction, and can separate the pricing term from the damages term even though the author did not label these sections. A computer, however, does not see these sections. Data scientists must tell the computer these sections exist and what text falls into each section. To a computer, a text document is simply a long string of characters that tell it what to display or print.

To data mine a text document, structure needs to be applied to the text. Data scientists call this process "parsing" the document. A person could parse a document by marking sections such as the title, the introduction, and each paragraph. The person could go further, by giving a tag to each word in the document, just you may have done in school if you learned to diagram a sentence. The sentence "Tom sees a dog" could be parsed by tagging "Tom" and "dog" as nouns, "sees" as a verb, and "a" as a determiner. The person could go even further and assign a number to each paragraph, each sentence, and each letter. The numbers would provide a coordinate system for referring to a paragraph, sentence, word, or character. In "Tom sees a dog," "dog" is the fourth word consisting of characters 11 through 13 (including spaces as characters).

Having a person parse each document would be costly, tedious, and time consuming. Instead, there is software that will parse the document. Many software programs, available as open-source programs, will parse documents. For example, Stanford University allows anyone to use its CoreNLP parsing program.[35] Some of these programs can do many tasks in addition to basic parsing, such as identifying dependencies between words, and can work with languages other than English (CoreNLP also works with Arabic, Chinese, French, German, and Spanish).

The data scientist can store information generated from parsing a text document in two basic ways: (1) as part of the main document or (2) separate from the main document. Individuals who know the structure of html or xml documents (document types used on the Internet) will recognize parsing information in the main document.

---

[34] In 2009, the US Securities and Exchange Commission mandated that certain filers file their documents using eXtensible Business Reporting Language (XBRL). The filer tags the financial data in its documents. These tags give structure to the documents, allowing users to compare, for example, revenue or cost of goods sold across companies without having to manually extract the data from documents and reenter it into a spreadsheet. See "Structured Disclosure at the SEC: History and Rulemaking," available at https://www.sec.gov/structureddata/historyandrulemaking.

[35] See Stanford CoreNLP which is available under a GNU General Public License, available at http://stanfordnlp.github.io/CoreNLP/http://stanfordnlp.github.io/CoreNLP/.

Using our simple sentence "Tom sees a dog" and storing parsing information in the main document, the finished document would look like this: "<noun>Tom<\noun><space><\space><verb>sees<\verb><space><\space><determiner> a<\determiner><space> <\space><noun>dog<\noun>." While this approach works for very simple parsing, it also creates many problems.[36]

Data scientists prefer to leave the original document intact and create one or more separate documents, linked to the original document, which includes the parsing information. Think of this as creating the text and then creating indices. Each index tells you where to find the main text and what information to apply to that text. An index could tell us that if we go to the sentence "Tom sees a dog" the fourth word in the sentence is a noun and another index could tell us that the noun "dog" is the object of the verb "sees." The parser could create many indices and allow the computer to combine various indices as needed, while keeping the original document unchanged. The separate document approach makes it easier to manipulate data and to combine the data with data from other sources.

Data scientists parse documents at one of two points in the preparation process. First, they can parse a document as part of the document-saving process. Many knowledge management systems create a simple index for documents at that time. Software can parse documents quickly in the background and make the data available for immediate use. Second, they can parse (or reparse) any time after saving the document. For example, the data scientist could do simple part-of-speech parsing (identifying whether words are nouns, verbs, etc.) at the time the document is saved, and more sophisticated parsing (word dependency) at a future time when the organization needs the data.

Once the data scientist has parsed the document, the data becomes accessible for many uses. The data scientist could break a parsed document into legal terms (e.g., choice of law, indemnification) and compare the terms across documents or to a standard term library. The data scientist could use the comparison to answer questions, such as whether a contract term is common, whether certain phrasing for the term is common, or even whether the term increases the risk of an agreement beyond an acceptable level (e.g., contracts with that term lead to disputes more often). The data scientist can combine parsed text data with data about the frequency and type of lawsuits to generate risk models. A risk model can alert managers during negotiations that certain terms increase risk levels.

In litigation, analyses of briefs and court decisions can reveal information about which arguments work best with a judge. Legal service providers could analyze argument styles to evaluate their persuasiveness. Organizations also could build sophisticated legal argument libraries using fact combinations or cases. Searching such a library could elicit instances where a case had been used in a legal brief, and could even lead to appellate decisions where the judge had relied on the case.

---

[36] Adding multiple layers of parsed information to a document becomes problematic, with tags embedded within tags and tags crossing tags. Recreating the original document requires stripping out all the tags. It is also easier to make mistakes when tagging.

The New Legal Data Challenge

Data scientists use text and photos alone or in combination with other data sources. But, the volume and types of data sources available to data scientists and legal service providers extend beyond these traditional sources. We can start with the Internet of Things. The number of products with embedded sensors increases daily. Those sensors send data streams to whoever is permitted to listen (and, the subject of a separate risk area, those who aren't). If you have a wearable device, it may capture your heart rate and other information about your physical condition while you sit at your desk or drive your car. If another car collides with your car, that data could make a difference in a personal injury lawsuit. The legal service provider will need to collect that data and combine it with other data—for example, data from an automobile's sensor—to create a story: Did the victim have a heart attack before the crash or did the crash cause the heart attack?

The legal service provider—a personal injury lawyer—may want to go further. The lawyer may want to compile data on the physical conditions of drivers who have taken a certain prescription medication within four hours of driving a car. By piecing together various data sets, the lawyer may suspect that the medication causes health problems that show up hours after taking the medication and impair a driver's ability to pilot a car. While legal service providers have done these types of analyses, they have not done so by starting their work with the mindset that they compile data sets that give them insights into how the world interacts with law.

With projections that billions of devices will have sensors embedded by 2025, legal service providers need to collect data that comes in many different formats and supplies new types of information.[37] A legal service provider specializing in class actions may discover commonalities among potential class members, a contract lawyer may learn about systematic warranty issues, and an in-house legal service provider for a manufacturer may get an early warning of product performance issues. Connecting the data from the devices to the terms of contracts or statutory law becomes a task for computers, not just humans.

The list of what legal service organizations can do with data expands each day. Facial recognition software can pick individuals out of a crowd, allowing police

---

[37] Gartner, Inc., an information technology research and advisory company, predicts that by 2020, the number of connected things in use worldwide will reach 20.8 billion. Gartner, "Gartner says 6.4 Billion Connected 'Things' Will Be in Use in 2016, Up 30 Percent From 2015," available at http://www.gartner.com/newsroom/id/3165317. Some have predicted that the number of sensors in these things already exceeds 50 billion and could exceed 1 trillion within 10 years. If the growth continues as predicted, data from these embedded sensors could account for approximately 10 percent of the data in the digital universe. See IDC, "The Digital Universe of Opportunities: Rich Data and the Increasing Value of the Internet of Things," EMC Digital Universe (April 2014), available at http://www.emc.com/leadership/digital-universe/2014iview/internet-of-things.htm. Even assuming the estimates are considerably overstated, the amount of data from sensors will quickly overwhelm a legal system that today is unequipped to deal with any of that data.

to scan images captured from closed-circuit television in a mall, a gas station, or an Automated Teller Machine. Geospatial Positioning System information allows trucking companies to pinpoint the location of its trucks at any time, their speed, and, combined with sensors embedded in the road and traffic signals, the trucking company (and its legal service provider) can define conditions at the point of an accident.

The personal injury legal service provider will need these streams—plus the data from the wearable device, the victim's automobile, and the victim's smartphone—to reconstruct an accident. Combining those data streams with the legal service organization's unique data set built from other matters it has handled allows the provider to answer client questions based on a unique and large data set. It provides a way to differentiate a legal service organization. Most importantly, it enables legal service providers to give clients advice based on a deeper understanding of how the world works than any legal service provider can offer based solely on his experience.

Conclusion

Many aspects of providing legal services in the 21st century have not moved far beyond practices of the late 19th century. The quill pen may have given way to the typewriter, which in turn gave way to the computer, but the output of each tool remains text buried in files, not data collected and analyzed. Until the late 20th century, collecting and analyzing legal data, particularly text data, was difficult. In the 21st century, the rapid increase in data mining by corporations has been coupled with a rapid increase in the availability of sophisticated software for collecting and analyzing legal data. Thus, legal data practices that were already dated by the late 20th century have become antiquated and even harmful now that we have cleared the resource hurdle.

Consultants, accountants, tax advisors, and other professional service providers go beyond reviewing information and comparing it to personal experience when they advise clients. They collect data as part of their practices, just as Google and Amazon collect data when providing their services. Taking advantage of widely available software, these professional service providers combine proprietary data from past services with publicly available data and data from clients to construct the services they provide clients.

Legal service providers and organizations should follow the same path, starting by treating what they collect and create as data. Although legal service organizations can get software to transform data to information, the software is useless without accessible and quality-assured data. Legal service organizations should create DMPs and begin enforcing them throughout their organizations. They also should explore data analysis and external data sources relevant to their practices. Legal service providers should realize that gold mining in the 19th century and oil exploration in the 20th century have given way to data mining in the 21st century.

Chapter 3

Deconstructing Contracts: Contract Analytics and Contract Standards

---

Kingsley Martin

Contents

Introduction

Contracts are the *language of business.* They document our business relationships and govern the global exchange of trillions of dollars of goods and services each year. Yet, despite their importance and the fact that we live in an increasingly interconnected world, contract drafting and review is relatively unchanged and has failed to keep up with innovation in other business sectors.

The consequences of current drafting practices have recently been quantified. They are alarming. Tim Cummins of the International Association for Contract and Commercial Management observes that "[p]oor Contract Management and contracting process can lead to value leakage of, on average, 9.5% of annual revenue."[1] Similar studies by Ernst & Young report that "[b]y having commercially efficient contracts, effectively managing these throughout their operational life and minimising waste in business activities with suppliers, an organisation can typically save between 5% to 15% of contract spend."[2] Finally, according to research by KPMG, ineffective governance of provider contracts can cause value leakage ranging from 17% to 40%.[3]

Given the significant loss of value, many governments, corporations, universities, and individuals around the world are working on next-generation systems to automate

---

[1] Tim Cummins, Poor Contract Management Costs Companies 9%—Bottom Line, Oct. 23, 2012, Commitment Matters blog, https://commitmentmatters.com/2012/10/23/poor-contract-management-costs-companies-9-bottom-line/ (last visited Dec. 9, 2017).

[2] Ernst & Young, Supporting Local Public Services Through Contract Optimization, 2016, www.ey.com/Publication/vwLUAssets/Supporting_local_public_services_through_change_-_Contracts_optimisation/$FILE/EY_Contracts_optimisation.pdf (last visited Dec. 9, 2017).

[3] Sourcing Focus, How to Stop the Value Leakage, 2016, www.sourcingfocus.com/site/featurescomments/how_to_stop_the_value_leakage/ (last visited Dec. 9, 2017).

and streamline the contracting process. This chapter outlines some of the key initiatives. It divides the topic into four parts. The first part examines whether technology can truly be harnessed to perform contract-related tasks. The second part describes how theories of complexity can be applied to hierarchical deconstruction and simplification. The third part applies these theories to the practical technology of contract analytics. The fourth part describes the modularization and simplification of contract language.

Can Technology Perform Human Tasks?

Before examining contract analysis, we must first answer the question whether technology can successfully emulate human tasks. One of the most prominent proponents of Artificial Intelligence, Ray Kurzweil, author of *The Singularity Is Near*, popularized the concept that technology will exceed human capacity in the near future. Technology, Kurzweil prophecies, will help design its successors, at ever-increasing speeds, creating a technology singularity, or an event horizon, beyond which we cannot see. Kurzweil's insight, along with many others, is that technology innovates exponentially, not linearly. This rate of change, which is occurring across all aspects of the technology spectrum, produces explosive growth, sometimes called the "hockey stick effect." One way to think about accelerating innovation is to consider all prior innovations since the birth of the computer and to imagine that all such prior capabilities will be doubled in the next one-to-two years.

> Here's what the exponential curves told [Kurzweil]. We will successfully reverse-engineer the human brain by the mid-2020s. By the end of that decade, computers will be capable of human-level intelligence. Kurzweil puts the date of the Singularity—never say he's not conservative—at 2045. In that year, he estimates, given the vast increases in computing power and the vast reductions in the cost of same, the quantity of artificial intelligence created will be about a billion times the sum of all the human intelligence that exists today.[4]

Of course, there are many who doubt that computers can become truly intelligent. For example, Professors Dreyfus and Dreyfus describe five stages of learning in their book *Mind over Machine* as a process that cannot be emulated by silicon and logic.[5] A *New York Times* opinion post, in response to IBM's Watson computer

---

[4] Lev Grossman, 2045: The Year Man Becomes Immortal. We're fast approaching the moment when humans and machines merge. Welcome to the Singularity movement, TIME, Feb. 10, 2011.

[5] Hubert L. Dreyfus, Stuart E. Dreyfus & Tom Athanasiou, Mind over machine: The Power of Human Intuition and Expertise in the Era of the Computer (1988).

winning performance on Jeopardy, asserted that "Watson Still Can't Think."[6] But it does not matter whether or not we believe a machine is "thinking." It is the results that count. When we consider any situation from the perspective of outcome or results, what is the difference between intelligence, judgment, brute force, or deep learning?

Others, such as Microsoft cofounder Paul Allen, contend that although the singularity may very well occur; it is a very long way off.[7] Allen points out that achieving the singularity will require enormous developments in software (not just improvements in hardware capacity), and replicating human capacity is unlikely to occur at an accelerating pace. In fact, Allen asserts, we will likely hit a "complexity brake" because "[a]s we go deeper and deeper in our understanding of natural systems, we typically find that we require more and more specialized knowledge to characterize them, and we are forced to continuously expand our scientific theories in more and more complex ways."

Once again, the core doubt is based on the fact that the human brain is exquisitely complex and therefore cannot be replicated. But, as one comment to Allen's article states, the doubt whether a computer can perform human tasks is based on the "premise that singularity can only occur when human intelligence can be engineered. It's far more likely that the inevitable accumulation of thousands of smart objects that don't even attempt to mimic human cognition will lead to systems that have inhuman intelligence, with the ability to outperform humans on so many different tasks that the intellectual contributions of all but the most creative humans will simply be unnecessary."

Or, as another comment predicts: the singularity is "the point at which the productivity growth rate permanently surpasses the economic output growth rate. Once that occurs, the economy must continuously shed (human) jobs."

Even for proponents of advanced automation, the singularity is still many years in the future. Moreover, the progression should not be seen as an event horizon whereby at a certain point in time, machines become hyperintelligent. It is rather an evolution whereby technology advances in skill levels in a series of stages. The likely stages of automation are shown in Figure 3.1. The stages reflect the skills needed to answer a complex question, such as what form of agreement will best serve a client's needs.

The first step requires us to find relevant material, such as prior examples of an agreement. We can accomplish this task using traditional cataloging techniques or with more modern search tools. Once we have collected relevant material, we must next analyze the data and determine the full range of clause elements (and alternatives) that may be found in each type of agreement. Finally, once we have identified all the elements and reviewed alternative forms, we must determine the optimal configuration.

---

[6] Stanley Fish, Watson Still Can't Think, *The New York Times*, Feb. 28, 2011.
[7] Paul Allen, The Singularity Isn't Near, *MIT Technology Review*, Oct. 12, 2011.

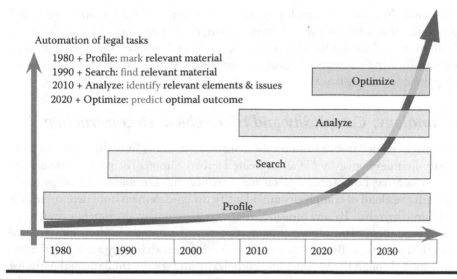

FIGURE 3.1   Stages of automation of legal tasks.

As shown in the illustration, technology does not yet have the capability to predict the best form of agreement. Technology, in itself, therefore, should not be seen as a current threat to take away jobs. Today, the state of the art is more like the magnetic resonance imaging machine used by the surgeon to augment the physician's insight. In the case of contract analytics, today's technology can analyze vast collections of agreements, create a checklist of items for the lawyer to consider, and offer examples of how other lawyers have drafted contract terms. Think of it as similar to a spell or grammar checker. When you draft a document, the checker compares what you wrote to its library of every correctly spelled word and grammar rule. It clearly shows you a comparison between what you wrote and what the standard is, and then allows you choose which one to use. Contracts analysis does something similar, but instead of just comparing simple spelling and grammar, it compares the complex clauses and language of your contract (either one you wrote or one someone else wrote that you need to review) with the clauses and language of a vast library of successfully executed contracts. It clearly shows you how your contract compares to the standard and allows you to quickly and easily make changes to improve the quality and comprehensiveness of your document.

Theory

The theoretical underpinnings of this chapter are founded on two main hypotheses. First: all complex systems can be examined through the process of hierarchical deconstruction, whereby the common building blocks or patterns can be discovered. Second: all complex systems—over time—follow a maturity model from one-off to commodities. In combination, deconstruction and maturity models allow us to "see the forest through the trees" and simplify the overall process, without limiting the capabilities of the resulting system to adapt to the full range of applicable circumstances.

Technology: Complexity and Hierarchical Deconstruction

The insight gained from hierarchical deconstruction draws from the science of complexity first developed by Nobel Laureate Herbert Simon. The goal of deconstruction, which has been applied to science, engineering, art, and literature, is to see through the cloud of complexity and identify the core elements and determine how they piece together. By any measure, contracts are complex documents. Seen as an assemblage of words, each agreement appears to be unique, and custom tailored to each transaction. But are they truly more different than they are similar? How can we see through the variance and complexity and see the fundamental patterns?

The first step is to examine the structure of agreements. Complexity theory "unlike traditional 'cause and effect' or linear thinking... is characterized by nonlinearity."[8] It addresses problems—like contracts—that are dynamic, unpredictable, and multidimensional, consisting of a collection of interconnected relationships and parts where certainty is replaced by probability. The thought leader of complexity, Herbert Simon, observed that all complex systems can be decomposed into a nested hierarchy of subsystems.[9] "Critically, however, not all these subsystems are of equal importance (i.e., centrality). In particular, some subsystems are 'core' to system performance, whereas others are only 'peripheral.' "[10] Contracts have similar attributes. Not all terms are equally important. In many cases just a small number of clauses are critical.[11]

An empirical analysis confirms that at the structural or building block level there is a high degree of similarity. This is not surprising since contracts document business relationships that have been performed millions of times. Over the years the manner and means of buying, selling, licensing, and engaging services has been documented into a knowable set of norms. For example, there are a finite number of ways to deliver goods, perform services, or pay for something. In fact, there is consistency across all agreements, as depicted in by the ContractStandards unified

---

[8] Complexity Science in Brief, 2012 (www.uvic.ca/research/groups/cphfri/assets/docs/Complexity_Science_in_Brief.pdf (last visited Dec. 8, 2017).

[9] Herbert A. Simon, The Architecture of Complexity, Proceedings of the American Philosophical Society, Vol. 106, No. 6. (Dec. 12, 1962), pp. 467–482.

[10] Alan MacCormack, Carliss Baldwin, and John Rusnak, The Architecture of Complex Systems: Do Core-periphery Structures Dominate? Harvard Business School Working Paper 10-059, Jan. 19, 2010.

[11] Kingsley Martin, Some Observations on the Nature of Contract Drafting, Feb. 28, 2011 (http://contractanalysis.blogspot.com/2011/02/some-observations-on-nature-of-contract.html, last visited Dec. 8, 2017).

contract framework.[12] Of course, there are the very rare situations where a transaction is performed for the first time, but such rarities should not obscure the general rule. They are simply exceptions.

Content: Automation and Standardization

A Wikipedia page describes maturity as "a measurement of the ability of an organization for continuous improvement in a particular discipline."[13] Different maturation stages can often be observed through the lens of other industries to better understand the process of commoditization. For example, Henry Ford revolutionized automobile manufacturing by introducing both the technology of assembly line and the introduction of modular, standardized components. Ford would not have met with success if he just introduced the automated assembly line. The line will quickly stall if each component of a car were designed differently without any thought how they will fit together.

In the legal industry, the trajectory is described by Richard Susskind in *The Future of Law.*[14] He categorized the phases as a journey from one-off, to standardized, to systemized, to packaged, and finally to commoditized. Unfortunately, law, for the most part, is still stuck on the bespoke phase, where all matters are treated as unique requiring custom-tailored solutions (Figure 3.2).

Contract Analysis

Evolution of Contract Technology

Over the next few years, technology will likely evolve from point solutions—automating particular tasks—to fully integrated platforms enabling a contract automation assembly line, orchestrating all phases of the contract lifecycle. The

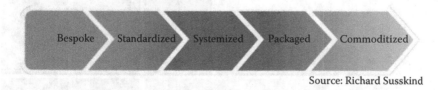

Bespoke Standardized Systemized Packaged Commoditized

Source: Richard Susskind

FIGURE 3.2 Evolution of legal services.[15]

[12] www.contractstandards.com/resources/csframework.
[13] https://en.wikipedia.org/wiki/Maturity_model (last visited Dec. 8, 2017).
[14] Richard Susskind, *The Future of Law,* Clarendon Press Publication, 1998.
[15] Richard Susskind, "Susskind on the Evolution of Legal Services," The Am Law Daily, Oct. 10, 2017

overall trend is to introduce more standardized processes and then to integrate such standards across all systems both internal and external. Today, the majority of contract tasks are performed by professionals with limited application of technology. Over time, this pattern is likely to reverse with more tasks handled by standard procedures and fewer tasks performed by skilled individuals undertaking nonstandard tasks. As illustrated in Figure 3.3, the trend line portends a decreasing percentage of tasks will be performed by professionals in a one-off manner and an increasing percentage performed by technology and systems.

Tools of Contract Analysis

Recently, contract analysis has emerged to offer promising tools to give us insights into individual contracts and portfolios of thousands of agreements. At its core, contract analytics is a suite of technologies and processes capable of parsing ones, tens, hundreds, thousands, or even millions of contracts and identify patterns within and across all agreements.

The overall approach is a hierarchical deconstruction. First, the algorithms deconstruct agreements into their component clauses (or building blocks). Second, each clause is broken down into sentences, and the software analyzes the precise language of each provision. Finally, sentences are examined at the word level to identify key contract variables, such as names, places, dates, and amounts. The overall approach is illustrated in Figure 3.4.

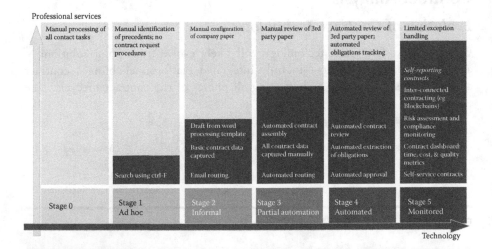

FIGURE 3.3 Contract technology maturity model.[16]

[16] Kingsley Martin, Contract Maturity Model (Part 2): Technology Assembly Line—from Active to Passive Systems, June 16, 2016, http://legalexecutiveinstitute.com/contract-maturity-technology-assembly-line/ (last visited Dec. 8, 2017).

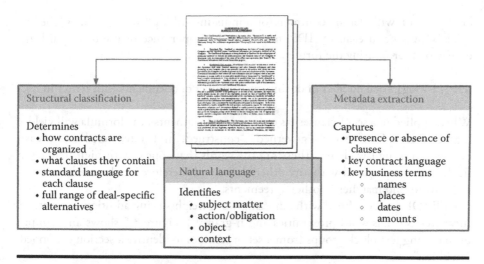

FIGURE 3.4 Suite of contract analysis tools.

Structural Classification

Contract analysis applies inductive reasoning techniques in order to identify the elements of a particular type of agreement. Algorithms first deconstruct a sample set of agreements into base components, such as clauses and sentences. Next, the software looks for similar components in other documents. Finally, the tools aggregate the components in a single organizing framework and capture key statistical information.

Deconstruction

Deconstruction may generate a flat list of clause paragraphs in the case of a simple agreement or a hierarchical outline of articles, sections, clauses, and subclauses in the case of longer and more complex agreements. One key advantage of deconstruction by contract sections is that the output can take advantage of captions that serve as outline headings and group-related concepts. For example, the software can group all representations, warranties, and covenants into sections of related concepts.

Matching

For each clause block or sentence, software next finds the closest match to such block or sentence in all other agreements. Typically, closest match algorithms apply some form of term frequency (TF)–inverse document frequency (IDF). The formula is composed of two elements. First, TF measures how frequently a term occurs in a document or a text block in a set of documents, using the formula:

$$\mathrm{TF}(t) = \big(\text{Number of times term } t \text{ appears in a document}\big)\big/$$
$$\big(\text{Total number of terms in the document}\big).$$

However, TF will identify common (or nondistinguishing) words, such as "the" or "and." The second element, IDF, measures the importance or the distinguishing nature of a term, using the formula:

$$IDF(t) = \log\left(\text{Total number of documents/Number of documents with term } t \text{ in it}\right).$$

When applied to a set of clauses (as opposed to documents), the formula will yield a high IDF score for the words "governed," "construed," and "interpreted" in the case of the governing law clause. These are the words that appear with high frequency in the clause compared with any other clause and therefore can be used as search patterns to find matches in other agreements.

TF-IDF can be refined with adjusting word weights using additional statistical measures (such as word proximities and n-grams[17]). Figure 3.5 shows an example of matching text block groups from a set of resumes to identify a section captioned "hobbies."

Aggregation

The process of aggregation reassembles all the matched elements into a single, common outline. A method of matching blocks is shown in in Figure 3.6. The resulting outline is shown in Figure 3.7. The process is typically iterative. It is similar to the

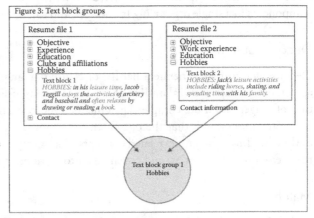

FIGURE 3.5   Matching text block groups.[18]

---

[17] An n-gram is a contiguous sequence of n items from a given sequence of text or speech, such as "hold harmless."

[18] Illustrations from US Patent 8606796: Method and system for creating a data profile engine, tool creation engines and product interfaces for identifying and analyzing files and sections of files.

By analyzing the shared characteristics of each text block groups, sets of text block groups are identified

Example: Three resume files

Text block captioned "other interests" is found and would likely match similar text blocks in further files and generates a text block group for "other interests".

By comparing the text block groups for "hobbies" and "other interests," the engine determines that "hobbies" and "other interests" share sufficient common attributes to be treated as a text block group set

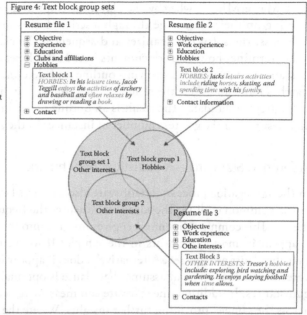

Figure 4: Text block group sets

Resume file 1
⊞ Objective
⊞ Experience
⊞ Education
⊞ Clubs and affiliations
⊟ Hobbies

Text block 1
HOBBIES: In his leisure time, Jacob Teggill enjoys the activities of archery and baseball and often relaxes by drawing or reading a book.

⊞ Contact

Resume file 2
⊞ Objective
⊞ Work experience
⊞ Education
⊟ Hobbies

Text block 2
HOBBIES: Jacks leisurs activities include riding horses, skating, and spending time with his family.

⊞ Contact information

Text block group set 1
Other interests

Text block group 1
Hobbies

Text block group 2
Other interests

Resume file 3
⊞ Objective
⊞ Work experience
⊞ Education
⊟ Othe interests

Text Block 3
OTHER INTERESTS: Tresor's hobbies include: exploring, bird watching and gardening. He enjoys playing football when time allows.

⊞ Contacts

FIGURE 3.6   Matching text block groups.[19]

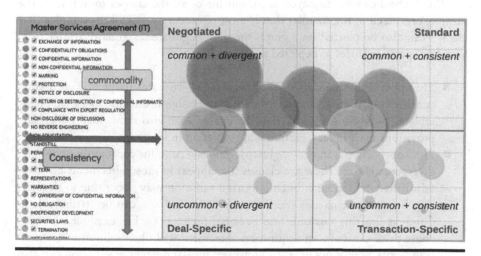

Master Services Agreement (IT)	Negotiated	Standard
☑ EXCHANGE OF INFORMATION		
☑ CONFIDENTIALITY OBLIGATIONS	*common + divergent*	*common + consistent*
☑ CONFIDENTIAL INFORMATION		
☑ NON-CONFIDENTIAL INFORMATION		
☑ MARKING		
☑ PROTECTION	commonality	
☑ NOTICE OF DISCLOSURE		
☑ RETURN OR DESTRUCTION OF CONFIDENTIAL INFORMATIO		
☑ COMPLIANCE WITH EXPORT REGULATION		
NON-DISCLOSURE OF DISCUSSIONS		
NO REVERSE ENGINEERING		
NON-SOLICITATION		
STANDSTILL		
PERM	Consistency	
☑ RE		
☑ TERM		
REPRESENTATIONS		
WARRANTIES		
☑ OWNERSHIP OF CONFIDENTIAL INFORMATION	*uncommon + divergent*	*uncommon + consistent*
NO OBLIGATION		
INDEPENDENT DEVELOPMENT		
SECURITIES LAWS		
☑ TERMINATION	**Deal-Specific**	**Transaction-Specific**
INDEMNIFICATION		

FIGURE 3.7   Contract analysis visualization.

---

[19] *Id* US Patent 8606796.

game MasterMind™, whereby the players attempt to decode a pattern sequence by building up their knowledge through a series of questions and binary answers. At each pass, the software organizes and sequences the clauses in a particular order and determines how many documents in the sample set will it match. It then reorders and resequences the evolving outline and determines whether the structure matches more (or less) of the samples. Each time it matches more, it moves closer to the aggregate standard. The result is an outline of the hierarchical building blocks that best match the greatest number of instances in the sample provided.

Reference Standard—A Statistical Benchmark

In the aggregation process, the software also captures key statistics for each branch in the common outline. The software measures the frequency of each clause across the set. This commonality number gives insights into the use of the provision. Does it appear in most agreements in the sample? If so, we can make the assumption that the clause as required. Alternatively, does it appear in some, but all the sample agreements? If so, we can assume that clause is optional to be used in specific circumstances. In addition, the software can measure the consistency of the language across the sample, providing further insights. Where the language is generally consistent, we can consider the term standard (or perhaps boilerplate). Where the term is highly variant, we can classify the term as highly negotiated or one to be configured to particularly deal circumstances.

The analysis can be displayed as an outline of all the clauses found in all the sample, organized in the manner that is most representative of all the samples. The clauses can also be plotted on a graph showing negotiated, standard, transaction, and deal-specific clauses as depicted in Figure 3.7.

- ■ The upper-right quadrant—*standard clauses*—contains frequently occurring, consistent clauses. Examples of such clauses should include so-called "boilerplate" provisions. However, as the analysis can also show, such boilerplate provisions may, in fact, exhibit wide variation in language.
- ■ The upper-left quadrant—*negotiated clauses*—contains commonly occurring, divergent clauses. These are clauses that appear in most agreements but contain different language. Such language variation may occur due to negotiation between the parties creating different terms or it can be attributable to different drafting customs and personal preferences. For example, the purchase price clause in an acquisition agreement will likely exhibit wide variation across a set of documents. However, similar degrees of variation can also be found in a severability clause.
- ■ The lower-right quadrant—*transaction-specific clauses*—contains clauses that do not occur frequently, but when they are found contain consistent language. A good example of a transaction-specific clause is "The Offer" term found in a set of merger agreements. This term may appear in about 20% of

the agreements—indicating that such transactions are structured as a tender offer. In these cases, the language will likely be consistent.

▪ Finally, the lower-left quadrant—*deal-specific clauses*—contains infrequently occurring clauses that display wide language variation. These are clauses that are custom-tailored to a particular transaction.

However, not all clauses fit neatly into this schema. Clauses that should contain consistent language are often, in practice, highly variable. In large part, this background divergence can be attributed to custom and personal drafting preferences. Indeed, this is very evident when analyzing documents from a large number of different organizations, compared with a set from a single law firm or corporate legal department. The more varied the source of the documents, the more diverse the clauses and the language. Of course, the fact that divergence increases with the diversity of the source set should not be surprising because they will contain a broader range of drafting customs and personal preferences. The key point is that as divergence increases above a certain threshold, the usefulness of the statistics is reduced.

Language (Legal Terms)

After identifying the structural clause blocks, technology can next examine the language of each provision, capture context, and some understanding of its meaning.

Supervised Deconstruction (Break-It-Down Checklists)

Just as the software analyzes entire agreements and identifies the clause building blocks, algorithms investigate the common elements of complex provisions in a manner similar to deconstructing entire agreements into clauses, but now at a more granular level. For example, an indemnity clause can be broken down into the core, highlighted elements: who indemnifies whom, for what, and under what circumstances. The approach can be applied to a recent merger agreement, where the highlighted text shows the common elements.

Once again, an empirical analysis confirms that the core concepts in each provision are highly consistent in substance, while the precise words may change semantically from one clause example to another.

Programmatic Deconstruction

Today, "break-it-down" analysis is done in a semiautomated manner whereby experts review program output and craft comprehensive checklists identifying the core and optional elements for an indemnity and all other clauses. At the same time, technologists are working on further automating the process to create detailed checklists for all agreement types. Most of this work builds on Natural Language

> **X. <u>Indemnification</u>.** *Subject to the terms and conditions of this Article...,
> upon the Closing of the Transactions,* **Parent shall indemnify and hold
> harmless each of the Company Securityholders** and each of their
> respective Affiliates, and the representatives, Affiliates, successors,
> and assigns of each of the foregoing Persons (each, a "Seller
> Indemnified Party"), **from,** against and in respect of any and **all
> Damages** incurred or suffered by the Seller Indemnified Parties **as a
> result of**, arising out of or relating to, directly or indirectly:
> (a) **any breach or inaccuracy of any representation or warranty** of Parent
> or Merger Sub set forth in this Agreement or the certificate of Parent
> or Merger Sub delivered at the Closing pursuant to Section... (or the
> assertion by any third party of claims which, if successful, would give
> rise to any of the foregoing); and
> (b) **the breach of any covenant or agreement of Parent or Merger Sub** in
> this Agreement or any other agreement contemplated by this
> Agreement to which Parent or Merger Sub is party (or the assertion by
> any third party of claims which, if successful, would give rise to any of
> the foregoing) and the breach by the Company of the covenant set
> forth in Section... hereof.

Processing (or NLP). NLP is the ability of a computer program to understand human communications in written and oral forms. It is composed of numerous subspecialties.[20] At its core, NLP parses sentences into their lexical components by tagging words with parts of speech, finding the relationships between the words, and resolving ambiguities.

One of the best known—and widely used—NLP platforms is Stanford's parser. For example, the Stanford parser can tag the words with parts of speech and identify word relationships, as shown in Figure 3.8.

Fortunately, contracts typically use a narrow lexicon compared with common parlance. They are written as a series of declarative statements in the form of subject, verb, and object. This gives NLP a framework to determine who is the actor (or subject), what is the action (or verb), and what is the nature of the action (the

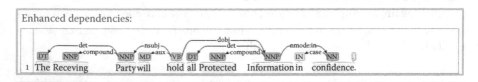

FIGURE 3.8   Stanford NLP parser.[21]

---

[20] Introduction to Natural Language Processing (NLP), Algorithmia Blog, Aug. 11, 2016, https://blog.algorithmia.com/introduction-natural-language-processing-nlp/ (last visited Dec. 8, 2017).

[21] Visualization provided using brat visualization/annotation software.

object). Of course, this can be complicated (and open to greater interpretation or ambiguity) when attempting to parse long, compound, or very complex sentences. However, it should also be said that humans will equally struggle to find definitive meaning in sentences exceeding a few hundred words.

Data (Business Terms)

Identifying Business Terms

Finally, within each sentence, the software can examine the words and identify key variable terms—often representing the business terms of the agreement—such as names, places, dates, values, etc. For example, in the following sentence, key terms are highlighted.

"	This Master Services Agreement is made on January 1, 2017, between ABC Inc., Delaware corporation (the "Seller") and XYZ, Inc., a California limited liability partnership (the "Buyer").

The extractions can be summarized in a term sheet capturing key variables such as the type of agreement, names of parties and law firms, consideration, governing jurisdiction, and notice periods.

Tools for Metadata Extraction

The programmatic tools used for automated data extraction are typically a combination of technologies including regular expressions and NLP. A regular expression or regex for short is a sequence of characters that define a search pattern. In some cases, they can be words or parts of words. But they can also be character patterns, such as three numbers followed by a dash, followed by two numbers, followed by a dash, and followed by four numbers: a pattern that describes a social security number.

This pattern can be expressed in regex as: $\land\backslash d\{3\}\text{-}\backslash d\{2\}\text{-}\backslash d\{4\}\$$. Where \d represents a number from 0 to 9 and {3} means repeat the last instruction three times.

But even relatively predictable patterns such as social security numbers can get complex when, for example, dashes are replaced with spaces or dots. In the case of something like an address, significant variability requires programmatic solutions to detect likely parts of an address and apply probabilistic solutions to predict how likely the text is, in fact, an address.

Despite the complexity, significant advances are made each year with many resources, such as the Stanford NLP parser being shared with a global community of developers. Such open sourcing is fueling increased innovation. For example, Figure 3.9 shows what the Stanford named entity parser captures in the sample opening sentence.

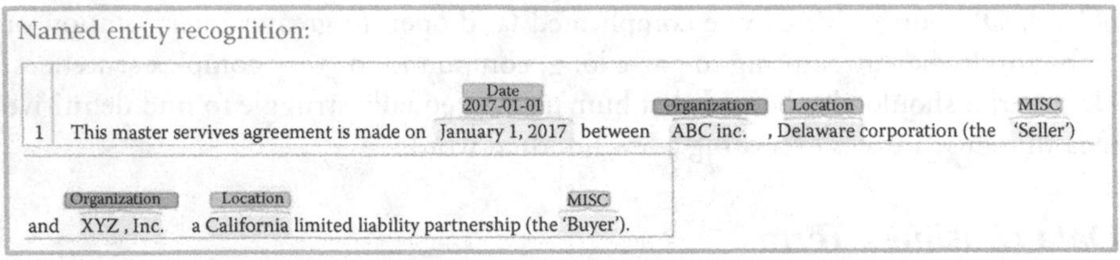

Named entity recognition:

| | Date 2017-01-01 | | | Organization | Location | | MISC |
| 1 | This master servives agreement is made on | January 1, 2017 | between | ABC inc. | , Delaware corporation (the | 'Seller') |

| | Organization | Location | | MISC |
| and | XYZ , Inc. | a California limited liability partnership (the 'Buyer'). |

FIGURE 3.9   Results from the Stanford named entity parser.

Training Approaches

The most significant developments in contract automation have been in the area of machine training. This work, as shown in the table, focuses on creating the elements of a particular type of contract and matching similar elements in other agreements. It has progressed from a largely manual set of procedures to one that is increasingly automated.

Approach	Outline	Matching
Manual	Manual identification of clauses	Rule-based matching
Supervised	Structural matching	Machine learning/ TF-IDF
Automated	Deep learning	Machine learning/ TF-IDF

Manual: Rule-Based Learning

In the early days, contract analysis was mostly a manual undertaking. Experts, often with the use of search tools, manually created a checklist of terms. Then for each term, programmers developed if-else-then, rule-based scripts to find sample clauses. For example, using a regular expression, a search pattern, such as the governing law example shown in the table later, can attempt to find matching sentences.

| </> | th(?:e|is)\s+{AGREEMENT}.*?(?:governed|construed).*?laws.*?of.*?({STATE}) |
| | Where {AGREEMENT} and {STATE} are macros that expand out to a list of alternatives. |

The challenge for such an approach is that an expert created, manually constructed pattern is unlikely to find all instances of a governing law clause. In technical terms, it may yield high precision, but its recall may be low due to high variation found in contract language. Moreover, the patterns will need to be manually created for all languages.

Supervised: Machine Learning

To overcome the limitations inherent in rule-based techniques, machine learning tools (such as TF-IDF) train the computer to identify the matching characteristics. Experts define the relevant blocks, provide exemplars or guidance, and the machine identifies the relevant characteristics that distinguish one text block from another.

"	Machine learning is an application of artificial intelligence (AI) that provides systems the ability to automatically learn and improve from experience without being explicitly programmed.[22]

Machine learning is explained by Tom Mitchell as "[a] computer is said to learn from experience E with respect to some class of tasks T and performance measure P if its performance at tasks in T as measured by P improves with experience E."[23]

Automated: Deep Learning

Deep learning takes this process one step further. Algorithms automatically identify the building blocks and which features are important for classification (Figure 3.10).

"	Deep learning is a particular kind of machine learning that achieves great power and flexibility by learning to represent the world as nested hierarchy of concepts, with each concept defined in relation to simpler concepts, and more abstract representations computed in terms of less abstract ones.[24]

"	The hierarchy of concepts allows the computer to learn complicated concepts by building them out of simpler ones. If we draw a graph showing how these concepts are built on top of each other, the graph is deep, with many layers. For this reason, we call this approach to AI deep learning.[25]

---

[22] What is Machine Learning? A definition, Expert System blog, www.expertsystem.com/machine-learning-definition/ (last visited Dec. 8, 2017).

[23] Tom M. Mitchell, *Machine Learning*. McGraw-Hill, 1997.

[24] Faizan Shaik, Deep Learning vs. Machine Learning – the essential differences you need to know! Analytics Vidhya Blog, April 8, 2017, www.analyticsvidhya.com/blog/2017/04/comparison-between-deep-learning-machine-learning/ (last visited Dec. 9, 2017).

[25] Ian Goodfellow, Yoshua Bengio and Aaron Courville, *Deep Learning*, MIT Press, 2016.

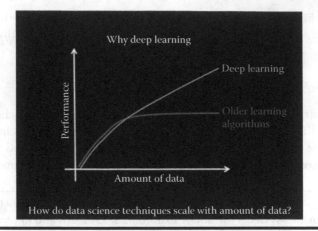

FIGURE 3.10 Comparison of deep learning.

Deep learning is best performed holistically, giving the software the entire agreement as a basis for examination. As a result, deep learning systems (as shown in Figure 3.9)[26] take much longer to train and require far more computing power. However, once trained, testing can be performed faster compared with traditional machine learning techniques as testing time increases with the amount of data.

The challenge for the analysis of transactional agreements is often a lack of high volumes of samples and a high variability in content. Indeed, this is the main reason why training in contract analytics has been based on supervised, machine learning techniques.

Contract Standards—Modularization, Standardization, and Simplification

Evolution of Content Standards

As Richard Susskind observed, the journey from one-off contracts to systematized and packaged systems starts with establishing standards.[27] This trend toward standards is a path followed by all businesses. Of course, law presents a more challenging technical exercise compared to automated manufacturing, where the subject matter is the full breadth of human and business interactions expressed in language. Nonetheless, as Figure 3.11 shows, the trend line evolves from one-off

---

[26] Andrew Ng (www.slideshare.net/ExtractConf).
[27] Richard Susskind, *The End of Lawyers?* 2008.

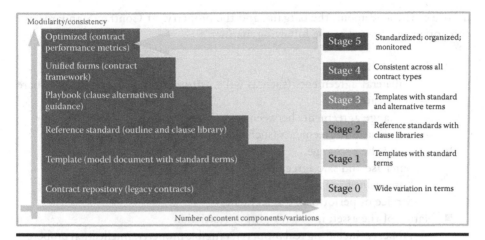

FIGURE 3.11   Evolution of content from one-offs to modular components.²⁸

contracting—where every agreement is slightly different—to portfolios of contracts built from standard, modular and reusable components, configured by input variables.

The methodology of content standardization and modularization follows a similar course as the approaches to technology. It also applies the technique of hierarchical deconstruction. We first organize all contract types into modular classes, then standardize the clause building blocks,²⁹ and finally simplify the language.³⁰

Consistent Organization—Unified Forms Library

The first step towards a unified forms library is to collect and organize all contract types in a single taxonomy or complementary set of taxonomies. This can be done by collecting the titles of all agreements filed on, for example, the U.S. Securities and Exchange Commission's Electronic Data Gathering, Analysis, and Retrieval (EDGAR) system or other publicly available resource. In such an exercise, an analysis of EDGAR filings yielded approximately 750 agreement types (although this list can be further refined to remove overlapping types and limit the list to about 500). These agreements can then be organized into a taxonomy organized by the

²⁸ Kingsley Martin, *Contract Maturity Model (Part 3): Evolution of Content from One-Offs to Modular Components*, Legal Executive Institute Blog, July 20, 2016 (http://legalexecutiveinstitute.com/contract-maturity-modular-components/ (last visited Dec. 9, 2017).

²⁹ See ContractStandards Unified Contract Framework, www.contractstandards.com/resources/csframework (last visited Dec. 9, 2017).

³⁰ See ContractStandards Style Guide, www.contractstandards.com/resources/style-guide (last visited Dec. 9, 2017).

nature of the agreement, the bargain, and the property. At ContractStandards, we categorize agreements in the following manner.

■ Nature of the agreement
  − unilateral agreements (such as wills, trusts, insurance agreements, share certificates, etc.)
  − exchange agreements between two or more parties
  − organization agreements (such as bylaws, operating agreements, etc.)
■ Nature of the exchange
  − purchase and sale agreements
  − lease or license agreements
  − Service or performance agreements
■ Nature of the asset, interest, right, or restriction
  − Property (including real property, tangible property, intellectual property)
  − Interest or right
■ Temporal nature of the asset, interest, right, or restriction
  − Existing rights
  − Future rights
  − Contingent rights

Consistent Contract Terms—Unified Contract Framework

Within each contact type, software and experts can identify the common clauses. Some may be unique to a particular agreement type, others may be found in many different agreements. While a definitive empirical study has yet to be completed, the total number of distinct clauses can be estimated with the following formula.

$$\text{Estimated number of exchange agreements}(500)$$
$$* \text{average number of clauses per agreement}(50)$$
$$* \text{percentage of unique clauses per agreement}(0.3) = 7,500.$$

Accordingly, it is estimated that with a library of 7,500 clauses (a relatively small number for computers) any agreement can be assembled.

The clauses can be further organized into a common or unified framework, as shown in Figure 3.12. The exchange framework is composed of a grid of three rows and three columns. The first row of terms describes the business agreement. It details the nature of the transaction (describing the value given and received by each party), the mechanics of the exchange (detailing how the consideration will be exchanged or received), and the period of time during which the parties are bound by the terms of the agreement. The second row describes the statements, actions, and circumstances that each party requires to assure that they

	Bargain What are the parties buying or exchanging? Service products, a license, property, etc?		Exchange What are the mechanics of exchange? How will the parties give and receive value?		Term What is the time period of the agreement? When does it start? When does it end? Can the agreement be extended?
	Reps, warranties and acknowledgements What statements, facts and actions are material to the bargain?		Conditions What actions, facts or circumstances must occur for the parties to close the transaction?		Obligations What actions of forbearances must each party continue to perform during the term of the agreement?
	Rights What actions can the parties take to protect their interest in the bargain? Rights to terminate, adjust services or costs, etc.		Remedies What can the parties do in the event the other does not perform its obligations?		General provisions How are disputes resolved? What laws apply? Who is benefited and bound by the agreement? How is the contract interpreted?

FIGURE 3.12   ContractStandards unified contract framework.[31]

receive the benefits of their bargain. Finally, the third row describes what happens in the event of a breach of the agreement or other circumstances preventing the parties from realizing the benefits of the bargain and how the agreement is interpreted.

Clause Variables: Playbooks

For each clause in the agreement, the software further identifies variations. In general, such clause variations are driven by three main factors: the nature of the transaction, the degree to which the clause favors one party or the other, and the requirements of the governing jurisdiction (in that order of importance). It is commonly believed that contract terms must be carefully crafted to the meet the mandates of each governing jurisdiction. In truth, this is significantly overstated. There are relatively few contract terms that must be specifically worded to comply with local laws. A contract is a private bargain, enforceable by law. The parties are free to enter into any terms of agreement, provided they are not illegal or contrary to public policy. Terms that are clear, fair, and balanced are more likely to be enforced by the courts—and less likely to be litigated in the first place.

Clause variations can be provided in the form of a playbook, which provides contract professionals with guidance on the use of each clause alternative, marking them in terms of preference. For example, some businesses use a PADU system, tagging clauses as Preferred, Acceptable, Discouraged, and Unacceptable.

---

[31] ContractStandards Framework, www.contractstandards.com/resources/csframework (last visited Dec. 9, 2017).

Deal Variables: Term Sheets

In addition to clause variations, text variables data (identified through metadata extraction tools) capture key contract or business terms. As noted earlier, these variables identify names of parties, dates, amounts, and places. In combination with all clause variations, software can outline all the choices that need to be made to configure a contract to the needs of a transaction. The process can be viewed as reverse engineering legal logic from a sample set of agreements.[32] While this may sound like an intrusion or even a usurpation of human intellect, it simply mirrors that way we learn. The main difference is that we can learn faster by training machine with inductive reasoning methods.

Monster Matrix

The ultimate goal is to create a resource for all contract types and a library of modular clauses (together with their deal-specific variations) that can, in combination, create every contract type and tailor each instance to the particular needs of any transaction. I sometimes refer to the final construct as the "monster matrix." It captures every contract type in the horizontal dimension and each contract clause the vertical (Figure 3.13).

Consistent Language—Style Guide

Contact consistency is perhaps best achieved through a style guide, ensuring that all agreements are written in a consistent manner and written in a form that can

1. Organization: Follow a consistent, logical organizational structure
2. Headings: Use informative headings that serve as a summary of the contents
3. Clauses: Break text into smaller units with one substantive topic per clause
4. Sentences: Draft in short, declarative sentences
5. Words: Use standard language, without jargon or legalese
6. Punctuation: Use punctuation to aid readability

FIGURE 3.13   ContractStandards drafting principles.

---

[32] Kingsley Martin, Waston J.D.—Breaking the Subjectivity Barrier, Reinvent Law Channel, www.reinventlawchannel.com/kingsley-martin-watson-jd-breaking-the-subjectivity-barrier (last visited Dec. 9, 2017).

be read by both humans and machines.[33] The style guide is used to draft contract sentences in a consistent manner. Applying a consistent approach to drafting, contractual sentences can be classified into three basic forms of sentences, each written in the form of subject–verb–object.

- Statements of the Parties
    - Obligations (what the parties must do): Party…will…verb…object.
    - Restrictions (what the parties can't do): Party…will not…verb…object.
    - Permissions (what the parties can do): Party…may…verb…object.
    - Statements (what the parties agree to): Party…[copula]…verb…object.
- Statements of the Agreement
    - Positive = This agreement will be…verb…object.
    - Negative = This agreement may not be…verb…object
- Definitions
    - Term… ("means"/"includes")…definition

Numerous agreements contain a fourth type of sentence, namely sentences about other subject matter topics. However, many of these sentence forms are the form of passive statements and should be avoided.

Obligations, restrictions, and permissions can be further refined and classified by NLP as being

- Dated (such as an obligation to deliver or pay on a particular date),
- Ongoing (such as a monthly payment obligation), or
- Contingent (such as an obligation conditional on another action or event).

In addition, contractual statements can be subject to qualifications (such as requirements, exceptions, minimums, maximums, or other restrictions).

Consistent Wording—Controlled Contract Language

The final level of consistency may be achieved through the creation of a controlled contract vocabulary, where contractual statements are crafted from a limited lexicon of words. Key contractual statements are generally expressed through a modal verb and a main verb. In the English language, there are 12 modal verbs of which just five commonly occur in agreements (can, may, must, shall, and will). The process of generating a controlled contract language can be aided with technology to examine the frequency of verb usage for each clause type and use the generated list to select the clearest verbs for each contractual obligation.

---

[33] See Auditable Contracts: Moving from Literary Prose to Machine Code, Legal Executive Institute Blog, http://legalexecutiveinstitute.com/auditable-contracts-moving-from-literary-prose-to-machine-code/ (last visited Dec. 9, 2017).

Many will doubt the feasibility of such narrowing of contract terms to a limited and controlled list. Lawyers may view it as a severe restriction on the need to custom-craft languages to nuances of each transaction. However, a recent exercise shows how the approach can offer real value. The study analyzed a large number of nondisclosure agreements and identified the core confidentiality obligations. The analysis found wide variations in wording empirically measured through Levenshtein distance vectors, which measures the similarity between two blocks of text. However, when captured as a checklist of concepts, the software found four main confidentiality obligations:

- To use the information solely for the purpose of the disclosure (87%)
- To keep the information confidential (93%)
- To protect the information from loss or unauthorized disclosure (42%)
- To notify the disclosing party in the event of loss or unauthorized disclosure (12%)

The software further captured how frequently each obligation appeared in the set (shown in parentheticals). With this information, a new simplified standard can be proposed using a controlled contract language with the benefit of significantly reducing contract length, while increasing readability. A sample set of obligations is illustrated as follows.

Use of Information. The receiving party will use the Protected Information solely for the [Purpose]. **Confidentiality Obligation**. The receiving party will hold the Protected Information in confidence.
Protection of Information. The receiving party will exercise reasonable care to protect the Protected Information from any loss or unauthorized disclosure. **Notification of Disclosure**. The receiving party will immediately notify the disclosing party upon discovery of any loss or unauthorized disclosure of Protected Information.

Conclusion: The Future of Contracts

The world of contracts, which has been largely unchanged for hundreds of years, is about to enter a period of rapid transition fueled by a global economy. Agreements that in the past were solely rendered in printed form may now be prepared, executed, and delivered in electronic form. Indeed, some terms may be linked to information on websites that may be amended with or without notice.

The combination of contract automation and contract standards will likely trigger the rise of contract apps. Not just applications to assemble and review contract terms, but rather technologies to link contract terms to applications. The best known is the blockchain designed to securely manage the ledger of obligations and payment terms. We will also see the integration of insurance applications to protect against loss (such as title insurance or reps and warranty insurance), to manage assurances (such as escrows), compliance applications to manage interparty obligations, and to ensure conformity with rapidly changing regulatory standards.

Chapter 4

The Big Move Toward Big Data in Employment

Aaron Crews[1]

Contents

---

[1] This chapter was adapted from a Littler Mendelson white paper co-authored by Marko Mrkonich, Allan King, Rod Fliegel, Philip Gordon, Harry Jones, Tamsen Leachman, Michael Lotito, Garry Mathiason, Michael McGuire, Natalie Pierce, Paul Weiner, Corinn Jackson, Zoe Argento, Shiva Shirazi Davoudian, Chad Kaldor, Elaine Lee, Catherine Losey, Joseph Wientge, Jr. It was published with permission from the firm.

Introduction to Big Data and Its Potential Uses in the Workplace

Numbers have always been used to monitor human activity. From primitive tallies etched onto the walls of ancient caves to multivolume reports generated by computer programs operating "in the cloud," humans have always tried to deploy the power of mathematics and numbers to help understand and guide our behavior. We are not surprised, for example, when actuaries use data regarding life expectancy and health risks to set life insurance premiums. We are also not taken aback when our neighborhood bank or car dealer asks a series of questions and assigns us a credit score before deciding whether to lend us money. And it is expected that an employer will evaluate the performance of its sales force by examining the numbers it generates. Not surprisingly, in today's era of supercomputing and digitalized information, our ability to acquire and use large quantities of data has expanded exponentially, and each day brings new developments in both what we know (or stated more precisely, what we can know if we choose to) and how we can use that data.

The world of Big Data has arrived, and it is beginning to affect employers and their decision making in ways undreamed of even a few years ago. Employers can access more information about their applicant pool than ever before, and have an ability to correlate data gleaned from the application itself, perhaps supplemented by publicly available social media sources, to determine how long a candidate is likely to stay on a particular job. Similarly, by combing through computerized calendar entries and e-mail headers, Big Data can tell us which employees are likely to leave their employment within the next 12 months. At the same time, new tools and methods that rely on concepts of Big Data are becoming part of the daily landscape in human resource departments, and employers continue to operate in a legal environment based on precedent and history with few guideposts that translate seamlessly into the world of Big Data. The issues that can arise either are brand new or develop in a context that makes yesterday's compliance paradigm difficult to apply.

The purpose of this chapter is to help provide employers with an introduction to the world of Big Data and what its arrival means for their daily activities. It has become axiomatic to observe that the digitalization of information has resulted in the creation of more data in recent years than in the prior combined history of humankind, and that at the same time we have acquired all of this data, our ability to apply advanced computer-based techniques to use the information has likewise expanded exponentially. It has also become cheaper and more readily accessible to do so for virtually everyone. For employers, these developments create both opportunities and novel issues of concern, and they generate new questions about long-time problems. Big Data potentially affects every aspect of employment decision making for employers of all sizes in virtually every industry, from the selection and hiring process, through performance management and promotion decisions, and up to and beyond the time termination decisions are made, whether for performance reasons or as part of a reorganization.

Employers, in essence, need to understand how to balance the opportunities and risks in the brave new world of Big Data. Big Data means that employers can theoretically analyze every aspect of every decision without worrying about a need to rely only on a partial sample, and Big Data allows employers to find (or, in some cases, to disprove) correlations between characteristics and outcomes that may or may not have a seeming connection. As a result, employers need to understand what Big Data means for background checks and employee privacy, to know the implications of the employer's data security obligations, to use Big Data to reduce the risks of traditional discrimination claims without giving rise to new varieties of such claims, and to know how the employers need to manage litigation with expanded eDiscovery and new theories of liability and new defenses based on statistical correlations.

Big Data and the Arrival of Artificial Intelligence in the Workplace

> In general, applications are still designed to perform predetermined functions or automate business processes, so their designers must plan for every usage scenario and code the logic accordingly. They don't adapt to changes in the data or learn from their experiences. Computers are faster and cheaper, but not much smarter.[2]

---

[2] Judith Hurwitz, Marcia Kaufman, Adrian Bowles, *Cognitive Computing and Big Data Analytics* (Apr. 8 2015), kindle cloud location 289.

The computer makes no decisions; it only carries out orders. It's a total moron, and therein lies its strength.[3]

This is the picture of Big Data analytics before cognitive computing. Big Data exists, but there can be challenges to its accessibility.

Computing makes simple analysis faster and easier, but requires substantial human guidance.

When cognitive computing is applied to Big Data, the picture changes: "Acting as partners or collaborators for their human users, [cognitive computing]... systems derive meaning from volumes of natural language text and generate and evaluate hypotheses in seconds based on analysis of more data than a person could absorb in a lifetime."[4] The application of these insights to the workplace has the potential to both create and alleviate legal challenges.

What Is Cognitive Computing?

Cognitive computing works by identifying associative connections between data points and reasoning from them.[5] The process by which a cognitive computing system reaches insights about the world is, on a very simple level, similar to that which can enable people to walk into a dark room and intuitively find a light switch.[6] Over time, humans have noted a pattern in the placement of light switches and have extrapolated an insight about their usual location.[7] Cognitive computing systems seek to replicate this process of observation-based learning.

Cognitive computing is hypothesis-driven. This means that a cognitive system can form a hypothesis, test and modify it, and reach an insight about the nature of something in the world. This distinguishes the algorithms grounding cognitive computing from other types of algorithms.[8]

Historically, cognitive computing is an outgrowth of the broader field of Artificial Intelligence (AI).[9] Unfortunately, because AI has been varyingly defined,[10] there are different ways of distinguishing between AI and cognitive computing.

---

[3] Peter Drucker, *Technology, Management, and Society* (Sep. 10, 2012), p. 147.

[4] *Supra* note 1.

[5] www.techrepublic.com/article/cognitive-computing-leads-to-the-next-level-of-big-data-queries/ (last visited July 14, 2015).

[6] *Id.*

[7] *Id.*

[8] *Supra* note 1 at 585.

[9] *See generally id.* at 503–590.

[10] AI is a very broad field and one where there is not a universally accepted definition, as people continue to discuss and debate exactly what constitutes intelligence. Certainly there is a high degree of overlap between cognitive computing and AI in areas such as machines learning algorithms, knowledge representation, natural language processing, and so on.

One proposed distinction is that AI "thinks," while cognitive computers "learn."[11] Others characterize cognitive computing as a branch or subset of AI. Depending on how you conceive of AI, cognitive computing is either the branch of AI being adapted to learn from and process Big Data or it is being used instead of AI for this purpose.

How Does Cognitive Computing Enable Big Data Analytics?

Cognitive computing enhances Big Data analysis by unlocking large portions of the world's data and by providing a more sophisticated and dynamic means of analyzing it.

Cognitive computing and Big Data benefit from each other. Cognitive computing systems require large data sets to "learn."[12] Big Data can provide these data sets. In turn, the ability of the cognitive computing systems to interpret unstructured data and data from analogous sources, such as articles, videos, photos, and human speech, has dramatically increased machine access to reams of unstructured data involved in some of the most important human interactions. Eighty percent of all data is unstructured.[13] Cognitive computing gives computers access to this information.

Allowing machines to access this 80 percent of data gives them the full picture they need to reach accurate insights about the world. For example, streaming and moving data has been traditionally difficult to analyze. Such information includes the movement of a body across a sensor, fluctuations in temperature, video feeds, and the movement of the stock market. Until cognitive computing, there was no effective way for computers to access and interpret this data in real time.

The other advantage of cognitive computing is its ability to learn from this data once it has access. Some potential uses of cognitive computing proposed in *Cognitive Computing and Big Data Analytics* are as follows:

■ Providing greater security to job sites by enabling analysis of movements detected by motion sensors to parse threats from innocuous incidents. For example, distinguishing between a human intruder and a rabbit.
■ Using sensors on medical instruments to detect malfunctions and alert physicians.
■ Interpreting the context of incidents in at-risk physical locations to determine whether there is a problem.[14]

---

[11] www.computerworld.com.au/article/522302/watson_future_cognitive_computing/ (last visited July 14, 2015).
[12] *Supra* note 1 at 1568–1588.
[13] *Id.* at 1652.
[14] *Id.* at 1850.

Thus, cognitive computing can overcome some of the human limitations on memory and observational capacity while mimicking the aspects of human cognition that permit learning.

Employment Law Consequences of Applying Cognitive Computing to Big Data

Equal Employment Opportunity Issues

If bias is the product of the human mind, must it also be the product of the mechanical mind? Not necessarily.

If cognitive computing algorithms are used to make employment decisions, it is possible that some of those decisions can constitute impermissible discrimination. As discussed later in "Big Data: Is There a Defense to a Potential Adverse Impact?," to prevail under a disparate impact theory of discrimination, a plaintiff must show the algorithm used to make an employment decision adversely impacts a protected group or, if the employer succeeds in establishing legitimate business reasons for using the algorithm, by demonstrating there exists a less discriminatory alternative

Who Uses Social Networking Sites % of Internet Users Within Each Group Who Use Social Networking Sites	
All internet users	74%
a. Men	72
b. Women	76
a. 18–29	89
b. 30–49	82
c. 50–64	65
d. 65+	49
a. High school grad or less	72
b. Some college	78
c. College+	73
a. Less than $30,000/year	79
b. $30,000–$49,999	73
c. $50,000–$74,999	70
d. $75,000+	78

that is equally efficient at serving the employer's legitimate business needs. Because cognitive computing is algorithm-based, a cognitive computing algorithm could conceivably be the basis of such a claim. However, the algorithms that enable cognitive computers to "learn" would only have an impact on employees if the insights they derived were used in creating the algorithms later used in making hiring decisions. It would therefore be far more likely that these insight algorithms would be the subject of legal challenges for disparate impact. The associations between high job performance and, for example, visiting a particular website or participation in certain social media, are the kinds of insight algorithms that could be produced by a cognitive computing process.

If relied on for hiring decisions, these insight algorithms could become the basis for disparate impact claims. For example, participation in social media varies based on a number of protected factors. The below chart, created by the Pew Research Center, shows that social media participation varies based on the legally protected categories of age and sex.

Pew Research Center's Internet Project January Omnibus Survey, January 23–26, 2014.

Note: Percentages marked with a superscript letter (*e.g.,* a) indicate a statistically significant difference between that row and the row designated by that superscript letter, among categories of each demographic characteristic (*e.g.,* age).

The likelihood of a cognitive computing process producing an algorithm with an unlawful disparate impact could increase if the data used in creating this algorithm is itself biased. The veracity of Big Data is fundamental to its utility.[15] A recent white paper by a management consulting firm McKinsey & Company stressed that "'garbage in, garbage out' applies as much to supercomputers as it did 50 years ago to the IBM System/360."[16]

Bearing this in mind, disparities in the type and volume of data available about different cross sections of the population could cause cognitive computing systems to produce incorrect hypotheses. For example, relying on the earlier chart, if a cognitive computing system concluded that individuals with glasses were more successful in a given position, and 18- to 29-year-old posted pictures of themselves at the same rate as people above 65, a cognitive computing system could mistakenly conclude that 18- to 29-year-old wear glasses almost twice as frequently as persons over 65.[17] The results could be even further skewed if younger social media users post more pictures of themselves on average than those over the age of 65. Conceivably, cognitive computing software could be programmed to evaluate whether the

---

[15] *Supra* note 1 at 1588–1610.

[16] Martin Dewhurst and Paul Willmott, *Manager and Machine: The New Leadership Equation* McKinsey & Company (Sept. 2014) available at www.mckinsey.com/insights/leading_in_the_21st_century/manager_and_machine (last visited July 14, 2015).

[17] This assumes, very conservatively, that people below the age of 29 wear glasses at the same rates as those above 65.

information it receives is skewed and to correct for this, or at least flag it, but its architects would need to be aware of these possibilities to avoid these kinds of results.

Workplace Safety and Automation

Cognitive computing's ability to analyze motion and streaming data to interpret what is happening in the physical world has obvious applications to workplace safety and management. The simplest example is using cognitive computing software to interpret a continuous stream of video and audio to identify illegal activities occurring there. Just as cognitive computers might be used to identify intruders on the jobsite and to distinguish between an unauthorized person and a rabbit, this software may be able to identify dangerous activity, such as failing to wear Occupational Safety and Health Administration-required safety gear, or sexual harassment occurring over email or even in person. This could make it possible for managers to intervene earlier to head off discrimination or injury.

While cognitive computing could become the focus of discrimination claims, it could also help to reduce workplace discrimination. Cognitive computers could be used to identify disparate impacts resulting from their very own insight algorithms. One interviewee in an article in *Fortune* noted, "If machine learning algorithms working on big data result in racial discrimination, then other algorithms can measure the effect of discrimination."[18]

Cognitive computing could eventually streamline the employment law process by making answers about the law easier for employers to obtain. If cognitive systems are able to produce results of comparable quality to those produced by human researchers, they could obviate the role of lawyers as advisors in some instances.

Gathering and Using Big Data in the Hiring and Selection Process

Background Data

The application and scope of the Fair Credit Report Act ("FCRA") is often confusing.[19] Even the Act's name is misleading because the FCRA governs many kinds of background check reports, not just true credit reports from one of the credit bureaus (*e.g.*, Experian, Trans Union, and Equifax). Add Big Data to this mix, where online employers or their Big Data companies can have virtually instant access to a wealth of information on employees and applicants, and the FCRA's application becomes even more complicated.

---

[18] http://fortune.com/2015/01/15/will-big-data-help-end-discrimination-or-make-it-worse/ (last visited July 14, 2015).
[19] 15 U.S.C. § 1681 *et seq.*

When employers use Big Data to obtain information for "employment purposes," the same FCRA strictures may apply along with the same risks, including potential class-action exposure for noncompliance.[20]

To summarize, the FCRA is widely known as the federal law that regulates the exchange of consumer credit information between credit bureaus and creditors in connection with mortgage lending and other consumer credit transactions (*e.g.,* true credit reports). By its terms, however, the FCRA also regulates the exchange of information between *employers* and "consumer reporting agencies"[21] (CRAs) that provide "consumer reports"[22] (*i.e.,* background reports). The obligations the FCRA imposes on employers are *not only* triggered when an employer orders a credit report from a CRA, but the employers must also comply with the FCRA when they order virtually any type of consumer report from a CRA, including criminal and motor vehicle record checks.

The FCRA typically does not apply when an employer *itself,* without engaging a CRA, obtains criminal and other background information directly from its primary source, such as when an employer procures publicly available court records.[23] Following this concept, up until the last few years, it remained uncertain whether employers could perform in-house internet research on applicants and employees without triggering the FCRA. Recent actions by the Federal Trade Commission (FTC)[24] in the Big Data context and court decisions taking expansive views of the FCRA's definitions of "consumer reports" and "CRAs" have suggested that this may no longer be the case (at least in the eyes of the FTC) depending on *how* that research is performed.

Given the swelling tide of FCRA class action litigation against employers and other risks from noncompliance with the FCRA, it is important for employers to

---

[20] 15 U.S.C. § 1681a(h) ("The term 'employment purposes'... means a report used for the purpose of evaluating a consumer for employment, promotion, reassignment, or retention as an employee.").

[21] 15 U.S.C. § 1681a(f) ("The term 'consumer reporting agency' means any person which, for monetary fees, dues, or on a cooperative nonprofit basis, regularly engages in whole or in part in the practice of assembling or evaluating consumer credit information or other information on consumers for the purpose of furnishing consumer reports to third parties, and which uses any means or facility of interstate commerce for the purpose of preparing or furnishing consumer reports.").

[22] 15 U.S.C. § 1681a(d) ("Consumer reports are any written, oral or other communication of any information by a consumer reporting agency bearing on a consumer's credit worthiness, credit standing, credit capacity, character, general reputation, personal characteristics, or mode of living, which is used or expected to be used or collected in whole or in part for the purpose of serving as a factor in establishing the consumer's eligibility for ... employment purposes."). "The term 'employment purposes'... means a report used for the purpose of evaluating a consumer for employment, promotion, reassignment or retention as an employee." 15 U.S.C. § 1681a(h).

[23] *But see* Cal. Civ. Code § 1786.53, which is one of the rare laws that may apply as to certain, defined "public records" even if no CRA is used to assemble the information.

[24] The sometimes controversial Consumer Financial Protection Bureau (CFPB) now shares oversight of the FCRA with the FTC. *See* Rod M. Fliegel and Jennifer Mora, *Employers Must Update FCRA Notices for Their Background Check Programs Before January 1, 2013,* Littler Insight (Sept. 4, 2012) available at www.littler.com/publication-press/publication/employers-must-update-fcra-notices-their-background-check-programs-jan.

understand the potential pitfalls in this area.[25] Even when employers think in-house searches are not subject to the FCRA, they could still inadvertently trigger the Act. The line will continue to be drawn as district courts continue to wrestle with how the FCRA may be implicated in new methods of information sharing and otherwise. This section summarizes FCRA obligations on employers that use consumer reports, summarizes recent FCRA trends in the Big Data context, and provides practical insights for mitigating the risks that have developed from those trends.

Summary of FCRA Obligations on Employers That Use Consumer Reports

The FCRA imposes requirements on employers who use "consumer reports" or "investigative consumer reports" for employment purposes.[26] A consumer report is known as a credit report or a background report prepared by a CRA, whereas an investigative consumer report is a special type of consumer report whereby the CRA obtains information through *personal* interviews (*e.g.*, an in-depth reference check).[27]

Before an employer may obtain a consumer report from a CRA, typically it must make a "clear and conspicuous" written disclosure to the consumer in a document that consists "solely" of the disclosure.[28] The applicant or employee must provide written permission for the employer to obtain a consumer report.[29] The employer must also make a certification to the CRA regarding its "permissible

---

[25] For a detailed discussion of the class action risks employers face under the FCRA, *see* Rod Fliegel, Jennifer Mora, and William Simmons, *The Swelling Tide of Fair Credit Reporting Act (FCRA) Class Actions: Practical Risk-Mitigating Measures for Employers*, Littler Report (Aug. 1, 2014) available at www.littler.com/publication-press/publication/swelling-tide-fair-credit-reporting-act-fcra-class-actions-practical-r.

[26] For a detailed discussion of the FCRA's requirements, *see* Rod Fliegel and Jennifer Mora, *The FTC Staff Report on "40 Years of Experience with the Fair Credit Reporting Act" Illuminates Areas of Potential Class Action Exposure for Employers*, Littler Report (Dec. 12, 2011), available at www.littler.com/publication-press/publication/ftc-staff-report-40-years-experience-fair-credit-reporting-act-illumin.

[27] 15 U.S.C. §§ 1681a(d) and (e).

[28] 15 U.S.C. § 1681b(b). But *see* 15 U.S.C. § 1681a(y) (related rules for misconduct investigations) and 15 U.S.C. § 1681b(b)(2)(B)(i) (different disclosure requirements for certain commercial drivers regulated by the federal Department of Transportation). If the employer procures an "investigative consumer report," additional disclosures are necessary. The employer must allow the employee to request information about the "nature and scope" of the investigation, and the employer must respond in writing to any such request within five days. 15 U.S.C. § 168 *ld*.

[29] 15 U.S.C. §§ 1681b(a)(3)(B) and 1681b(b). For Department of Transportation-regulated motor carriers, and where the applicant applies for employment by mail, telephone, computer, or other similar means, consent may be oral, written, or electronic. 15 U.S.C. § 1681b(b)(2)(B)(ii). In addition, the FTC issued an opinion letter in 2001 indicating that it believed that a "consumer's consent is not invalid merely because it is communicated in electronic form," under the FCRA. *See* FTC Opinion Letter May 24, 2001 (Brinckerhoff).

purpose" for the report and its compliance with relevant FCRA provisions and state and federal equal opportunity laws.[30]

After obtaining the consumer report or investigative consumer report on an employee or applicant, an employer must follow certain requirements *if* it intends to take "adverse action" against the applicant or employee based even in part on the contents of the report.[31] First, *before* the employer implements the adverse action against the applicant or employee, the employer must provide a "preadverse action" notice to the individual, which must include a copy of the consumer report and the statutory Summary of Rights.[32] This requirement affords the applicant or employee with an opportunity to discuss the report with the employer before the employer takes adverse action.[33] If the employer ultimately decides to take an adverse action against the applicant or employee, it must then provide to the individual an adverse action notice with certain information specified in the FCRA.[34]

Recent trends in FCRA enforcement in the Big Data context and decisions expansively interpreting the FCRA's definitions of "consumer reports" and "CRAs" have changed the traditional perception of how the foregoing employer obligations may be triggered.

---

[30] 15 U.S.C. § 1681b.

[31] An adverse action broadly includes "a denial of employment or any other decision for employment purpose that adversely affects any current or prospective employee." 15 U.S.C. § 1681a(k)(l)(B)(ii).

[32] 15 U.S.C. § 1681b(b). If an individual contacts the employer in response to the pre-adverse action notice to say there was a mistake (inaccuracy or incompleteness) in the consumer report, the employer may exercise its discretion whether to move forward with the hiring decision or engagement; the FCRA does not dictate a course of action. DOT-regulated motor carriers are not required to provide a "pre-adverse action" notice to applicants or employees if the applicant applied for employment by mail, telephone, computer or other similar means. 15 U.S.C. § 1681b(b)(3)(B). Rather, motor carriers must provide to the individual, within three days of taking adverse action, an oral, written or electronic notification that adverse action has been taken, which must include the same disclosures required in "adverse action" notices for non-trucking employers. Id.

[33] Obabueki v. IBM and Choicepoint, Inc., 145 F. Supp. 2d 371, 392 (S.D.N.Y. 2001). The text of the FCRA does not dictate the minimum amount of time an employer must wait between mailing the pre-adverse action and adverse action notices. One fairly accepted standard is five business days. *See, e.g.,* Beverly v. Wal-Mart Stores, Inc., No. 3:07cv469 (E.D. Va. 2008); *see* also Johnson v. ADP Screening and Selection Services, 768 F. Supp. 2d 979, 983–984 (D. Minn. 2011).

[34] 15 U.S.C. § 1681m(a) (requiring employers to provide: (1) the name, address and telephone number of the CRA that provided the report; (2) a statement the CRA did not make the adverse decision and is not able to explain why the decision was made; (3) a statement setting forth the person's right to obtain a free disclosure of his or her report from the CRA if he or she makes a request for such a disclosure within 60 days; and, (4) a statement setting forth the person's right to dispute directly with the CRA the accuracy or completeness of any information in the report).

Big Data Enforcement Trends and Potential Impact on Employer Obligations under the FCRA

The FTC has recently expanded the view of what constitutes a CRA. Traditionally, CRAs were thought of as major credit bureaus or background screening companies compiling and generating hard copy reports for employers on specific applicants and employees. The FTC has gone beyond that traditional notion, finding that certain online data brokers and even mobile application developers were acting as CRAs without adhering to the strictures of the FCRA. Because at least some of these companies may now be considered CRAs (depending on the range and nature of their product offerings), the information employers obtain from them may also be considered consumer reports.[35] This, in turn, potentially would trigger the employer's obligations under the FCRA for procuring and using such reports for employment purposes.

The FTC filed an administrative complaint against two companies that developed mobile applications by allowing users to conduct unlimited searches of criminal history information on individuals.[36] The companies had *specific* disclaimers that the information from the apps should not be considered employment screening tools and were not covered by the FCRA. The FTC found the disclaimers ineffective, noting that the companies also and concurrently had *advertising,* suggesting that the apps could be used to screen potential employees.[37] The FTC considered the companies to be CRAs, subject to the FCRA, and in violation of the FCRA.[38]

---

[35] Several courts have also adopted expansive views of what constitutes a consumer report under the FCRA, going beyond traditional notions of a paper report compiled and provided by a background screening company. *See* Ernst v. Dish Network, LLC, 49 F.Supp.3d 377 (S.D.N.Y. 2014) (finding that the report at issue was a consumer report even though the named defendant did not use the report for employment purposes); Dunford v. American Data Bank, LLC, No. C 13-03829 WHA (N.D. Cal. Aug. 12, 2014) (finding that the report at issue was a consumer report under the FCRA even though the CRA provided it only to the consumer herself and not to any prospective employer or other person).

[36] In the Matter of Filiquarian Publishing, et al., FTC Matter/File Number 112 3195 (filed Jan. 10, 2013) available at www.ftc.gov/enforcement/cases-proceedings/112-3195/filiquarian-publishing-llc-choice-level-llc-joshua-linsk.

[37] *See* Federal Trade Commission, Analysis of Proposed Consent Order to Aid Public Comment in the Matter of Filiquarian Publishing, LLC; Choice Level, LLC; and Joshua Linsk, individually and as an officer of the companies, (File No. 112 3195) available at www.ftc.gov/enforcement/cases-proceedings/112-3195/filiquarian-publishing-llc-choice-level-llc-joshua-linsk.

[38] Although the FTC did not impose monetary penalties on these companies, it did require them to follow stringent reporting and records preservation requirements to establish their compliance with the FCRA for several years after the matter was resolved.

In another action, the FTC sued a data broker that compiled information profiles on individuals from internet and social media sources.[39] The FTC alleged that the data broker *marketed* the profiles on a subscription basis to human resource professionals, job recruiters, and others as an employment screening tool. The FTC further asserted the company was a CRA and the profiles were consumer reports.[40] The matter was resolved with the company paying $800,000 to the FTC.[41] This case illustrates how murky this area can be, as the data broker arguably was nothing more than a search engine, like Google. One difference was the data broker provided *targeted* searches of individuals' online identities, whereas a person can search for anything on Google.

Although the FTC targeted data brokers in these cases, the agency's actions arguably have significant implications for many employers. Because the FTC considered the data brokers to be CRAs, the information they were providing also would be considered a consumer report. Any employer using that information to make hiring decisions arguably would have been obligated to provide a disclosure to the applicant that it would be seeking the information and obtain the applicant's authorization before viewing the information. The employer also arguably would have had to provide the preadverse and adverse notices if it denied the applicant employment based even in part on the information. Most employers may not think that the FCRA would even apply when they obtain information through internet data brokers like the ones discussed earlier. The FTC's position, as one view of the law, indicates otherwise.

An example further illustrates the blurred line between triggering the FCRA and not triggering the FCRA in the world of Big Data. Suppose an internal recruiter for an employer goes to the Facebook and Instagram pages of an applicant and decides not to hire him or her because of offensive posts and inappropriate Instagram photos. The employer arguably did not trigger the FCRA because it went directly to the separate sources of information without any third party compiling the information for the employer. Suppose instead that the same internal recruiter had an account to a website that compiled the same Facebook and Instagram pages for the applicant

---

[39] United States of America v. Spokeo, Inc., U.S. District Court Case No. 12-cv-05001 (C.D. Cal. filed June 7, 2012).

[40] *See id.*; *see also* FTC Staff Closing Letter to Renee Jackson (May 9, 2011) available at www. ftc.gov/enforcement/cases-proceedings/closing-letters-and-other-public-statements/staff-closing-letters?title=Social+Intelligence&field_matter_number_value=&field_document_description=&date_filter%5Bmin%5D%5Bdate%5D=&date_filter%5Bmax%5D%5Bdate %5D=&=Apply (finding that a similar data broker that compiled information from social networking sites was a consumer reporting agency).

[41] *See* Federal Trade Commission, Press Release: Spokeo to Pay $800,000 to Settle FTC Charges Company Allegedly Marketed Information to Employers and Recruiters in Violation of FCRA (June 12, 2012) available at www.ftc.gov/news-events/press-releases/2012/06/ spokeo-pay-800000-settle-ftc-charges-company-allegedly-marketed.

in one place, and the recruiter logged into the account to view the information. The recruiter is viewing the exact same information as in the first example, but this conduct could trigger the employer's FCRA obligations because the information may have been compiled by a CRA under the FTC's expansive view of that term.

Mitigating Measures

There are several practical steps employers can take to mitigate the risks of noncompliance with the FCRA in the Big Data context, including the following:

1. Employers should consider reviewing their current policies and practices regarding employment-purposed internet searches by recruiters and other personnel, including those with direct involvement in the hiring process, such as managers and supervisors.
2. Employers should also consider taking steps to help ensure that they have provided the required disclosure and have a signed authorization from applicants and employees before they obtain background information that may be subject to the FCRA.[42] (Likewise as to efforts to comply with state and local laws, which are beyond the scope of this section.)
3. Employers should consider sending or arranging to send preadverse and adverse action notices whenever they take adverse action against job applicants and employees based, in whole or in part, on background information compiled by any third-party.

In the age of Big Data, employers have instantaneous access to information on employees and applicants. When employers use Big Data for employment purposes, the same FCRA strictures may apply along with the same risks for noncompliance. Employers should be mindful of recent developments expanding the FCRA's application into the world of Big Data, and should consider taking measures to mitigate the risks associated with that expansion.

---

[42] An exemption to the FCRA's coverage, added a decade ago in the Fair and Accurate Credit Transactions Act Amendment (FACTA), provides that if a communication from a CRA is made to an employer in connection with an investigation of either "suspected misconduct" or compliance with "Federal, State, or local laws and regulations, the rules of a self-regulatory organization, or any preexisting written policies of the employer" the communication is not a "consumer report." Under this exception, an employer does not have to provide the required disclosure or obtain authorization to obtain a consumer report when conducting these types of investigations. FACTA still requires that employers provide a "summary containing the nature and substance of the communication" after taking an adverse action against an individual based on the communication. For a detailed discussion of the FACTA, *see* Rod Fliegel, Jennifer Mora and William Simmons, Fair Credit Reporting Act Amendment Offers Important Protections rom Lawsuits Targeting Background Check Programs, Littler Report (Sep. 10, 2013) available at www.littler.com/publication-press/publication/fair-credit-reporting-act-amendment-offers-important-protections.

How Big Data Affects the Numbers: OFCCP and EEOC Implications

Investigations by both the Equal Employment Opportunity Commission (EEOC) and the Office of Federal Contract Compliance Programs frequently are numbers driven, particularly when allegations concern disparities in hiring, promotion, pay, or terminations. Investigators are trained to obtain data regarding the decision-making process that is challenged and to subject that data to elementary statistical analyses, as explained in the agencies' compliance manuals. This often is referred to as "standard deviation analysis," because the statistic on which the decision to accept or reject the null hypothesis of "no adverse impact" is based on the number of "standard deviations" by which the estimated disparity between the protected and favored group differs from zero.[43]

An alternative measure of an adverse impact derives from the Uniform Guidelines on Employee Selection Procedures (UGESP).[44] These guidelines suggest that

> A selection rate for any race, sex, or ethnic group which is less than four-fifths (4/5) (or eighty percent) of the rate for the group with the highest rate will generally be regarded by the Federal enforcement agencies as evidence of adverse impact, while a greater than four-fifths rate will generally not be regarded by Federal enforcement agencies as evidence of adverse impact.[45]

These alternatives do not necessarily yield the same result. That is, an employer may select members of a disfavored group at a rate below 80 percent of the favored group, yet the disparity may not be statistically significant. On the other hand, a result may be statistically significant but the selection ratio may be greater than 80 percent. The parties, of course, can be expected to advocate the test that puts their data in the most favorable light. Courts have been less predictable, but it is fair to say that the majority have advocated statistical significance as the litmus test for determining when a disparity is materially different and therefore legally meaningful.[46]

Citations to the line of cases that supply the "two standard deviation" criterion employed by most courts generally begin with the U.S. Supreme Court's decision in *Castaneda v. Partida*.[47] Yet *Castaneda* was not an employment discrimination

---

[43] Watson v. Ft. Worth Bank & Trust, 487 U.S. 977, 995 (1988).

[44] 29 C.F.R. § 1607.

[45] 29 C.F.R. § 1607.4(D).

[46] But *see, e.g.*, Matrixx Initiatives, Inc. v. Siracusano, 131 S. Ct. 1309, 1321 (2011) (factors other than statistical significance must be considered in determining materiality); and Clady v. Los Angeles Co., 770 F.2d 1421, 1428 (9th Cir. 1985) (rejecting the 80% test), cert. denied, 475 U.S. 1109 (1986).

[47] 430 U.S. 482 (1977).

case, much less a disparate impact case. At issue was whether a South Texas county's method of convening a grand jury unfairly excluded Mexican-Americans, resulting in the discriminatory adjudication of Mexican-American defendants in criminal cases.[48]

In reviewing this claim, the Court compared the percentage of Mexican-Americans among those summoned to serve on the county's grand juries, to Mexican-American representation in the county's eligible population. The Court noted that there were only 339 Mexican-Americans among 870 grand jurors summoned during the relevant timeframe, and that strictly proportional representation would have seated 688 Mexican-American grand jurors.[49] The Court considered this disparity of nearly 100 percent to be material, observing that "if the difference between the expected value and the observed number is greater than two or three standard deviations, then the hypothesis... would be suspect to a social scientist."[50] Yet in *Castaneda*, the difference between the actual and expected number of Mexican-American grand jurors was approximately 29 standard deviations.[51] Based in part on that comparison, the Court affirmed the district court's finding that Mexican-Americans discriminatorily were excluded from grand jury service.[52]

The Court again referenced the benchmark of "two or three standard deviations" in *Hazelwood School District v. United States*.[53] *Hazelwood* was a pattern and practice suit alleging that a school district engaged in the discriminatory hiring of African-American teachers.[54] The Court compared the percentage of teachers in the district who were African-Americans to the percentage in the relevant labor market. Noting that the disparity exceeded six standard deviations in one year and five standard deviations in the following year, the Court concluded that the statistical evidence reflected a "gross" disparity that was probative of a pattern and practice of discrimination.[55] Relying in part upon this finding, the Court remanded the case

---

[48] Id. at 482.

[49] Id. at 496 n.17.

[50] Id.

[51] Id. "The 'standard deviation' is a unit of measurement that allows statisticians to measure all types of disparities in common terms. Technically, a 'standard deviation' is defined as 'a measure of spread, dispersion, or variability of a group of numbers equal to the square root of the variance of that group of numbers.'" Palmer v. Shultz, 815 F.2d 84, 92 n.7 (1987) (quoting David Baldus & James Cole, Statistical Proof of Discrimination 359 (1980)). Case law often erroneously interchanges this term with the more technically appropriate term, "standard error," which describes the distribution of sample estimators, such as the mean, around its true value. *See* David H. Kaye & David A. Freedman, Reference Guide on Statistics, Federal Judicial Center, Reference Manual on Scientific Evidence 174 (2d ed. 2000).

[52] *Castenada*, 430 U.S. at 517.

[53] 433 U.S. 299, 308 n.14 (1977).

[54] Id. at 299.

[55] Id. at 308 n.14.

with instructions that the district court crafts an acceptable remedy, which was to include injunctive as well as other equitable relief.

In *Watson v. Fort Worth Bank & Trust*, Justice O'Connor reviewed the Court's statistical criteria in employment-discrimination cases.[56] Although she acknowledged the prevalence of the *Castaneda-Hazelwood* test of "two or three standard deviations," she noted that the Court never instructed lower courts to apply the standard mechanistically.[57] Rather, courts should evaluate statistical evidence in relation to the disputed issues and determine the appropriateness of such evidence case-by-case. Justice O'Connor observed:

> We have emphasized the useful role that statistical methods can have in Title VII cases, but we have not suggested that any particular number of "standard deviations" can determine whether a plaintiff has made out a prima facie case in the complex area of employment discrimination. Nor has a consensus developed around any alternative mathematical standard. Instead courts appear generally to have judged the "significance" or "substantiality" of numerical disparities on a case-by-case basis. At least at this stage of the law's development, we believe that such a case-by-case approach properly reflects our recognition that statistics "come in infinite variety and... their usefulness depends on all of the surrounding facts and circumstances."[58]

Nevertheless, many lower courts have adopted the *Castaneda-Hazelwood* criterion of "two or three standard deviations" as a bright-line rule. In doing so, they have noted that this criterion, when applied to the commonly assumed bell-shaped, normal distribution corresponds to the 0.05 level of "statistical significance" prevalent in the scientific literature.[59] This criterion—the 5 percent probability threshold—corresponds, in turn, to the probability of "Type I error," the probability of mistakenly rejecting the null hypothesis of nondiscrimination when it is true. Generally, the lower the probability of Type I error, the more confident the researcher is that he or she is not mistakenly claiming a statistical finding to be important. The Seventh Circuit has explained:

> In addition to describing statistical significance in terms of levels of standard deviation, statistical significance also may be expressed as a probability value (P) on a continuous or relative scale ranging from 0 to

---

[56] 487 U.S. 977 (1988).

[57] Id. at 995 n.3.

[58] Id. (internal citations omitted).

[59] In *Castaneda*, the Supreme Court noted that, when dealing with large numbers, social scientists reject the "hypothesis of equality"—that the chances of an event are "equally" likely to result from chance or a proposed cause—if a disparity between actual and expected representation exceeds two or three standard deviations. 430 U.S. at 496 n.17.

1.0. The level of statistical significance rises as the value of the (P) level declines... A (P) value below .05 is generally considered to be statistically significant, i.e., when there is less than a 5% probability that the disparity was due to chance. For large samples, statistical significance at a level in the range below 0.05 or 0.01 is "essentially equivalent" to significance at the 2 or 3 standard deviation level.[60]

This reasoning has led many courts to adopt a *per se* rule that statistical evidence failing to meet the 0.05 level of significance is inadmissible.[61]

For example, in *Palmer v. Shultz*, the U.S. Court of Appeals for the District of Columbia Circuit extensively considered the rather esoteric question of whether it should apply a one-tailed or two-tailed test of statistical significance.[62] Its decision to apply the two-tailed test ultimately was outcome-determinative and led to rejecting the plaintiff's statistical evidence.[63] Similarly, in *Bennett v. Total Minatome Corp*, the Fifth Circuit explicitly discussed the relationship between the number of standard deviations, and the "*p*-value"—the probability of Type I error associated with that disparity.[64] It reaffirmed its rule that only statistical results corresponding to a *p*-value of 0.05 or less are admissible. In the same vein, the Eleventh Circuit has opined:

> The "general rule" is that the disparity must be "greater than two or three standard deviations" before it can be inferred that the employer has engaged in illegal discrimination under Title VII. The Court has also called that sort of imbalance a "gross statistical disparit[y]."[65]

Whether the 80-percent rule or the statistical significance test is likely to favor either party depends in large measure on the number of decisions at issue. Other

---

[60] *Griffin v. Bd. of Regents of Regency Univs.*, 795 F.2d 1281, 1291 n.19 (7th Cir. 1986) (citing *Coates v. Johnson & Johnson*, 756 F.2d 524, 537 n.13 (7th Cir. 1985)).

[61] *See, e.g., Bennett v. Total Minatome Corp.*, 138 F.3d 1053, 1062 (5th Cir. 1998).

[62] *Palmer*, 815 F.2d 84, 92 (D.C. Cir. 1987).

[63] Id. at 94–95.

[64] *Total Minatome*, 138 F.3d at 1062 (and cases cited therein).

[65] *Peightal v. Metropolitan Dade Co.*, 940 F.2d 1394, 1406 (11th Cir. 1991) (internal citations omitted), cert. denied, 502 U.S. 1073 (1992) (citing: *Casteneda*, 430 U.S. at 497 n.17; *Hazelwood*, 433 U.S. at 308; and *City of Richmond v. J.A. Croson Co.*, 488 U.S. 469, 501 (1989)). *See also Smith v. Xerox Corp.*, 196 F.3d 358, 364–366 (2d Cir. 1999) (finding that a disparity of two or three standard deviations equals a gross statistical disparity); *Ottaviani v. State Univ. of N.Y. at New Paltz*, 875 F.2d 365, 370–374 (2d Cir. 1989) (same), cert. denied, 493 U.S. 1021 (1990); *Palmer*, 815 F.2d at 96–97 (same); *NAACP v. Town of East Haven*, 892 F. Supp. 46, 48, 50–51 (D. Conn. 1995) (same).

things the same, the greater the number of decisions, the greater the statistical significance of any disparity:[66]

> For example, if the average wage rate is $10.00 per hour, a wage differential between men and women of $0.10 per hour is likely to be deemed practically insignificant because the differential represents only 1% ($0.10/$10.00) of the average wage rate. That same difference could be statistically significant, however, if a sufficiently large sample of men and women was studied. The reason is that statistical significance is determined, in part, by the number of observations in the data set.[67]

As a result, small employers whose selection disparities are below 80 percent, suggesting a legally meaningful difference, are prone to emphasize that the disparity is not statistically significant. In contrast, a large employer, by virtue of the number of decisions analyzed, is likely to advocate the 80-percent rule, because with enough data even numerically small differences may be statistically significant. Accordingly, as employers have grown and the data available for analysis has increased, plaintiffs and the government have urged that statistical significance is the standard by which disparities should be evaluated, rather than the agencies' own rule of thumb.

Big Data pushes this statistical framework to its limits and perhaps beyond. As more and more data is brought to bear on the selection process, disparities between demographic groups are bound to become increasingly significant, in the statistical sense, as a natural consequence of super-sized databases. At the extreme, even differences most would find negligible nevertheless may exceed the "two standard deviation" criterion. A prominent example is the statistical analysis reported in *Wal-Mart Stores, Inc. v. Dukes*, which considers one of the largest data sets to be analyzed in an employment discrimination suit.[68] In his comparison of pay differences between men and women, the plaintiffs' expert reported a standard deviation of one-tenth of one percent. The implication is that a gender difference in pay of just two-tenths of a percent—the difference between a male employee paid $10 per hour and a female paid $9.99 per hour would be judged "statistically significant."

---

[66] "[L]arger sample sizes give more reliable results with greater precision and [statistical] power..." The Importance and Effect of Sample Size, Select Statistical Services, www.select-statistics. co.uk/ article/blog-post/the-importance-and-effect-of-sample-size.

[67] *See* Daniel L. Rubenfeld, Reference Guide on Multiple Regression, Federal Judicial Center, Reference Manual on Scientific Evidence 191 (2d ed. 2000).

[68] 131 S. Ct. 2541 (2011). In this suit, the nationwide class consisted of approximately 1.5 million female employees. Id. at 2544.

When data sets grow to that size, statistical criteria risk trivializing the important question of what may constitute discrimination.[69]

After decades of increasing comfort and growing sophistication with statistical criteria, courts now have to confront the problem that the criteria for identifying discrimination honed in a small-data world may be unhelpful in a world of Big Data. Precisely because it is "big," Big Data makes it highly likely that any difference between demographic groups in selection rates, be it with respect to promotion, hiring, or termination, will be statistically significant no matter how slight. A reasonable response by the courts may be to resurrect a rule of thumb—an arbitrary, but reasonable, threshold for determining when a disparity is of legal consequence.

Rules of thumb are common in cases of age discrimination litigation. For example, several circuits have declared that disparities in the treatment of employees who differ by less than five, six, or even eight years are not probative of discrimination.[70] Analogously, the Eighth Circuit holds that reductions in force that fail to reduce the percentage of the workforce aged 40 and older by more than 4 percentage points are *per se* not discriminatory.[71] Although courts are receptive to statistical proof beyond those thresholds, these standards of proof reflect the view of many courts that, notwithstanding statistical significance, minimal differences lack probative value and should be ignored. More generally, perhaps it is time to revive the 80-percent threshold of the Uniform Guidelines and recognize that, in the era of Big Data, statistical significance is the norm and therefore a poor indicator of legal relevance.

---

[69] *See, e.g.*, Mark Kelson, Significantly misleading, Significance Magazine (Oct. 22, 2013), www.statslife.org.uk/the-statistics-dictionary/1000-the-statistics-dictionary-significantly-misleading ("Imagine if an environmentalist said that oil contamination was detectable in a sample of water from a protected coral reef. The importance of that statement would change drastically depending on whether they were referring to a naked-eye assessment of a water sample or an electron microscope examination. The smaller the amount of oil, the harder we would have to look. The same is true for a clinical study that detects a statistically significant treatment effect. If the study is huge, then issues of statistical significance become unimportant, since even tiny and clinically unimportant differences can be found to be statistically significant.").

[70] *See, e.g.*, *Holowecki v. Fed. Exp. Corp.*, 644 F. Supp. 2d 338, 357–358 (S.D.N.Y. 2009) aff'd, 392 F. App'x 42 (2d Cir. 2010) (vague allegations of preferential treatment to someone three years younger is insufficient to give rise to inference of age discrimination as matter of law); *Grosjean v. First Energy Corp.*, 349 F.3d 332, 339 (6th Cir. 2003) (adopting bright-line rule that "in the absence of direct evidence that the employer considered age to be significant, an age difference of six years or less between an employee and a replacement is not significant"); *Aliotta v. Bair*, 576 F. Supp. 2d 113, 125 n.6 (D.C. Cir. 2008) (age difference of seven years insignificant without further evidence showing age was a determining factor) (citing *Dunaway v. Int'l Bhd. Of Teamsters*, 310 F.3d 758, 767 (D.C. Cir. 2002)).

[71] *See Clark v. Matthews Intern. Corp.*, 639 F.3d 391, 399 (8th Cir. 2011).

Big Data and the Americans with Disabilities Act

The Americans with Disabilities Act of 1990 ("ADA") as amended by the ADA Amendments Act of 2008,[72] poses special challenges for Big Data. Unlike other antidiscrimination laws that merely prohibit certain conduct, the ADA imposes affirmative obligations on employers.[73] Yet, the statute and its regulations reflect the screening and hiring processes as they were configured over 20 years ago. The regulations require employers:

> to select and administer tests concerning employment in the most effective manner to ensure that, when a test is administered to a job applicant or employee who has a disability that impairs, sensory, manual or speaking skills, the test results accurately reflect the skills, aptitude or whatever other factor of the applicant or employee that the test purports measure, rather than reflecting the impaired sensory, manual, or speaking skills of such employee or applicant....[74]

The Interpretive Guidance explains: "The intent of this provision is to further emphasize that individuals with disabilities are not to be excluded from jobs that they can actually perform merely because a disability prevents them from taking a test, or negatively influences the results of a test, that is a prerequisite to the job."[75]

Big Data does not easily fit within this regulation for at least two reasons. First, one of the advantages claimed for Big Data is that the information input into its algorithms is gleaned from activities engaged in voluntarily by individuals, which frequently are unrelated to any work requirement.[76] Thus, Big Data may use visits to particular websites to screen applicants, but that type of activity is not traditionally regarded as a test.

---

[72] 42 U.S.C. § 12101, *et seq.* (2009).

[73] Employers have a duty to engage an employee or applicant in the interactive process to determine whether the employee or applicant with a known disability can perform a position's essential functions with reasonable accommodations. 42 U.S.C. §§ 12111(8), (9), 12112(a) & (b)(5) (2009); 29 C.F.R. §§ 1630.2(o), 1630.9 & Pt. 1630, App. §§ 1630.2(o) & 1630.9; *Humphrey v. Memorial Hosps. Ass'n*, 239 F. 3d 1128, 1137 (9th Cir. 2001) ("Once an employer becomes aware of the need for accommodation, that employer has a mandatory obligation under the ADA to engage in an interactive process with the employee to identify and implement appropriate reasonable accommodations."); *see Equal Employment Opportunity Comm'n v. Sears, Roebuck & Co.*, 417 F. 3d 789, 805–808 (7th Cir. 2005).

[74] 42 U.S.C.§ 12112(b)(7) (2009).

[75] Section 1630.11 Administration of Tests, 29 C.F.R. Pt. 1630.

[76] *See e.g., How Big Data is Taking Recruiters from "I Think" to "I Know."* Theundercoverrecruiter. com, available at http://theundercoverrecruiter.com/big-data-recruiters/ (last visited July 14, 2015).

Second, because some of the information relied upon by Big Data is generated by individuals in the normal course of living, they are unaware their extracurricular activities may be the basis on which their suitability for a position will be judged. Disabled individuals, impaired in the activities monitored by Big Data, cannot request reasonable accommodations if they are unaware how they are being screened. On the other hand, an employer also may not know that an applicant, whose data has been gleaned from the web, has an impairment that might require accommodation. Not only may the employer be unaware the applicant is disabled but may also be ignorant of the behaviors tracked by Big Data that influence how an applicant is assessed. Although it is unfair to require employers to accommodate unknown disabilities, it is equally unfair to base hiring decisions on criteria that reflect an applicant's disability. However, unless a "test" is construed to include Big Data algorithms and applicants are informed of their elements, disabled applicants may be denied reasonable accommodation in the application process.

The ADA provides disabled individuals a cause of action regarding policies and practices that have a disparate impact,[77] but that theory may be unsuited to litigating questions of reasonable accommodation. The disabled are a heterogeneous group and the elements of an employer's Big Data algorithm that affect one disabled applicant may have no impact on other disabled applicants. As a result, the paucity of numbers might not permit a disabled applicant to prove a class-wide impact. Indeed, there are few reported cases of a successful disparate impact claim under the ADA.[78] In contrast, a disabled applicant is entitled to a reasonable accommodation[79] irrespective of how anyone else is affected by a particular facet of the screening procedure.

A potential solution is to require Big Data to disclose the data input into its algorithms, so disabled applicants have notice of the activities that are monitored. However, these algorithms are proprietary and reflect extensive development efforts by Big Data. Public disclosure, of course, would greatly devalue this intellectual property. Alternatively, employers might be required to disclose that they premise their employment decisions on data gleaned from external sources. This might trigger a dialogue in which a disabled applicant explains his or her physical or mental limitations, and a reasonable alternative may be to evaluate such candidates independent of the Big Data algorithm.

---

[77] 42 U.S.C. § 12112(b)(3) (2009); *Raytheon Co. v. Hernandez,* 540 U.S. 44, 52 (2003).

[78] *See e.g., McGregor v. National R.R. Passenger Corp.,* 187 F. 3d 1113, 1116 (9th Cir. 1999) (policy requiring employees to be "100% healed" or "fully healed" in order to return to work after an injury is facially discriminatory and constitutes a *per se* violation of the ADA); *Bates v. United Parcel Service, Inc.,* 511 F. 3d 974, 994–995 (9th Cir. 2007) (hearing standards not otherwise mandated by law constitute *per se* violation of the ADA because the policy screens out hearing- impaired individuals who are otherwise qualified to perform the job. Employer therefore has the burden to establish the affirmative defense of business necessity to show that "performance cannot be established by reasonable accommodation.")

[79] 42 U.S.C. § 12112(a), (b)(1) & (b)(5) (2009).

Big Data Use in Performance Management and Discipline

How Invasive Is Too Invasive: Big Data and Privacy in the Workplace

Companies using Big Data in employment (referred to in this section alternately as "Big Data analytics" and "human resources analytics") claim they can increase employee productivity and morale and decrease turnover.[80] While the claims are compelling, employers must address privacy and data security concerns if they engage these services. First, collecting information about employees could potentially violate employees' privacy rights. Second, employers must protect the security of any sensitive information collected about employees. In addition, privacy and data security concerns become quite complex if the employer collects and analyzes the data of international employees.

Privacy

With regard to privacy, federal and state statutes and the common law restrict the information that employers can collect about employees and how they can use it. While these restrictions are particularly onerous when it comes to the collection and use of employees' health information, employers have a surprisingly high degree of latitude with respect to employee data unrelated to health, such as performance and compensation information.

Health Data

Many employers likely would be interested in conducting Big Data analysis on the health of their employees and their employees' family members because employees' and their family members' health can have a significant impact on the employer's bottom line. An employee or an employee's family member with a serious health condition is more expensive to insure. In addition, the employee likely would miss more work due to this condition or his or her performance might suffer. However, employers are effectively precluded from using health information about employees to conduct Big Data analysis, the results of which could be used to make employment decisions.

There are several federal laws designed to protect health information in general, and employee (and their family members') medical information, in particular.[81]

---

[80] Steven Pearlstein, *People analytics: 'Moneyball' for human resources*, Wash. Post, Aug. 1, 2014, available at www.washingtonpost.com/business/people- analytics-moneyball-for-human-resour ces/2014/08/01/3a8fb6ac-1749-11e4-9e3b-7f2f110c6265_story.html (last visited July 14, 2015).

[81] Employers should also be aware of the myriad of state laws that protect employee medical information, such as the California Confidentiality of Medical Information Act, which prohibits employer misuse of medical information. Ca. Civ. Code §§ 56.20–56.245.

These laws recognize that employers may receive health information about employees for a specific purpose and are designed to prevent access to, and use of, that information for a different purpose. The Health Insurance Portability and Accountability Act of 1996 (HIPAA), the Health Information Technology for Economic and Clinical Health Act, and their implementing regulations, are the most comprehensive of these laws. HIPAA regulations govern the use and disclosure of individually identifiable health information and significantly restrict access to information and the ways employers can use the information that becomes available. Companies with self-insured health plans are most directly impacted by HIPAA and require the most comprehensive privacy safeguards to ensure that information used to administer health benefit claims is not utilized for other purposes, including making employment decisions.[82]

The ADA also imposes tight restrictions on the collection and use of employees' health information. The ADA precludes employers from asking applicants and employees about medical conditions or disabilities, with limited exceptions, such as when an employee or applicant is seeking an accommodation. In the case of more intrusive inquiries, such as requiring examinations, the examination must be "job-related and consistent with business necessity."[83] In addition, the results of permitted health exams and other health information collected from employees for purposes of addressing disabilities that impact work must be kept confidential in a file separate from the employees' personnel file and may be disclosed only to very limited categories of individuals within and outside the employer's organization.[84]

The Family Medical Leave Act also has strong privacy protections in that it incorporates, by reference, the ADA's confidentiality language. Consequently, information concerning an employee's request for Family Medical Leave Act leave would be off limits to employers for purposes other than administering leave.[85]

The Genetic Information Nondiscrimination Act (GINA), despite what its name might suggest, protects far more than genetic test results. GINA defines as "genetic information" and protects any information related to the manifestation of a disease or disorder in a family member to the fourth degree.[86] GINA tightly restricts employers' collection and use of genetic information for employment purposes and imposes substantial confidentiality obligations.[87] These restrictions likely would effectively preclude an employer's use of genetic information for Big Data analytics.

---

[82] 45 C.F.R. § 164.504(f)(2)(ii)(C).
[83] 42 U.S.C. § 12112(d)(4).
[84] *See* 42 U.S.C. § 12112(d)(3).
[85] 29 C.F.R. § 825.500(g).
[86] 42 U.S.C. § 2000ff(4); 29§ C.F.R. § 1635.3(c).
[87] *See generally* 42 U.S.C. § 2000ff-1, 2000ff-5.

Information Unrelated to Health

Putting aside employees' health data, employers are becoming interested in compiling and analyzing information other than health information about employees to make better decisions or gain perspective about their current or prospective employees. The following types of data are of particular interest to employers:

■ Compensation information
■ Performance evaluation
■ Job progression
■ Tenure
■ Business expense reimbursement and compliance with reimbursement and documentation policies

Employers generally can use these categories of information about their own employees to conduct Big Data analytics virtually without legal restriction. However, if the employer maintains a privacy policy for employee data, the employer should confirm that any Big Data analytics using this information complies with the employer's own privacy policy.

As human resources data analytics becomes more prevalent, employers may find themselves receiving more requests for the categories of information listed earlier about former employees during calls by a prospective employer of an applicant who is a former employee. While these categories of information generally are not protected by statute or otherwise protected as private, employers considering whether to disclose these categories of information to prospective employers of former employees should consider whether disclosure would be consistent with the Company's own policies about the confidentiality of employee information. For example, disclosing personnel information to prospective employers likely would be inconsistent with a policy that describes personnel records as confidential company property and significantly restricts access to the information in the file.

Looking over the Employee's Shoulder

The past several years have seen massive changes in the rules and attitudes toward privacy and the use of data. While individual privacy may be at an all-time low, the expectations that employers will respect applicants' and employees' personal life are incrementally increasing each year. One illustration of this trend with particular relevant for human resources analytics is the recent wave of "password protection" legislation.

While employers may be interested in using social media content to build profiles of individuals likely to succeed in their workplace, these laws impose substantial limitations on employers' access to online content that is not publicly available. Currently, 21 states have enacted laws aimed at protecting applicants' and employees' personal social media content: Arkansas, California, Colorado, Connecticut, Illinois, Louisiana, Maine, Maryland, Michigan, Nevada, New Hampshire, New Jersey, New Mexico, Oklahoma, Oregon, Rhode Island, Tennessee, Utah, Virginia, Washington, and Wisconsin.[88] All 21 laws prohibit employers from requesting or requiring that applicants or employees[89] disclose their user name, password, or other information needed to access a personal social media account and most of them impose other restrictions on access by employers to personal online content, such as prohibitions on "shoulder surfing." These laws would effectively prohibit employers from "harvesting" nonpublic online content of applicants and employees for purposes of conducting data analytics.

Electronic Communication Review

Employers seeking to gather information from employees' electronic communications for purposes of human resources analytics should also be aware of the restrictions imposed by the federal Stored Communications Act ("SCA"). The SCA prohibits accessing electronic communications stored in a "facility through which an electronic communications service (ECS) is provided."[90] The legislative history identifies telephone companies and email providers as examples of providers of ECS.[91] Over the years, courts have not hesitated to apply the term to new forms of service providers, from internet service providers and bulletin board services[92] to Gmail,[93] Skype,[94] and Facebook.[95] As a result, accessing an employee's messages, for example, those stored in an employee's Gmail account, without permission could violate the SCA.

A crucial point for employers is that the SCA creates an exception for *providers* of an ECS to access communications stored on that own service.[96] This means that employers do not violate the SCA when they access communications stored on electronic communication systems they provide themselves, such as emails on their own company's email server.[97]

---

[88] For more discussion of password protection statutes, *see* Philip L. Gordon & Joon Hwang, *Virginia's Password Protection Law Continues the Trend Toward Increasing Legislative Protection of Personal Online Accounts*, Littler Insight (Mar. 30, 2015) *available at* www.littler. com/publication-press/publication/virginias-password-protection-law-continues-trend-toward-increasing-le#sthash.bo3qapdM.dpuf.

[89] The notable exception is New Mexico, which applies the prohibition only to applicants.

[90] 18 U.S.C. § 2701(a)(1).

[91] S. Rep. No. 99-541, at 14.

[92] *Garcia v. City of Laredo*, 702 F.3d 788, 792 (5th Cir. 2012).

[93] *Lazette v. Kulmatycki*, 949 F.Supp.2d. 748 (N.D. Ohio 2013).

[94] *Snyder v. Fantasy Interactive, Inc.*, No. 11 Civ. 3593 (S.D.N.Y. 2012).

[95] *Crispin v. Christian Audigier, Inc.*, 717 F. Supp. 2d 965, 981–982 (C.D. Cal. 2010).

[96] 18 U.S.C. § 2701(c)(1).

[97] *See, e.g., Fraser v. Nationwide Mut. Ins. Co.*, 352 F.3d 107, 115 (3d Cir. 2003); *Bohach. v. City of Reno*, 932 F. Supp. 1232, 1236 (D. Nev. 1996).

Location Tracking Devices

Collecting data about employees' location, using Global Positioning System ("GPS") technology, involves risks too. Several states have passed laws prohibiting GPS tracking of vehicles without the consent of the vehicle's owner.[98] In addition, employers face risks of common law invasion of privacy claims. The law in this area is just beginning to emerge. However, the Supreme Court held in *U.S. v. Jones* that the government's use of a location-tracking device to track the vehicle of an individual suspected of drug trafficking for one month was an unreasonable search under the Fourth Amendment because it was conducted without a warrant.[99]

The Fourth Amendment does not apply to employee searches conducted by private employers, but the "reasonable expectation of privacy" standard in the common law invasion of privacy tort closely parallels the "reasonable expectation of privacy" standard under the Fourth Amendment.[100] As a result, courts may follow the Supreme Court's decision in *Jones* to find that similar tracking of employees invades their privacy under the common law.

A recent case illustrates how courts may analyze claims based on an employer's use of location-tracking devices. In *Matter of Cunningham v. New York State Dept. of Labor*, the New York Court of Appeals held that agency officials acted unreasonably when they ordered the tracking of an employee's vehicle without his or her knowledge or consent to investigate whether he or she was taking unauthorized absences and falsifying time records.[101] After one month of tracking, the agency terminated the employee for misconduct, based, in part, on the GPS data. The employee later sued, claiming the termination was improper and that the GPS data should not have been collected without his consent. The appellate court found that the agency officials' use of GPS technology was reasonable at the inception because there were "ample" grounds to suspect the employee of submitting false time records.[102] However, the court held that use of GPS was unreasonable in scope because "[i]t examined much activity with which the State had no legitimate concern—*i.e.*, it tracked [the employee] on all evenings, on all weekends, and on vacation."[103] The court noted that the state removed the GPS device twice to replace it with a new device, but did not bother to remove it when the employee was about to start his annual vacation.[104]

---

[98] *See, e.g.*, Cal. Penal Code § 637.7. The California statute, however, creates an exception for a location-tracking device placed by an employer on an employer- owned vehicle. *Id.* at § 637.7(b).

[99] 132 S. Ct. 945 (2012).

[100] *See, e.g.*, *Smyth v. Pillsbury Co.*, 914 F. Supp. 97, 101 (E.D. Pa. 1996) (holding that a claim of invasion of privacy under the tort of intrusion upon seclusion against an employer requires a showing that the employer invaded a reasonable expectation of privacy).

[101] 21 N.Y.3d 515, 974 N.Y.S.2d 896, 997 N.E.2d 468.

[102] 21 N.Y.3d at 522.

[103] *Id.*

[104] *Id.*

The primary lesson from the *Cunningham* case is that, while GPS tracking can serve as a helpful tool for human resources analytics, it should be used only for an appropriate purpose and within a defined and limited scope, particularly where the employee's work and home life necessarily overlap.[105] Moreover, providing employees with robust notice of the location tracking and obtaining their prior consent should effectively eliminate an employer's exposure to a claim under state laws restricting the use of location-tracking devices under a common law invasion of privacy theory.

Data Security

Multiple federal and state laws and regulations protect the security of personal information. The law in this area tends to focus on information that could be used to commit identify theft—Social Security numbers, driver's license numbers, credit and debit card numbers, and financial account numbers, for example—and on information generally understood to be private, such as health information. Critically, the employer retains responsibility for the data even when the employer outsources the data analysis to a third party. Consequently, the employer may be liable for the missteps of a service provider handling the data on the employer's behalf.

To reduce the risk of outsourcing data analysis, employers should deidentify personal data where possible. "Deidentification" refers to the process of removing individually identifying information—name and Social Security number, for example—from a data set. Several studies have thrown into question the extent to which standard deidentification steps actually sever the link between the data and an identifiable individual.[106] Nevertheless, there can be no question that deidentifying personal data at least makes it harder to use the data for identity theft or other harmful purposes. Moreover, deidentifying data can provide a safe harbor under some laws, such as the Health Information Portability and Accountability Act, as long as the deidentification process meets accepted standards.[107] Even where a statutory ore regulatory scheme does not include an express safe harbor, deidentification can effectively create a safe harbor because virtually all data protection and information security laws apply only to information that is individually identifiable.

If the service provider must use identified data, the employer should conduct due diligence on the service provider to confirm that it can protect the data and obtain

---

[105] Justice Sotomayor expressed a similar sentiment in her 2012 concurring opinion in *U.S. v. Jones*, 565 U.S. 945, 957 (2012) (Sotomayor Concurring), "[I]t may be necessary to reconsider the premise that an individual has no reasonable expectation of privacy in information voluntarily disclosed to third parties[.]" "This approach is ill suited to the digital age, in which people reveal a great deal of information about themselves to third parties in the course of carrying out mundane tasks."

[106] *See* Paul Ohm, Broken Promises of Privacy: Responding to the Surprising Failure of Anonymization, 57 UCLA L. Rev. 1701, 1716–1723 (2010).

[107] 45 C.F.R. 164.514(a).

written assurances that the service provider will provide reasonable safeguards for that information. In some circumstances, the employer may be legally required to address information security in the service agreement. California, for example, has enacted a statute requiring any business that owns or licenses personal information regarding a California resident and that shares such information with a third party to "require by contract that the third party implement and maintain reasonable security procedures and practices appropriate to the nature of the information, to protect the personal information from unauthorized access, destruction, use, modification, or disclosure.[108] Massachusetts and Oregon have enacted similar statutes regarding their residents.[109]

Employers also should note that HIPAA mandates data security provisions regarding protected health information in contracts between any employer covered by HIPAA and a third-party service provider, a "business associate" in HIPAA parlance, which will handle the employer's protected health information.[110] Such contracts must establish the permitted and required uses and disclosures of the protected health information, including appropriate safeguards to prevent unauthorized disclosures, and reporting requirements in the event of any such unauthorized disclosure.[111]

For those employers that are not required by law to address information security in service agreements with data service providers, a good practice is to require that service providers safeguard data by contract anyway. One third of states require companies to implement general safeguards to protect some forms of personal information.[112] Forty-seven states require notification of a breach of security, including when the personal information is held by a service provider.[113] Consequently, employers in many states could be liable not only for failing to report a breach, but also for the absence of safeguards that led to the breach, even if the breach was caused by a service provider.

Indeed, a company could theoretically face penalties from government regulators for a service provider's failure to apply reasonable security measures even without a breach. In practice, government regulators are unlikely to crack down on a company for its service providers' failure to maintain the required safeguards. If a company fails to conduct due diligence, however, and the service provider suffers a data breach, the company may find itself facing an enforcement action. The company may also become the target of class actions alleging negligence. Although negligence claims in cases of data breaches have generally foundered on the elements of harm and causation, defending against the claims can be costly.[114] Leaving aside legal liability, a breach may be embarrassing for the company and undermine

---

[108] *See* Cal. Civ. Code 1798.81.5(c).
[109] M.G.L. c. 93H as implemented by 201 C.M.R. 17.00; Or. Rev. Stat. 646A.622(2)(d).
[110] 45 C.F.R. 164.504(e).
[111] Id.
[112] *See, e.g.,* Fla. Stat. § 501.171(2); Tex. Bus. & Com. Code Ann. § 521.052(a).
[113] *See, e.g.,* 815 Ill. Comp. Stat. 530/5 et seq.; Mich. Comp. Laws § 445.72; N.Y. Bus. Law § 899-aa; Ohio Rev. Code § 1349.19.
[114] Douglas H. Meal & David T. Cohen, Private Data Security Litigation in the United States, in Inside the Minds: Privacy and Surveillance Legal Issues (Aspatore 2014).

employee morale.[115] Security breaches also can be costly due to the expenses involved in providing notification in accordance with breach notification laws.[116]

The company can delegate breach notification to the service provider by contract, but the company retains the responsibility under breach notification laws to ensure that notifications are provided to affected individuals.[117] Therefore, in addition to requiring that the service provider implement reasonable data security safeguards, the employer should require the service provider to promptly report any data breach to the employer and to cooperate with the employer in the data breach investigation. The contract should also provide that the service provider will reimburse the employer for all costs incurred by the employer when responding to a security breach involving personal information in the service provider's possession and indemnify the employer from any third-party claims arising out of the security breach. Finally, the contract should clearly indicate which party will provide breach notifications and give the employer the right to supervise the notification process.

International Data Protection

Although a full discussion of international data protection regimes is beyond the scope of this chapter, employers should exercise particular caution when analyzing the data of non-U.S. employees, especially employees who reside in the European Union (E.U.). All countries in the E.U. have enacted laws to implement the E.U. Data Protection Directive, which tightly regulates the processing of personal data.[118] Many other countries have adopted data protection laws similar to those of the E.U.[119]

The Data Protection Directive is broad. For instance, "personal data" is defined as "any information relating to an identified or identifiable natural person ('data

---

[115] According to the Ponemon Institute's 2014 survey on data breach costs, businesses lost over 3 million dollars' worth of business on average after experiencing a data breach. Ponemon Institute, 2014 Cost of Data Breach Study: Global Analysis, 16 (May 2014).

[116] The Ponemon Institute also estimated that the average cost of breach notification in the United States in 2014 was over $500,000. Id. at 15.

[117] For example, New York, like many other states, imposes a duty to notify affected individuals on the party that "owns or licenses" the data. N.Y. Gen. Bus. Law § 899-aa(2). A party that "maintains" the data only has the obligation to notify the data's owner or licensor. Id. at § 899-aa(3).

[118] *See* Commission Directive 95/46/EC, of the European Parliament and the Council of 24 October 1995 on the Protection of Individuals with Regard to the Processing of Personal Data and the Free Movement of Such Data, 1995 O.J. (L281) 31 [hereinafter E.U. Data Protection Directive].

[119] A few examples of non-E.U. countries with broad data protection laws are Australia (The Privacy Act 1988 (Cth)), India (Information Technology Act, 2000, No. 21 of 2000, as amended by Information Technology (Amendment) Act, 2008 and Information Technology (Reasonable Security Practices and Procedures and Sensitive Personal Data or Information) Rules, 2011, G.S.R. 313(E) (Apr. 11, 2011)), Mexico (Ley Federal de Protección de Datos Personales en Posesión de los Particulares, 5 de Julio de 2010), and South Korea (Personal Information Protection Act, Act No. 10465, Mar. 29, 2011).

subject'); an identifiable person is one who can be identified, directly or indirectly, in particular by reference to an identification number or to one or more factors specific to his physical, physiological, mental, economic, cultural or social identity."[120] This definition covers a much wider array of information than most U.S. legal definitions of personal information, which limits protection to specific data points, such as Social Security numbers or protected health information subject to HIPAA. In the context of data analytics, the broader definition is particularly noteworthy because categories of information that generally are not protected under U.S. law, such as performance appraisals, records of discipline, and compensation information, are protected under the directive.

Critically, when discussing data analytics, the E.U. Data Protection Directive forbids decisions based on the automated processing of personal data except in certain circumstances.[121] Making decisions based on data-driven analysis of employee personal data could potentially violate this prohibition. As a result, "Moneyball"-like techniques[122] may court considerable risk in the E.U. even if all the other requirements discussed later are met.

Among other points, the E.U. Data Protection Directive requires notice regarding the processing of personal data, and unless an exception applies, also requires consent.[123] This means that employers must provide notice to employees regarding how their personal data is processed, including the processing of their personal data to conduct data analytics. Employers would have to notify their employees about the purpose of the analysis and whether a third party was conducting the analysis.[124] Employees generally have the right to object to data processing, and could refuse to let the employer conduct the analysis.[125]

In addition to granting the subjects of personal data the right to object to processing, the E.U. Data Protection Directive grants them the right to access, correct, and delete their personal data.[126] The Directive also requires reasonable security for personal data.[127] Consequently, just as it should when sharing the personal data of U.S. employees with a service provider, the employer should conduct due diligence on service providers and execute agreements containing data security provisions and provisions addressing these obligations before disclosing the personal data of E.U.-based employees to a service provider.

---

[120] E.U. Data Protection Directive, ch. I, art. 2(a).

[121] *Id.*, ch. II, art. 15.

[122] In an approach made famous by the book *Moneyball* and the movie of the same name, the Oakland Athletics baseball team used data-driven analytical techniques to determine what quantifiable measures made baseball players successful and then recruited players based on these statistics.

[123] *Id.*, ch. II, arts. 10, 14.

[124] *See id.*, ch. II, arts. 10(a), (b).

[125] *See id.*, ch. II, art. 14.

[126] *Id.*, ch.II, art. 12.

[127] *Id.*, ch. II, art. 17.

Employers cannot simply bypass the E.U.'s restrictions by processing the data on U.S. territory. The E.U. Data Protection Directive forbids the transfer of E.U. residents' data to countries where the local law does not provide "an adequate level of protection."[128] As of now, the E.U. has determined that the U.S. law generally does not ensure an adequate level of protection.[129] Companies, however, may provide an adequate level of protection for data transferred to the U.S. by implementing one of three mechanisms to assure that the personal data will continue to be subject to E.U.-like protections once transferred to the U.S.: model data transfer agreements;[130] Binding Corporate Rules;[131] or certifying to the U.S.-E.U. Safe Harbor.[132] The most commonly used of these approaches is the U.S.-E.U. Safe Harbor. Certifying to the U.S.-E.U. Safe Harbor effectively requires the certifying company to implement a privacy framework for transferred personal data and to implement information security safeguards that mirror those required by the Data Protection Directive.[133]

The FTC enforces the Safe Harbor.[134] Until now, the FTC's enforcement has been relatively lax; the agency has focused principally on companies that represent that they are still Safe Harbor-certified after their certification has expired. Recently, the FTC has come under pressure from European regulators for inadequately enforcing the Safe Harbor. As a result, the FTC may step up enforcement efforts and target more substantive violations.

The E.U. is also likely to tighten rules on processing personal data. The European Commission has proposed comprehensive reform of the Data Protection Directive to bolster privacy protections for personal data.[135] Among other points, the latest proposal calls for fines of 2–5 percent of a noncompliant company's global annual turnover, a right of consumers to have unnecessary data deleted (the "right to be forgotten"), and mandatory reporting of data breaches to state authorities.[136]

---

[128] *Id.*, ch. IV, art. 25(1).

[129] The E.U. Commission's list of countries with an adequate level of protection is available here: http://ec.europa.eu/justice/data-protection/document/international-transfers/adequacy/index_en.htm.

[130] Commission Decision 2001/497/EC Controller to Controller Transfers (amended by Commission Decision C(2004) 5271).

[131] Working Document: Transfers of personal data to third countries: Applying Article 26 (2) of the EU Data Protection Directive to Binding Corporate Rules for International Data Transfers (Adopted June 3, 2003).

[132] Commission Decision 2000/520/EC of 26 July 2000 Pursuant to Directive 95/46/EC of the European Parliament and of the Council on the Adequacy of the Protection Provided by the Safe Harbor Privacy Principles and Related Frequently Asked Questions Issued by the US Department of Commerce, 2000 O.J. (L 215) 7–47.

[133] *See id.* at Art. 1, § 3. 134 *Id.*, Annex VII.

[134] European Commission, *Data Protection Day 2015: Concluding the EU Data Protection Reform essential for the Digital Single Market* (Jan. 28, 2015) *available here*

[135] http://europa.eu/rapid/press-release_MEMO-15-3802_en.htm.

[136] *Id.*

The Commission opted for a Regulation instead of a Directive, because no transposition into local law will be required, and the Regulation will directly and equally apply in all Member States.[137]

The exact wording of the draft Regulation is being negotiated by the members of the European Parliament and the member state delegations. A final text is expected by the end of 2015.[138] After official publication, a two-year transitional period will apply.[139] The new data protection regime likely will have a significant impact on employers' ability to use the personal data of E.U.-based employees to conduct data analytics.

Big Data: Is There a Defense to a Potential Adverse Impact?

Title VII of the Civil Rights Act of 1964, as amended (Title VII),[140] the Age Discrimination in Employment Act,[141] and the ADA,[142] all prohibit disparate impact discrimination. The gist of this claim is the same under each statute—a *prima facie* case requires a plaintiff to (a) identify a facially neutral policy or practice, (b) prove that this policy or practice adversely impacts members of a specific protected group, and then (c) demonstrate that this causes an adverse employment action affecting the plaintiff.[143] Big Data lends itself to this proof.

One of the consequences of Big Data is that small differences between groups may be "statistically significant." "Statistical significance" is the criterion many courts use to assess proof of an adverse impact.[144] However, statistical significance is a flexible yardstick and, other things equal, any disparity between two groups will increase in statistical significance the larger the sample on which the analysis is based.[145] Thus, Big Data may identify selection criteria that are statistically significant,

---

[137] *Id.*

[138] On June 15, 2015, the EU Council agreed on a "general approach" to proposing a final draft of the Regulation. www.consilium.europa.eu/en/press/press-releases/2015/06/15-jha-data-protection/ (last visited July 14, 2015).

[139] European Parliament, *Q&A on EU data protection reform*, Mar. 3, 2014, *available at* www.europarl.europa.eu/news/en/news-room/content/20130502BKG07917/html/QA-on-EU-data-protection-reform.

[140] Title VII of The Civil Rights Act, 42 U.S.C. § 2000e, *et seq.*

[141] Age Discrimination in Employment Act of 1967 ("ADEA"), 29 U.S.C. §§ 621–634 (2000).

[142] Americans with Disabilities Act of 1990 ("ADA"), 42 U.S.C. §§ 12101–12213 (2000).

[143] Courts apply the burden-shifting framework to claims under each of these statutory frameworks. *See e.g.,* 42 U.S.C. § 2000e-2(k) (Title VII of The Civil Rights Act); *Shelley v. Geren,* 666 F.3d 599, 607–608 (9th Cir. 2012) (ADEA); *Roggenbach v. Touro College of Osteopathic Medicine,* 7 F. Supp. 3d 338, 343–344 (2014) (ADA).

[144] *See, e.g., Contreras v. City of Los Angeles,* 656 F.2d 1267 (9th Cir. 1981); *Waison v. Port Authority,* 948 F.2d 1370, 1376 (2d Cir. 1991); *Ottaviani v. State Univ. of N.Y. at New Paltz,* 875 F.3d 365, 370–371 (1989); *Sobel v. Yeshiva Univ.,* 839 F.2d 18 (1988).

[145] "[L]arger sample sizes give more reliable results with greater precision and [statistical] power..." *The Importance and Effect of Sample Size,* Select Statistical Services, www.select-statistics.co.uk/article/blog-post/the-importance-and-effect-of-sample-size.

although in practical terms the difference between success and failure may be quite small. In the landmark case of *Wal-Mart Stores, Inc. v. Dukes*,[146] the large number of promotions would cause a disparity in the number of men and women promoted of just seven-tenths of one percent to be judged "statistically significant."[147]

Once the adverse impact of the selection criterion is established, the plaintiff next must prove the algorithm caused her to suffer an adverse employment action.[148] The question is whether, if the algorithm had valued this candidate more highly, the plaintiff would have been more likely to be selected? This too can be established statistically, by comparing the selection rate among those who score more favorably than the plaintiff with those who score no more favorably. If a statistically significant difference exists, a fact finder may reasonably conclude that the algorithm caused an adverse employment action.

If a plaintiff makes this proof, the burden shifts to the employer to prove that the challenged algorithm is job related for that position and consistent with business necessity.[149] This may be Big Data's greatest challenge. Some of its most vocal advocates contend Big Data is valuable precisely because it crunches data that are ubiquitous and *not* job related. The employer's reliance on the algorithm may be job related, but the algorithm itself is measuring and tracking behavior that has no direct relationship to job performance. Its value derives solely from a correlation between the information gleaned from all sources and job performance. The legal question is whether an employer can meet its burden to prove job-relatedness on the basis of evidence that is strictly correlational.

The Uniform Guidelines on Employee Selection Procedures, although published in 1978, continue to inform how courts view validation.[150] An overarching principle is that an employer generally will not be able to establish validity based upon the job performance of employees who work elsewhere, except in particular circumstances. To "transport" statistical findings from one workplace to another, the employer must demonstrate its own employees and those who are the subject of the validation study "perform substantially the same work behaviors, as shown by appropriate job analyses."[151] The regulations contemplate a comparison between the job duties of the subjects of the validation study and the job duties of those the selection procedure will screen, which should be similar in material respects.[152]

---

[146] 131 S. Ct. 2541 (2011).

[147] Allan G. King, *"Gross Statistical Disparities" as Evidence of a Pattern and Practice of Discrimination: Statistical versus Legal Significance*, 22 The Labor Lawyer 271, 280 (2007).

[148] *McDonnell Douglas Corp. v. Green*, 411 U.S. 792, 802–804 (1973).

[149] *Id.*; 42 U.S.C. § 2000e-2(k)(1)(A)(i).

[150] "There are two sources of expertise upon which the courts often rely in deciding whether a test has been properly validated... Perhaps the most important source of guidance is the Equal Employment Opportunity Commission's 'Uniform Guidelines on Employment Selection Procedures'..." *Gulina v. N.Y. State Educ. Dept.*, 460 F.3d 361, 383 (2d Cir. 2006).

[151] 29 C.F.R. § 1607.7(B)(2).

[152] *Id.*

The Uniform Guidelines approve three types of validation studies: criterion, content, and construct validity studies.[153] Content validity is the most straightforward, but the least relevant to Big Data. It relies on a close correspondence between the skills tested and those required to succeed in that job.[154] The typing test given to a prospective typist is the paradigm, although even here it would be important to demonstrate that the text on which the examination is given is similar to the text that must be typed by a proficient employee.

But this close correspondence is anathema to Big Data. The contribution claimed for Big Data is that the information fed to the algorithm may be entirely unrelated to the job requirements, so long as it is predictive of job performance. On its face, the data relied upon by the algorithm, and the algorithm itself, are likely to be far removed from the tasks the job requires. Thus, content validity is an unlikely method for validating Big Data.

Construct and criterion validity are closely related. Construct validity measures the degree to which candidates have "identifiable characteristics which have been determined to be important for successful job performance."[155] Sometimes these traits may be apparent. Other things the same, speed is likely to be a substantial asset to a football player. In other settings, identifying the salient traits is more challenging. Accordingly, the Uniform Guidelines caution employers that "[t]he user should be aware that the effort to obtain sufficient empirical support for construct validity is both an extensive and arduous effort involving a series of research studies..."[156] Thus, an employer must first establish that the construct in question contributes significantly to success on the particular job, and that the procedure or test accurately identifies those who possess that construct.[157]

Criterion validity, or predictive validity as it sometimes is known, differs in that the objective is to predict ultimate success on the job, rather than traits believed to lead to success. Because this method of validation was longstanding when the Uniform Guidelines were formulated, the regulations governing criterion validity are more detailed than those pertaining to construct validity. The Guidelines list several steps they deem "essential," many of which pertain to a "job analysis."[158] A job analysis should identify the behaviors or outcomes that are critically important, the proportion of time spent on each, their difficulty, the consequences of errors, and the frequency with which various tasks are performed.[159] The purpose in systematizing this information is to determine which jobs reasonably may be grouped to rate employees for their proficiency and identify a common test or screen for selecting

---

[153] *See generally* 29 C.F.R. § 1607.14.
[154] 29 C.F.R. § 1607.14(C).
[155] 29 C.F.R. § 1607.16(E).
[156] 29 C.F.R. § 1607.14(D).
[157] *Id.*
[158] 29 C.F.R. § 1607.15(B)(3).
[159] *Id.*

them.[160] Employers must also explain the bases for selecting the success measures and the means by which they were observed, recorded, evaluated, and quantified.[161]

The Uniform Guidelines provide that "a selection procedure is considered related to the criterion, for the purposes of these guidelines, when the relationship between performance on the procedure and performance on the criterion measure is statistically significant at the 0.05 level of significance."[162] Generally, there are two methods of establishing either construct or criterion validity. One is "concurrent validity"; the other is "predictive validity."[163] In a concurrent study, both the selection procedure score, *e.g.*, a test score, and the performance score it is intended to predict are collected at the same time. For example, an incumbent workforce, whose job performance can be evaluated, may be administered a proposed test to see whether the test scores are correlated with a measure of on-the-job performance. In a predictive validity study, selection scores are obtained for a group of applicants but not used in hiring decisions. Some portion of the applicant pool is hired and subsequently evaluated in terms of on-the-job performance. The selection scores are then correlated with measures of performance to assess whether selection scores predicted performance accurately.[164]

Both methods of validation pose challenges for Big Data solutions based largely on correlations. Because the relationships relied upon by Big Data are entirely empirical, and both concurrent and predictive validity are time dependent (as will be explained), there is no reason the correlations that underlie Big Data solutions should persist beyond the sample period. Because concurrent validity is based upon information regarding incumbent employees, the correlations uncovered regarding these individuals will be relevant to the applicant pool only if incumbents and applicants are similar in the dimensions measured by Big Data. For example, if incumbents are older than applicants, then the social media profile of this older group may differ markedly from that of younger job applicants. Accordingly, an algorithm highly accurate in sorting a generation of *incumbents* may yield *applicants* notable only for their "retro" tastes and lifestyles.

Similarly, a predictive validity study, in which applicants are first screened in the dimensions relevant to Big Data, and then have their job performance assessed after they are employed for a reasonable time,[165] will be relevant only if patterns observed in the past continue to be relevant to job performance. If in January the best programmers have flocked to a particular website, but by July a different website is the hottest draw, an algorithm that continues to rely on visits to the

---

[160] *Id.*

[161] 29 C.F.R. § 1607.15(B)(5).

[162] 29 C.F.R. § 1607.14B(5).

[163] 29 C.F.R. § 1607.14(B)(4).

[164] Richard Jeanneret, *Professional and Technical Authorities and Guidelines*, in Employment Discrimination Litigation: Behavioral, Quantitative, and Legal Perspectives 47, 58 (Frank Landy, 2005).

[165] Dr. Jeanneret recommends assessing performance no sooner than six months after hire. *Id.*

first website may be mistaking the very best applicants. Thus, the gold standard is not mere correlations, but stable correlations that yield reliable predictions over a relatively long time.

Underlying each validation method approved by the Uniform Guidelines is the requirement of a job analysis.[166] This reflects the common-sense view that to design a test or selection instrument that distinguishes those best able to perform a job from those who are least able requires some understanding of what the job entails. The Guidelines' technical standards require at a minimum that "[a]ny validity study should be based upon a review of information about the job for which the selection procedure is to be used."[167]

Big Data begins from the opposite perspective. The algorithm is uninterested in what any employee actually does, so long as the employer can identify who does it well and who does it poorly. The algorithm will identify the set of variables (the information available to it) that best distinguishes these groups. Consequently, the tests of statistical significance that ensure the ultimate validity of conventionally developed tests are far less relevant to Big Data. Well-conceived algorithms will eliminate every alternative that is not significantly related to job performance— that is the cornerstone of the methodology. As a result, applying conventional tests of validity to Big Data makes little sense because, by design, its algorithms identify the correlates that best fit the (job performance) data, without regard to why they are related.

This is the salient difference between predictions based upon theories of causation versus those solely based on correlations. The logic of "cause and effect" is that the associated theory is based on something believed to be fundamental to the relationship in question. For example, the logic that suggests faster athletes make better football players reflects the assumption that the faster a football player can run towards or away from an opponent, the more likely that player is to be in the right place at the right time. As long as the rules of the game remain the same, this proposition should remain true.

In contrast, suppose these players were selected on the basis of social media profiles and Internet activity. It well may be possible to achieve higher correlations using this information than relying on the player's speed, but there is no telling how long those correlations will be reliable. If a new fad sweeps college campuses, today's high correlation may quickly become tomorrow's zero correlation. Consequently, the correlation demanded by the Uniform Guidelines may be a poor criterion by which to judge the performance of Big Data.

Thus, Big Data effects a shift from selection criteria distilled from job-related knowledge, skills, and ability, which uses correlation to establish that the correct criteria were identified, to one in which correlation is established at the outset, independent of knowledge, skills, and ability, and leaves the duration of that correlation

---

[166] *See generally* 29 C.F.R. § 1607.15.
[167] 29 C.F.R. § 1607.14(A).

in question. Accordingly, rather than assessing Big Data in terms of correlation, which it will pass with flying colors, the relevant question is the probable duration of the correlations on which its algorithms are based. In terms of validation, this translates into a comparison between the time elapsed since the algorithm was first calibrated and the time it was applied to the plaintiff, relative to the probable duration of the correlation.

Because Big Data algorithms, by design, maximize the correlation between Big Data variables and some measure(s) of job performance, the correlation should be greatest when the algorithm initially is calibrated and should decay as time passes. But how much decay is tolerable before the algorithm is deemed too unreliable to pass legal scrutiny? An answer is suggested by the Uniform Guidelines: "Generally, a selection procedure is considered related to the criterion, for the purpose of these guidelines, when the relationship between performance on the procedure and performance on the criterion measure is statistically significant at the 0.05 level of significance..."[168] This suggests that the useful life of an algorithm should be measured by the time elapsed before the correlation is reduced in significance to the 0.05 level. This lifespan therefore is the critical inquiry in assessing how long a Big Data algorithm lawfully is applied to an employer's workforce.

Litigation in a World of Big Data

Class Action Risks and Exposure

Class actions pose significant risks to employers. On March 17, 2015, it was reported that "[t]op legal counsel at nearly 350 companies managed on average five class actions in 2014 and spent $2 billion on class actions."[169] The same survey reported that 23 percent of these cases are employment class actions.[170] Thus, whether Big Data adds to these risks should be an important inquiry for in-house counsel and employers. An important consideration, therefore, is whether classes challenging Big Data are more likely to be certified.

Class actions are driven by common questions with common answers.[171] The Supreme Court reversed class certification, in *Wal-Mart Stores, Inc. v. Dukes*, because the decisions that were challenged as discriminatory were decentralized, and did not reflect the effects of a policy that was commonly applied to class

---

[168] 29 C.F.R. § 1607.14(B)(5).

[169] Melissa Maleske, *GCs Facing More Class Actions, Higher-Exposure Cases*, Law 360 (Mar. 17, 2015) www.law360.com/articles/632403/gcs-facing-more-class-actions-higher-exposure-cases (last visited July 14, 2015).

[170] *Id.*

[171] *See, e.g.*, Fed. R. Civ. P. 23(a)(2); *Brinker Restaurant Corp. v. Super. Ct.*, 53 Cal. 4th 1004, 1022 n.5 (2012).

members.[172] Consequently, resolving these claims would have required determining whether each class member was treated in a discriminatory manner.[173]

The implication of *Dukes* is that policies that are more centralized, and applied uniformly, enhance the likelihood a class will be certified. This suggests that a Big Data algorithm, applied uniformly and consistently throughout an employer's workforce, potentially provides the "glue" missing from *Dukes*. However, that conclusion may be too facile.

Big Data is a methodology rather than a particular selection device. It is a data intensive means of distinguishing promising from unpromising employees, based upon correlations between measures of success and other information a developer can glean from various sources. If Big Data is the method, then the algorithm is the predictive model that is designed to select the most promising employees. As opposed to the Big Data methodology, the algorithm essentially is the equation that sorts applicants or incumbent employees into groups with greater or lesser promise. The algorithm, therefore, is a legitimate target of a discrimination lawsuit.[174]

In terms of class action litigation and the critical question of class certification, the corresponding issue is whether decision making by algorithms enhances the risk of class certification. Superficially, it may seem that the discriminatory impact of a commonly applied algorithm is precisely the question amenable to a common answer and a prime target of class action litigation. However, the "algorithm" may vary by day, week, or month, depending upon how long any one remains "best," and may have as many variations as the individualized decisions that caused *Dukes* to be decertified.

But first let's consider the simplistic case in which an employer adopts a single, unchanging algorithm it applies across the board to all applicants and those seeking promotion. Subject to a plaintiff discovering the demographic characteristics of applicants, this appears to be a practice that lends itself to class litigation.[175]

---

[172] *Wal-Mart Stores, Inc. v. Dukes*, 131 S. Ct. 2541, 2554–2555 (2011). In this suit, the U.S. Supreme Court reversed the class certification of a gender discrimination claim that included a class of 1.6 million women who currently worked or had worked for Wal-Mart stores. In particular, the plaintiff alleged that Wal-Mart engaged in discriminatory pay and promotion policy and practices.

[173] *Id.* at 2552 ("Without some glue holding the alleged reasons for all those decisions together, it will be impossible to say that examination of all the class members' claims for relief will produce a common answer to the crucial question why was I disfavored."). *See also, e.g., Duran v. US Bank Nat'l Ass'n*, 59 Cal. 4th 1, 25 (2014) ("Faced with the potential difficulties of managing individual issues... many trial courts have denied certification or decertified the class before trial... [S]uch decisions have been routinely upheld.").

[174] *See, e.g., Griggs v. Duke Power Co.*, 401 U.S. 424, 436 (1971) ("Nothing in the [Civil Rights] Act precludes the use of testing or measuring procedures; obviously they are useful. What Congress has forbidden is giving these devices and mechanisms controlling force unless they are demonstrably a reasonable measure of job performance.")

[175] "Claims alleging that a uniform policy consistently applied to a group of employees is in violation of the wage and hour laws are of the sort routinely, and properly, found suitable for class treatment." *Brinker*, 53 Cal. 4th at 531.

Although an employer might argue that it differentially impacts applicants for various positions, *e.g.*, engineers and accountants, this is likely to be viewed as an argument for subclasses rather than one that defeats certification.[176] Indeed, this scenario is very close to a common fact pattern in which an employer administers a standardized test to its applicants, and the test has an adverse impact on a protected group. Cases of that type frequently are certified.[177]

However, this hypothetical puts Big Data in an artificial straightjacket. One of the advantages of Big Data is the relatively low cost in mining data once it is harvested from the sources that feed it. Consequently, the cost of producing job-specific algorithms, which are likely to be more accurate than one "standard" model, may be just marginally greater than the cost of developing one grand algorithm. Thus, a class action plaintiff may be faced with challenging numerous algorithms.

The problem this creates is that no one plaintiff is likely to have been affected by each of the algorithms in use. As a result, that plaintiff may not have standing to challenge algorithms by which he or she was unaffected. If a court determines the scope of a class or subclass must be limited to those affected by the same algorithm, it may be infeasible to bring large class actions against employers whose decisions reflect an array of algorithms that differ by position.

Apart from algorithms specific to particular jobs, algorithms may, and probably should, change periodically. As a result, employees hired or promoted at different times may have been selected by different algorithms. Developers may find it useful to update algorithms—not to avoid litigation, but because Big Data algorithms are based on correlation and not causation.[178] This means that the algorithms they create are useful only as long as the correlations on which they are based remain substantial.

For example, an article in the *Atlantic* describes how one company searched for software engineers proficient in writing computer code:

> They assess the way coders use language on social networks from LinkedIn to Twitter; the company has determined that certain phrases and words used in association with one another can distinguish expert programmers from less skilled ones... [The company] knows these phrases and words are associated with good coding because it can correlate them with its evaluation of open-source code, and with the

---

[176] "When appropriate... a class may be divided into subclasses and each subclass treated as a class, and the provisions of this rule [23(c)(4)(B)] shall then be construed and applied accordingly." Fed. R. Civ. P. 23(c)(4)(B).

[177] *See, e.g., Griggs*, 401 U.S. 424 (certifying class action against employer that required a high school education or passing a standardized general intelligence test as condition of employment, when neither was significantly related to job performance and both disqualified black applicants at a substantially higher rate than white applicants).

[178] Chris Taylor, *Big Data's Slippery Issue of Causation vs. Correlation*, Wired (Jul. 15, 2013), available at http://insights.wired.com/profiles/blogs/big-data-s-slippery-issue-of-causation-versus-correlation#axzz3WY6JsHAy (last visited July 14, 2015).

language and online behavior of programmers in good positions at prestigious companies.[179]

The article explains this information, which can then identify promising programmers whose code is not available on the Internet by determining whether their social media footprint is similar to that of the best open-source programmers, by comparing their online histories.[180] The chief scientist with this company explained, "They're not all obvious, or easy to explain... [O]ne solid predictor of strong coding is an affinity for a particular Japanese manga site."[181] However, any website ultimately may be of passing interest to a group that once found it an obsession.

If correlations unearthed by Big Data are ephemeral, then their algorithms must be dynamic to maintain validity. This requires constantly updating the profiles of individuals best qualified for various positions, which may lead to new algorithms. Consequently, an employer's hiring decisions might be predicated on an ever-changing array of algorithms, with only minimal commonality. As a result, the likelihood of common answers is drastically diminished because each version of the algorithm may have different properties, in terms of both adverse impact and its degree of validity. In principle, one version might impact neutrally and another might be highly predictive, although its adverse impact is greater. Thus, the dynamic differences in Big Data may be the contemporary counterpart of the store-to-store differences that precluded class certification in *Dukes*.[182]

A Whole New World of Experts

Big Data changes the testimony necessary to admit expert evidence at trial and establish the business necessity of using a particular Big Data algorithm. To most employers, Big Data algorithms are a "black box," the inner workings of which are known largely by the developer. Although the employer may be in the dark about the algorithm, it nevertheless may be liable if the algorithm screens out members of a protected group and the employer is unable to explain how or why its results should be trusted. To prevail under a disparate impact theory of discrimination, a plaintiff must show that the algorithm adversely impacts a protected group or, if the employer succeeds in establishing the business reasons for using the algorithm, by

---

[179] Don Peck, *They're Watching You at Work*, The Atlantic (Nov. 20, 2013), www.theatlantic. com/magazine/archive/2013/12/theyre-watching-you-at-work/354681/ (last visited July 14, 2015).

[180] *Id.*

[181] *Id.* Manga are comics created in Japan, or by Japanese creators in the Japanese language, conforming to a style developed in Japan in the late 19th century. http://en.wikipedia.org/ wiki/Manga (last visited July 14, 2015).

[182] Some of the store-to-store differences cited in *Dukes* include the availability of women, qualified women, or interested women, as well as the nature and effects of sex-neutral, performance-based criteria in each specific location. *Dukes*, 131 S. Ct. at 2555.

demonstrating there exists a less discriminatory alternative that is equally efficient at serving the employer's legitimate business needs.

A Big Data algorithm is created by gathering data regarding the various dimensions of employee performance and correlating them with any and all information regarding those employees.[183] Because Big Data algorithms are entirely empirical—a case of measurement without theory—all information regarding each employee potentially is relevant until shown to add nothing to the algorithm's ability to distinguish between good and bad performers. After searching among all possible combinations of data, and allowing the search process to consider each item of information to maximum effect, the algorithm identifies the optimal combination. By design, the algorithm selected must bear a significant statistical relationship to the measure(s) of employee performance; otherwise, it would have been discarded in favor of a different algorithm that is a better predictor.

Given Big Data's dependence on information gathered from sources external to the employer, and indirectly from applicants and employees, a variety of novel issues arise. Particularly with respect to applicants, potential plaintiffs are confronted with the problem of identifying the applicants who have been evaluated unfavorably by the Big Data algorithm. The difficulty this presents is that neither the gender, race, and ethnicity of these rejected applicants may not be documented by employers nor is it likely to be known how any algorithm impacts more generally. For example, suppose an algorithm returns the result that applicants who drive standard-shift automobiles are the best and brightest employees—how is one to learn whether that criterion impacts a protected group adversely?

Litigants have tried various methods to identify the race of applicants who do not self-identify, sometimes with disastrous results. Perhaps the most notorious was the EEOC's efforts to use "race panels" to determine the race of applicants from driver's license photographs. In *EEOC v. Kaplan Higher Education Corporation*,[184]

---

[183] In some instances, the information has nothing to do with an employee's potential to perform a specific job. For example, Gild's Big Data algorithms found that one solid predictor of strong computer coding was an affinity for a specific Japanese manga site. "'Obviously, it's not a causal relationship'... But Gild does have 6 million programmers in its database, [Vivienne Ming, Gild's chief scientist] said, and the correlation, even if inexplicable, is quite clear." Don Peck, *They're Watching You at Work*, The Atlantic (Nov. 20, 2013), available at www.theatlantic.com/magazine/archive/2013/12/theyre-watching-you-at-work/354681/ (last visited July 14, 2015). Similarly, a different Big Data algorithm found that job applicants who completed online job applications using browsers that did not come with the computer (*e.g.*, Microsoft's Internet Explorer on a Windows OC) and instead had to be installed (*e.g.*, Firefox or Google Chrome) performed better at their jobs and have a lower level of turnover. *Robert recruiters: How software helps firms hire workers more efficiently*, The Economist, Apr. 6, 2013, available at www.economist.com/news/business/21575820-how-software-helps-firms-hire-workers-more-efficiently-robot-recruiters (last visited July 14, 2015).

[184] 748 F.3d 749 (6th Cir. 2014).

the Sixth Circuit affirmed the district court's decision striking the expert who relied on this methodology, in rather harsh terms. "The EEOC brought this case on the basis of a homemade methodology, crafted by a witness with no particular expertise to craft it, administered by persons with no particular expertise to administer it, tested by no one, and accepted only by the witness himself."[185]

However, other methods of imputing race have received a more favorable reception.[186] "Geocoding" is a methodology that relies on an individual's place of residence, and the racial or ethnic composition of others in that same location, to impute the racial and ethnic identity of any particular individual. For instance, if it is known that an applicant resides in a census block that is 50 percent Hispanic, that applicant is assigned a 50 percent probability of being Hispanic. By summing these probabilities over all applicants, the researcher arrives at an estimate of the composition of the entire group of applicants.[187]

Plaintiffs also have surveyed those identified as applicants to characterize the demographics of the applicant pool. Private survey research companies abound, and have been retained to provide expert testimony regarding the make-up of a pool of applicants. When survey methodologies conform to generally accepted principles, such as those followed by the U.S. Bureau of the Census, these surveys have been admitted into evidence.[188]

Accordingly, as Big Data relies increasingly on data sources that are external to the employer, employers who are not obligated to collect demographic data regarding their applicants may find themselves contesting with experts who purport to impute racial, ethnic, and gender characteristics to their applicant flow, using methodologies that may or may not withstand scientific scrutiny.

Just as Big Data elevates trivial differences to statistical significance, so too does it trivialize the concept of "validity," as conventionally defined. In traditional cases in which the challenged screening mechanism takes the form of a test, the standard controversy concerns whether the test is "valid," usually as that is defined by the Uniform Guidelines on Employee Selection Procedures.[189]

Instead of disputing validity, which Big Data should pass with flying colors because algorithms are selected precisely because they maximize correlations, much of the battle will be fought over an issue that rarely surfaces in litigation over conventional selection methods. Title VII provides that a plaintiff may prevail, despite the employer's proof that its selection criterion is valid, if it can demonstrate that there exists an alternative selection criterion that meets the employer's business

[185] *Id.* at 754.

[186] *See, e.g., Israel v. United States*, No. 09-CF-687, Dist. of Columbia Ct. of Appeals (Nov. 26, 2014) (citing geocoded estimates of potential jurors).

[187] *See, e.g., United States v. Reyes*, 934 F. Supp. 553, 560 (S.D.N.Y. 1996).

[188] *EEOC v. FAPS, Inc.*, Civil No. 10-3095 (JAP)(DEA) (D.N.J. Sep. 26, 2014) (unpublished op. citing cases admitting survey evidence).

[189] *See generally* 29 C.F.R. § 1607.

needs, but is less discriminatory in its impact.[190] But selecting among alternatives is precisely what Big Data is about.

The procedure for developing a Big Data algorithm is to assess the performance of all possible algorithms, within the limitations of the data available, and select the one that works best. The plaintiff 's rebuttal to the employer's defense of validity requires searching among those same algorithms and determining if any impacts the protected group less harshly. This sets up a contest among algorithms, necessitating experts skilled in developing and measuring how they perform. Although these comparisons may be assessed in statistical terms, the experts who will be in demand must be skilled in constructing and assessing algorithms, as well as applying the statistical tests by which this contest may be decided.

Preparing for Data-Enhanced Legal Services

Employers should prepare for a new human resources world dominated by data sets, analytics, and statistical correlations. Depending on the employer, that world either has already arrived or is in the process of arriving quickly and with momentum. Big Data is here to stay and will not easily be separated from effective human resources management techniques or from the legal world in which employers operate. Whether addressing the laws that govern the gathering and storage of information about candidates and employees or the tests used to determine whether illegal discrimination has occurred, or examining the ways in which parties manage data in litigation, employers need to know and understand the interplay between Big Data and the human resources laws that dictate what can and cannot be done.

The challenge for employers is to find a way to embrace the strengths of Big Data without losing sight of their own business goals and culture amidst potential legal risks. An important part of this process is finding and working with key business partners to assist in Big Data efforts and developing strategies that have the potential to make the workplace function more effectively for everyone. Employers also need to work with those business partners to establish a clear understanding regarding who is responsible for managing which risks and who bears the responsibility for any legal action that might arise.

Responsible employers will be mindful of the risks attendant upon collecting and storing Big Data from the perspectives of data collectors, privacy laws, and data security custodians, while simultaneously using Big Data to achieve key business goals and create a more cohesive and collegial working environment. To do that well, it is vital that human-resource professionals and their lawyers have a seat at the table when business decisions are made regarding how and when to use Big Data. The first step in securing that place in the decision-making process is to better understand what Big Data is and how it relates to the current legal system and human-resources framework.

---

[190] *See, e.g., Albemarle Paper Co. v. Moody*, 422 U.S. 405, 425 (1975); *Contreras v. City of Los Angeles*, 656 F.2d 1267, 1284–1285 (1981).

Chapter 5

Computational Law, Symbolic Discourse, and the AI Constitution

---

Stephen Wolfram[1]

Contents

---

[1] This chapter is based on an article originally posted on Stephen Wolfram's blog: http://blog.
stephenwolfram.com/2016/10/computational-law-symbolic-discourse-and-the-ai-constitution/.

Leibniz's Dream

Gottfried Leibniz—who died just more than 300 years ago in November 1716—worked on many things, but a theme that recurred throughout his life was the goal of turning human law into an exercise in computation. Of course, as we know, he didn't succeed. But three centuries later, I think we're finally ready to give it a serious try again. And I think it's a really important thing to do—not just because it'll enable all sorts of new societal opportunities and structures, but because I think it's likely to be critical to the future of our civilization in its interaction with artificial intelligence (AI).

Human law, almost by definition, dates from the very beginning of civilization—and undoubtedly, it's the first system of rules that humans ever systematically defined. Presumably, it was a model for the axiomatic structure of mathematics as defined by the likes of Euclid. And when science came along, "natural laws" (as their name suggests) were at first viewed as conceptually similar to human laws, except that they were supposed to define constraints for the universe (or God) rather than for humans.

Over the past few centuries we've had amazing success formalizing mathematics and exact science. And out of this there's a more general idea that's emerged: the idea of computation. In computation, we're dealing with arbitrary systems of rules—not necessarily ones that correspond to mathematical concepts we know, or features of the world we've identified. So now the question is: can we use the ideas of computation, in very much the way Leibniz imagined, to formalize human law?

The basic issue is that human law talks about human activities, and (unlike say for the mechanics of particles) we don't have a general formalism for describing human activities. When it comes to talking about money, for example, we often can be precise. And as a result, it's pretty easy to write a very formal contract for paying a subscription, or determining how an option on a publicly traded stock should work.

But what about all the things that typical legal contracts deal with? Well, clearly we have one way to write legal contracts: just use natural language (like English). It's often very stylized natural language, because it's trying to be as precise as possible. But ultimately it's never going to be precise. Because at the lowest level, it's always going to depend on the meanings of words, which for natural language are effectively defined just by the practice and experience of the users of the language.

A New Kind of Language

For a computer language, though, it's a different story. Because now the constructs in the language are absolutely precise: instead of having a vague, societally defined effect on human brains, they're defined to have a very specific effect on a computer. Of course, traditional computer languages don't directly talk about things relevant to human activities: they only directly talk about things like setting values for variables or calling abstractly defined functions.

But what I'm excited about is that we're starting to have a bridge between the precision of traditional computer languages and the ability to talk about real-world constructs. And actually, it's something I've personally been working on for more than three decades now: our knowledge-based Wolfram Language.

The Wolfram Language is precise: everything in it is defined to the point where a computer can unambiguously work with it. But its unique feature among computer languages is that it is knowledge based. It's not just a language to describe the low-level operations of a computer; instead, built right into the language is as much knowledge as possible about the real world. And this means that the language includes not just numbers like 2.7 and strings like "abc," but also constructs like the United States, or the Consumer Price Index, or an elephant. And that's exactly what we need to start talking about the kinds of things that appear in legal contracts or human laws.

I should make it clear that the Wolfram Language as it exists today doesn't include everything that's needed. We've got a large and solid framework, and we're off to a good start. But there's more about the world that we have to encode to be able to capture the full range of human activities and human legal specifications.

The Wolfram Language has, for example, a definition of what a banana is, broken down by all kinds of details. So if one says "you should eat a banana," the language has a way to represent "a banana." But as of now, it doesn't have a meaningful way to represent "you," "should," or "eat."

Is it possible to represent things like this in a precise computer language? Absolutely! But it takes language design to set up how to do it. Language design is a difficult business—in fact, it's probably the most intellectually demanding thing I know, requiring a strange mixture of high abstraction together with deep knowledge and down-to-earth practical judgment. But I've been doing it now for nearly four decades, and I think I'm finally ready for the challenge of doing language design for everyday discourse.

So what's involved? Well, let's first talk about it in a simpler case: the case of mathematics. Consider the function plus, which adds things like numbers together. When we use the English word "plus" it can have all sorts of meanings. One of those meanings is adding numbers together. But there are other meanings that are related, say, by various analogies ("product X plus," "the plus wire," "it's a real plus," …).

When we come to define plus in the Wolfram Language we want to build on the everyday notion of "plus," but we want to make it precise. And we can do that by picking the specific meaning of "plus" that's about adding things like numbers together. And once we know that this is what plus means, we immediately know all sorts of properties and can do explicit computations with it.

Now consider a concept like "magnesium." It's not as perfect and abstract a concept as plus. But physics and chemistry give us a clear definition of the element magnesium—which we can then use in the Wolfram Language to have a well-defined "magnesium" entity.

It's very important that the Wolfram Language is a symbolic language—because it means that the things in it don't immediately have to have "values"; they can just be symbolic constructs that stand for themselves. And so, for example, the entity "magnesium" is represented as a symbolic construct, that doesn't itself "do" anything, but can still appear in a computation, just like, for example, a number (like 9.45) can appear.

There are many kinds of constructs that the Wolfram Language supports. Like "New York City" or "last Christmas" or "geographically contained within." And the point is that the design of the language has defined a precise meaning for them. New York City, for example, is taken to mean the precise legal entity considered to be New York City, with geographical borders defined by law. Internal to the Wolfram Language, there's always a precise canonical representation for something like New York City (it's Entity["City", {"NewYork", "NewYork", "UnitedStates"}]). And this internal representation is all that matters when it comes to computation. Yes, it's convenient to refer to New York City as "nyc," but in the Wolfram Language, that natural language form is immediately converted to the precise internal form.

So what about "you should eat a banana"? Well, we've got to go through the same language design process for something like "eat" as for Plus (or "banana"). And the basic idea is that we've got to figure out a standard meaning for "eat." For example, it might be "ingestion of food by a person (or animal)." Now, there are plenty of other possible meanings for the English word "eat"—for example, ones that use analogies, as in "this function eats its arguments." But the idea—like for Plus—is to ignore these, and just to define a standard notion of "eat" that is precise and suitable for computation.

One gets a reasonable idea of what kinds of constructs one has to deal with just by thinking about parts of speech in English. There are nouns. Sometimes (as in "banana" or "elephant") there's a pretty precise definition of what these correspond to, and usually the Wolfram Language already knows about them. Sometimes it's a little vaguer but still concrete (as in "chair" or "window"), and sometimes it's abstract (like "happiness" or "justice"). But in each case one can imagine one or several entities that capture a definite meaning for the noun—just like the Wolfram Language already has entities for thousands of kinds of things.

Beyond nouns, there are verbs. There's typically a certain superstructure that exists around verbs. Grammatically, there might be a subject for the verb, and an object, and so on. Verbs are similar to functions in the Wolfram Language: each one deals with certain arguments, which, for example, correspond to its subject, object, etc. Now of course in English (or any other natural language), there are all sorts of elaborate special cases and extra features that can be associated with verbs. But basically we don't care about these because we're really just trying to define symbolic constructs that represent certain concepts. We don't have to capture every detail of how a particular verb works; we're just using the English verb as a way to give us a kind of "cognitive hook" for the concept.

We can go through other parts of speech. Adverbs that modify verbs; adjectives that modify nouns. These can sometimes be represented in the Wolfram Language by constructs like EntityInstance and sometimes by options to functions. But the important point in all cases is that we're not trying to faithfully reproduce how the natural language works; we're just using the natural language as a guide to how concepts are set up.

Pronouns are interesting. They work a bit like variables in pure anonymous functions. In "you should eat a banana," the "you" is like a free variable that's going to be filled in with a particular person.

Parts of speech and grammatical structures suggest certain general features to capture in a symbolic representation of discourse. There are a bunch of others, though. For example, there are what amount to "calculi" that one needs to represent notions of time ("within the time interval," "starting later," etc.) or of space ("on top of," "contained within," etc.). We've already got many calculi like these in the Wolfram Language; the most straightforward are ones about numbers ("greater than," etc.) or sets ("member of"), etc. Some calculi have long histories ("temporal logic," "set theory," etc.); others still have to be constructed.

Is there a global theory of what to do? Well, no more than there's a global theory of how the world works. There are concepts and constructs that are part of how our world works, and we need to capture these. No doubt there'll be new things that come along in the future, and we'll want to capture those too. And my experience from building Wolfram|Alpha is that the best thing to do is just to build each thing one needs, without starting off with any kind of global theory. After a while, one may notice that one has built similar things several times, and one may go in and unify them.

One can get deep into the foundations of science and philosophy about this. Yes, there's a computational universe out there of all the possible rules by which systems can operate (and, yes, I've spent a good part of my life studying the basic science of this). And there's our physical universe that presumably operates according to certain rules from the computational universe. But from these rules can emerge all sorts of complex behavior, and in fact, the phenomenon of computational irreducibility implies that in a sense there's no limit to what can be built up.

But there's not going to be an overall way to talk about all this stuff. And if we're going to be dealing with any finite kind of discourse it's going to only capture certain features. Which features we choose to capture is going to be determined by what concepts have evolved in the history of our society. And usually these concepts will be mirrored in the words that exist in the languages we use.

At a foundational level, computational irreducibility implies that there will always be new concepts that could be introduced. Back in antiquity, Aristotle introduced logic as a way to capture certain aspects of human discourse. And there are other frameworks that have been introduced in the history of philosophy, and more recently, natural language processing and AI research. But computational irreducibility effectively implies that none of them can ever ultimately be complete. And we must expect that as the concepts we consider relevant evolve, so too must the symbolic representation we have for discourse.

The Discourse Workflow

OK, so let's say we've got a symbolic representation for discourse. How's it actually going to be used? Well, there are some good clues from the way natural language works.

In standard discussions of natural language, it's common to talk about "interrogative statements" that ask a question, "declarative statements" that assert something and "imperative statements" that say to do something. (Let's ignore "exclamatory statements," like expletives, for now.)

Interrogative statements are what we're dealing with all the time in Wolfram|Alpha: "what is the density of gold?" "what is $3+7$?" "what was the latest reading from that sensor?" etc. They're also common in notebooks used to interact with the Wolfram Language: there's an input (In[1]:= $2+2$) and then there's a corresponding output (Out[1] = 4).

Declarative statements are all about filling in particular values for variables. In a very coarse way, one can set values ($x=7$), as in typical procedural languages. But it's typically better to think about having environments in which one's asserting things. Maybe those environments are supposed to represent the real world, or some corner of it. Or maybe they're supposed to represent some fictional world, where for example, dinosaurs didn't go extinct or something.

Imperative statements are about making things happen in the world: "open the pod bay doors," "pay Bob 0.23 bitcoin," etc.

In a sense, interrogative statements determine the state of the world, declarative statements assert things about the state of the world, and imperative statements change the state of the world.

In different situations, we can mean different things by "the world." We could be talking about abstract constructs, like integers or logic operations, that just are the way they are. We could be talking about natural laws or other features of our physical universe that we can't change. Or we could be talking about our local environment, where we can move around tables and chairs, choose to eat bananas, and so on. Or we could be talking about our mental states or the internal state of something like a computer.

There are lots of things one can do if one has a general symbolic representation for discourse. But one of them—which is the subject of this post—is to express things like legal contracts. The beginning of a contract, with its various whereas clauses, recitals, definitions, and so on tends to be dense with declarative statements ("this is so"). Then the actual terms of the contract tend to end up with imperative statements ("this should happen"), perhaps depending on certain things determined by interrogative statements ("did this happen?").

It's not hard to start seeing the structure of contracts as being much like programs. In simple cases, they just contain logical conditionals: "if X then Y." In other cases they're more modeled on math: "if this amount of X happens, that amount of Y should happen." Sometimes there's iteration: "keep doing X until Y happens." Occasionally there's some recursion: "keep applying X to every Y." And so on.

There are already some places where legal contracts are routinely represented by what amount to programs. The most obvious are financial contracts for things like bonds and options—which just amount to little programs that define payouts based on various formulas and conditionals.

There's a whole industry of using "rules engines" to encode certain kinds of regulations as "if then" rules, usually mixed with formulas. In fact, such things are almost universally used for tax and insurance computations. (They're also common in pricing engines and the like.)

Of course, it's no coincidence that one talks about "legal codes." The word code—which comes from the Latin codex—originally referred to systematic collections of legal rules. And when programming came along a couple of millennia later, it used the word "code" because it basically saw itself as similarly setting up rules for how things should work, except now the things had to do with the operation of computers rather than the conduct of worldly affairs.

But now, with our knowledge-based computer language and the idea of a symbolic discourse language, what we're trying to do is to make it so we can talk about a broad range of worldly affairs in the same kind of way that we talk about computational processes—so we put all those legal codes and contracts into computational form.

Code versus Language

How should we think about symbolic discourse language compared with ordinary natural language? In a sense, the symbolic discourse language is a representation in which all the nuance and "poetry" have been "crushed" out of the natural language. The symbolic discourse language is precise, but it'll almost inevitably lose the nuance and poetry of the original natural language.

If someone says "2+2" to Wolfram|Alpha, it'll dutifully answer "4." But what if instead they say, "hey, will you work out 2+2 for me." Well, that sets up a different mood. But Wolfram|Alpha will take that input and convert it to exactly the same symbolic form as "2+2," and similarly just respond "4."

This is exactly the kind of thing that'll happen all the time with symbolic discourse language. And if the goal is to answer precise questions—or, for that matter, to create a precise legal contract, it's exactly what one wants. One just needs the hard content that will actually have a consequence for what one's trying to do, and in this case, one doesn't need the "extras" or "pleasantries."

Of course, what one chooses to capture depends on what one's trying to do. If one's trying to get psychological information, then the "mood" of a piece of natural language can be very important. Those "exclamatory statements" (like expletives) carry meaning one cares about. But one can still perfectly well imagine capturing things like that in a symbolic way—for example by having an "emotion track" in one's symbolic discourse language. (Very coarsely, this might be represented by sentiment or by position in an emotion space—or, for that matter, by a whole symbolic language derived, say, from emoji.)

In actual human communication through natural language, "meaning" is a slippery concept that inevitably depends on the context of the communication, the history of whoever is communicating, and so on. My notion of a symbolic discourse language isn't to try to magically capture the "true meaning" of a piece of natural language. Instead, my goal is just to capture some meaning that one can then compute with.

For convenience, one might choose to start with natural language, and then try to translate it into the symbolic discourse language. But the point is for the symbolic discourse language to be the real representation: the natural language is just a guide for trying to generate it. And in the end, the notion is that if one really wants to be sure one's accurate in what one's saying, one should say it directly in the symbolic discourse language, without ever using natural language.

Back in the 1600s, one of Leibniz's big concerns was to have a representation that was independent of which natural language people were using (French, German, Latin, etc.). And one feature of a symbolic discourse language is that it has to operate "below" the level of specific natural languages.

There's a rough kind of universality among human languages, in that it seems to be possible to represent any human concept at least to some approximation in any language. But there are plenty of nuances that are extremely hard to translate—between different languages, or the different cultures that surround them (or even the same language at different times in history). But in the symbolic discourse language, one's effectively "crushing out" these differences—and getting something that is precise, even though it typically won't correspond exactly to any particular human natural language.

A symbolic discourse language is about representing things in the world. Natural language is just one way to try to describe these things. But there are others. For example, one might give a picture. One could try to describe certain features of the picture in natural language ("a cat with a hat on its head")—or one could go straight from the picture to the symbolic discourse language.

In the example of a picture, it's very obvious that the symbolic discourse language isn't going to capture everything. Maybe it could capture something like "he is taking the diamond." But it's not going to specify the color of every pixel, and it's not going to describe all conceivable features of a scene at every level of detail.

In some sense, what the symbolic discourse language is doing is to specify a model of the system it's describing. And like any model, it's capturing some features, and idealizing others away. But the importance of it is that it provides a solid foundation on which computations can be done, conclusions can be drawn, and actions can be taken.

Why Now?

I've been thinking about creating what amounts to a general symbolic discourse language for nearly 40 years. But it's only recently—with the current state of the

Wolfram Language—that I've had the framework to actually do it. And it's also only recently that I've understood how to think about the problem in a sufficiently practical way.

Yes, it's nice in principle to have a symbolic way to represent things in the world. And in specific cases—like answering questions in Wolfram|Alpha—it's completely clear why it's worth doing this. But what's the point of dealing with more general discourse? Like, for example, when do we really want to have a "general conversation" with a machine?

The Turing test says that being able to do this is a sign of achieving general AI. But "general conversations" with machines—without any particular purpose in mind—so far usually seem in practice to devolve quickly into party tricks and Easter eggs. At least that's our experience looking at interactions people have with Wolfram|Alpha, and it also seems to be the experience with decades of chatbots and the like.

But the picture quickly changes if there's a purpose to the conversation: if you're actually trying to get the machine to do something or learn something from the machine. Still, in most of these cases, there's no real reason to have a general representation of things in the world; it's sufficient just to represent specific machine actions, particular customer service goals, or whatever. But if one wants to tackle the general problem of law and contracts, it's a different story. Because inevitably one is going to represent the full spectrum of human affairs and issues. And so now there's a definite goal to having a symbolic representation of the world: one needs it to be able to say what should happen and have machines understand it.

Sometimes it's useful to do that because one wants the machines just to be able to check whether what was supposed to happen actually did; sometimes one wants to actually have the machines automatically enforce or do things. But either way, one needs the machine to be able to represent general things in the world—and so one needs a symbolic discourse language to be able to do this.

Some History

In a sense, it's an obvious idea to have something like a symbolic discourse language. And indeed, it's an idea that's come up repeatedly across the course of centuries. But it's proved a very difficult idea to make work, and it has a history littered with (sometimes quite wacky) failures.

Things in a sense started well. Back in antiquity, logic as discussed by Aristotle provided a very restricted example of a symbolic discourse language. And when the formalism of mathematics began to emerge, it provided another example of a restricted symbolic discourse language.

But what about more general concepts in the world? There'd been many efforts—between the Tetractys of the Pythagoreans and the I Ching of the Chinese—to assign symbols or numbers to a few important concepts. But around 1300 Ramon

Llull took it further, coming up with a whole combinatorial scheme for representing concepts—and then trying to implement this with circles of paper that could supposedly mechanically determine the validity of arguments, particularly religious ones.

Four centuries later, Gottfried Leibniz was an enthusiast of Llull's work, at first imagining that perhaps all concepts could be converted to numbers and truth then determined by doing something like factoring into primes. Later, Leibniz starting talking about a *characteristica universalis* (or, as Descartes called it, an "alphabet of human thoughts")—essentially a universal symbolic language. But he never really tried to construct such a thing, instead chasing what one might consider "special cases"—including the one that led him to calculus.

With the decline of Latin as the universal natural language in the 1600s, particularly in areas like science and diplomacy, there had already been efforts to invent "philosophical languages" (as they were called) that would represent concepts in an abstract way, not tied to any specific natural language. The most advanced of these was by John Wilkins—who in 1668 produced a book cataloging over 10,000 concepts and representing them using strange-looking glyphs, with the rendering of the Lord's Prayer as an example.

In some ways these efforts evolved into the development of encyclopedias and later thesauruses, but as language-like systems, they basically went nowhere. Two centuries later, though, as the concept of internationalization spread, there was a burst of interest in constructing new, country-independent languages—and out of this emerged Volapük and then Esperanto. These languages were really just artificial natural languages; they weren't an attempt to produce anything like a symbolic discourse language. I always used to enjoy seeing signs in Esperanto at European airports, and was disappointed in the 1980s when these finally disappeared. But, as it happens, right around that time, there was another wave of language construction. There were languages like Lojban, intended to be as unambiguous as possible, and ones like the interestingly minimal Toki Pona intended to support the simple life, as well as the truly bizarre Ithkuil, intended to encompass the broadest range of linguistic and supposedly cognitive structures.

Along the way, there were also attempts to simplify languages like English by expressing everything in terms of 1000 or 2000 basic words (instead of the usual 20,000–30,000)—as in the "Simple English" version of Wikipedia or the xkcd Thing Explainer.

There were a few, more formal, efforts. One example was Hans Freudenthal's 1960 Lincos "language for cosmic intercourse" (i.e. communication with extraterrestrials) which attempted to use the notation of mathematical logic to capture everyday concepts. In the early days of the field of AI, there were plenty of discussions of "knowledge representation," with approaches based variously on the grammar of natural language, the structure of predicate logic or the formalism of databases. Very few large-scale projects were attempted (Doug Lenat's Cyc being a notable counterexample), and when I came to develop Wolfram|Alpha, I was disappointed at how little of relevance to our needs seemed to have emerged.

In a way, I find it remarkable that something as fundamental as the construction of a symbolic discourse language should have had so little serious attention paid to it in the past. But at some level, it's not so surprising. It's a difficult, large project, and it somehow lies in between established fields. It's not a linguistics project. Yes, it may ultimately illuminate how languages work, but that's not its main point. It's not a computer science project because it's really about content, not algorithms. And it's not a philosophy project because it's mostly about specific nitty-gritty and not much about general principles.

There've been a few academic efforts in the last half century or so, discussing ideas like "semantic primes" and "natural semantic metalanguage." Usually such efforts have tried to attach themselves to the field of linguistics—but their emphasis on abstract meaning rather than pure linguistic structure has put them at odds with prevailing trends, and none have turned into large-scale projects.

Outside of academia, there's been a steady stream of proposals—sometimes promoted by wonderfully eccentric individuals—for systems to organize and name concepts in the world. It's not clear how far this pursuit has come since Ramon Llull—and usually it's only dealing with pure ontology, and never with full meaning of the kind that can be conveyed in natural language.

I suppose one might hope that with all the recent advances in machine learning there'd be some magic way to automatically learn an abstract representation of meaning. And, yes, one can take Wikipedia, for example, or a text corpus, and use dimension reduction to derive some effective "space of concepts." But, not too surprisingly, simple Euclidean space doesn't seem to be a very good model for the way concepts relate (one can't even faithfully represent graph distances). And even the problem of taking possible meanings for words—as a dictionary might list them—and breaking them into clusters in a space of concepts doesn't seem to be easy to do effectively.

Still, as I'll discuss later, I think there's a very interesting interplay between symbolic discourse language and machine learning. But for now my conclusion is that there's not going to be any alternative but to use human judgment to construct the core of any symbolic discourse language that's intended for humans to use.

Contracts into Code

But let's get back to contracts. Today, there are hundreds of billions of them being signed every year around the world (and vastly more being implicitly entered into)—though the number of "original" ones that aren't just simple modifications is probably just in the millions (and is perhaps comparable to the number of original computer programs or apps being written.)

So can these contracts be represented in precise symbolic form, as Leibniz hoped 300 years ago? Well, if we can develop a decently complete symbolic discourse language, it should be possible. (Yes, every contract would have to be defined relative to some underlying set of "governing law" rules, etc., that are in some ways like the built-in functions of the symbolic discourse language.)

But what would it mean? Among other things, it would mean that contracts themselves would become computable things. A contract would be converted to a program in the symbolic discourse language. And one could do abstract operations just on this program. And this means one can imagine formally determining—in effect through a kind of generalization of logic—whether, say, a given contract has some particular implication, could ever lead to some particular outcome, or is equivalent to some other contract.

Ultimately, though, there's a theoretical problem with this. Because questions like this can run into issues of formal undecidability, which means there's no guarantee that any systematic finite computation will answer them. The same problem arises in reasoning about typical software programs people write, and in practice it's a mixed bag, with some things being decidable, and others not.

Of course, even in the Wolfram Language as it is today, there are plenty of things (such as the very basic "are these expressions equal?") that are ultimately in principle undecidable. And there are certainly questions one can ask that run right into such issues. But an awful lot of the kinds of questions that people naturally ask turn out to be answerable with modest amounts of computation. And I wouldn't be surprised if this were true for questions about contracts too. (It's worth noting that human-formulated questions tend to run into undecidability much less than questions picked, say at random, from the whole computational universe of possibilities.)

If one has contracts in computational form, there are other things one can expect to do too. Like the ability to automatically work out what the contracts imply for a large range of possible inputs. The 1980s revolution in quantitative finance started when it became clear one could automatically compute distributions of outcomes for simple option contracts. If one had lots (perhaps billions) of contracts in computational form, there'd be a lot more that could be done along these lines—and no doubt, for better or worse, whole new areas of financial engineering that could be developed.

Where Do the Inputs Come From?

OK, so let's say one has a computational contract. What can one directly do with it? Well, it depends somewhat on what the form of its input is. One important possibility is that they're in a sense "born computational": that they're immediately statements about a computational system ("how many accesses has this ID made today?" "what is the ping time for this connection?" "how much bitcoin got transferred?" etc.). And in that case, it should be possible to immediately and unambiguously "evaluate" the contract—and find out if it's being satisfied.

This is something that's very useful for lots of purposes—both for humans interacting with machines and machines interacting with machines. In fact, there are plenty of cases where versions of it are already in use. One can think of computer security provisions such as firewall rules as one example. There are others that are gradually emerging, such as automated service-level agreements and automated terms of service. (I'm certainly hoping our company, for example, will be able to make these a routine part of our business practice before long.)

But, OK, it's certainly untrue that every input for every contract is "born computational": plenty of inputs have to come from seeing what happens in the "outside" world ("did the person actually go to place X?" "was the package maintained in a certain environment?" "did the information get leaked to social media?" "is the parrot dead?" etc.). And the first thing to say is that in modern times it's become vastly easier to automatically determine things about the world, not least because one can just make measurements with sensors. Check the global positioning system (GPS) trace. Look at the car counting sensor. And so on. The whole Internet of Things is out there to provide input about the real world for computational contracts.

Having said this, though, there's still an issue. Yes, with a GPS trace there's a definite answer (assuming the GPS is working properly) for whether someone or something went to a particular place. But let's say one's trying to determine something less obviously numerical. Let's say, for example, that one's trying to determine whether a piece of fruit should be considered "Fancy Grade" or not. Well, given some pictures of the piece of fruit, an expert can pretty unambiguously tell. But how can we make this computational?

Well, here's a place where we can use modern machine learning. We can set up some neural net, say in the Wolfram Language, and then show it lots of examples of fruit that's Fancy Grade and that's not. And from my experience (and those of our customers!), most of the time we'll get a system that's really good at a task like grading fruit. It'll certainly be much faster than humans, and it'll probably be more reliable and more consistent too.

And this gives a whole new way to set up contracts about things in the world. Two parties can just agree that the contract should say "if the machine learning system says X then do Y." In a sense it's like any other kind of computational contract: the machine learning system is just a piece of code. But it's a little different. Because normally one expects that one can readily examine everything that a contract says: one can in effect read and understand the code. But with machine learning in the middle, there can no longer be any expectation of that.

Nobody specifically set up all those millions of numerical weights in the neural net; they were just determined by some approximate and somewhat random process from whatever training data that was given. Yes, in principle we can measure everything about what's happening inside the neural net. But there's no reason to expect that we'll ever be able to get an understandable explanation—or prediction—of what the net will do in any particular case. Most likely, it's an example of the phenomenon I call computational irreducibility—which means there really isn't any way to see what will happen much more efficiently than just by running it.

What's the difference with asking a human expert, then, whose thought processes one can't understand? Well, in practice machine learning is much faster so one can make much more use of "expert judgment." And one can set things up so they're repeatable, and one can for example systematically test for biases one thinks might be there, and so on.

Of course, one can always imagine cheating the machine learning. If it's repeatable, one could use machine learning itself to try to learn cases where it would fail. And in the end it becomes rather like computer security, where holes are being found, patches being applied, and so on. And in some sense, this is no different from the typical situation with contracts too: one tries to cover all situations, then it becomes clear that something hasn't been correctly addressed, and one tries to write a new contract to address it, and so on.

But the important bottom line is that with machine learning one can expect to get "judgment-oriented" input into contracts. I expect the typical pattern will be this: in the contract there'll be something stated in the symbolic discourse language (like "X will personally do Y"). And at the level of the symbolic discourse language there'll be a clear meaning to this, from which, for example, all sorts of implications can be drawn. But then there's the question of whether what the contract said is actually what happened in the real world. And, sure, there can be lots of sensor data that gives information on this. But in the end there'll be a "judgment call" that has to be made. Did the person actually personally do this? Well—like for a remote exam proctoring system—one can have a camera watching the person, one can record their pattern of keystrokes, and maybe even measure their electroencephalogram. But something's got to synthesize this data, and make the judgment call about what happened, and turn this in effect into a symbolic statement. And in practice, I expect it will typically end up being a machine learning system that does this.

Smart Contracts

OK, so let's say we've got ways to set up computational contracts. How can we enforce them? Well, ones that basically just involve computational processes can at some level enforce themselves. A particular piece of software can be built to issue licenses only in such-and-such a way. A cloud system can be built to make a download available only if it receives a certain amount of bitcoin. And so on.

But how far do we trust what's going on? Maybe someone hacked the software or the cloud. How can we be sure nothing bad has happened? The basic answer is to use the fact that the world is a big place. As a (sometime) physicist, it makes me think of measurement in quantum mechanics. If we're just dealing with a little quantum effect, there's always interference that can happen. But when we do a real measurement, we're amplifying that little quantum effect to the point where so many things (atoms, etc.) are involved that it's unambiguous what happened—in much the same way as the Second Law of Thermodynamics makes it inconceivable that all the air molecules in a room will spontaneously line up on one side.

And so it is with bitcoin, Ethereum, etc. The idea is that some particular thing that happened ("X paid Y such-and-such" or whatever) is shared and recorded in so many places that there can't be any doubt about it. Yes, it's in principle possible that all the few thousand places that actually participate in something like bitcoin today could collude to give a fake result. But the idea is that it's like with gas molecules in a room: the probability is inconceivably small. (As it happens, my Principle of Computational Equivalence suggests that there's more than an analogy with the gas molecules, and actually, the underlying principles at work are basically exactly the same. And, yes, there are lots of interesting technical details about the operation of distributed blockchain ledgers, distributed consensus protocols, etc., but I'm not going to get into them here.)

It's popular these days to talk about "smart contracts." When I've been talking about "computational contracts" I mean contracts that can be expressed computationally. But by "smart contracts" people usually mean contracts that can both be expressed computationally and execute automatically. Most often, the idea is to set up a smart contract in a distributed computation environment like Ethereum, and then to have the code in the contract evaluate based on inputs from the computation environment.

Sometimes the input is intrinsic—like the passage of time (who could possibly tamper with the clock of the whole internet?) or physically generated random numbers. And in cases like this, one has fairly pure smart contracts, say for paying subscriptions, or for running distributed lotteries.

But more often, there has to be some input from the outside—from something that happens in the world. Sometimes one just needs public information: the price of a stock, the temperature at a weather station, or a seismic event like a nuclear explosion. But somehow the smart contract needs access to an "oracle" that can give it this information. And convenient enough, there is one good such oracle available in the world: Wolfram|Alpha. And indeed Wolfram|Alpha is becoming widely used as an oracle for smart contracts. (Yes, our general public terms of service say you currently just shouldn't rely on Wolfram|Alpha for anything you consider critical—though hopefully, soon those terms of service will get more sophisticated and computational.)

But what about nonpublic information from the outside world? The current thinking for smart contracts tends to be that one has to get humans in the loop to verify the information: that in effect one has to have a jury (or a democracy) to decide whether something is true. But is that really the best one can do? I tend to suspect there's another path, that's like using machine learning to inject human-like judgment into things. Yes, one can use people, with all their inscrutable and hard-to-systematically influence behavior. But what if one replaces those people in effect by AIs—or even a collection of today's machine-learning systems?

One can think of a machine-learning system as being a bit like a cryptosystem. To attack it and spoof its input, one has to do something like inverting how it works. Well, given a single machine-learning system there's a certain effort needed to achieve this. But if one has a whole collection of sufficiently independent systems, the effort goes up. It won't be good enough just to change a few parameters in the system. But if one just goes out into the computational universe and picks systems at random, then I think one can expect to have the same kind of independence as by having different people. (To be fair, I don't yet quite know how to apply the mining of the computational universe that I've done for programs like cellular automata to the case of systems like neural nets.)

There's another point as well: if one has a sufficiently dense net of sensors in the world, then it becomes increasingly easy to be sure about what's happened. If there's just one motion sensor in a room, it might be easy to cover it. And maybe even if there are several sensors, it's still possible to avoid them, Mission Impossible-style. But if there are enough sensors, then by synthesizing information from them one can inevitably build up an understanding of what actually happened. In effect, one has a model of how the world works, and with enough sensors one can validate that the model is correct.

It's not surprising, but it always helps to have redundancy. More nodes to ensure the computation isn't tampered with. More machine-learning algorithms to make sure they aren't spoofed. More sensors to make sure they're not fooled. But in the end, there has to be something that says what should happen—what the contract is. And the contract has to be expressed in some language in which there are definite concepts. So somehow from the various redundant systems one has in the world, one has to make a definite conclusion—one has to turn the world into something symbolic, on which the contract can operate.

Writing Computational Contracts

Let's say we have a good symbolic discourse language. Then how should contracts actually get written in it?

One approach is to take existing contracts written in English or any other natural language, and try to translate (or parse) them into the symbolic discourse language. Well, what will happen is somewhat like what happens with Wolfram|Alpha today. The translator will not know exactly what the natural language was supposed to mean, and so it will give several possible alternatives. Maybe there was some meaning that the original writer of the natural-language contract had in mind. But maybe the "poetry" of that meaning can't be expressed in the symbolic discourse language: it requires something more definite. And a human is going to have to decide which alternative to pick.

Translating from natural-language contracts may be a good way to start, but I suspect it will quickly give way to writing contracts directly in the symbolic discourse language. Today lawyers have to learn to write legalese. In the future, they're going to have to learn to write what amounts to code: contracts expressed precisely in a symbolic discourse language.

One might think that writing everything as code, rather than natural-language legalese, would be a burden. But my guess is that it will actually be a great benefit. And it's not just because it will let contracts operate more easily. It's also that it will help lawyers think better about contracts. It's an old claim (the Sapir–Whorf hypothesis) that the language one uses affects the way one thinks. And this is no doubt somewhat true for natural languages. But in my experience it's dramatically true for computer languages. And indeed I've been amazed over the years at how my thinking has changed as we've added more to the Wolfram Language. When I didn't have a way to express something, it didn't enter my thinking. But once I had a way to express it, I could think in terms of it.

And so it will be, I believe, for legal thinking. When there's a precise symbolic discourse language, it'll become possible to think more clearly about all sorts of things.

Of course, in practice it'll help that there'll no doubt be all sorts of automated annotation: "if you add that clause, it'll imply X, Y, and Z," etc. It'll also help that it'll routinely be possible to take some contract and simulate its consequences for a range of inputs. Sometimes one will want statistical results ("is this biased?"). Sometimes one will want to hunt for particular "bugs" that will only be found by trying lots of inputs.

Yes, one can read a contract in natural language, like one can read a math paper. But if one really wants to know its implications, one needs it in computational form, so one can run it and see what it implies—and also so one can give it to a computer to implement.

The World with Computational Contracts

Back in ancient Babylon, it was a pretty big deal when there started to be written laws like the Code of Hammurabi. Of course, with very few people able to read, there was all sorts of clunkiness at first—like having people recite the laws in order from memory. Over the centuries things got more streamlined, and then about 500 years ago, with the advent of widespread literacy, laws and contracts started to get more complex (which among other things allowed them to be more nuanced, and to cover more situations).

In recent decades the trend has accelerated, particularly now that it's so easy to copy and edit documents of any length. But things are still limited by the fact that humans are in the loop, authoring and interpreting the documents. Back 50 years ago, pretty much the only way to define a procedure for anything was to write it down and have humans implement it. But then along came computers, and programming. And very soon it started to be possible to define vastly more complex procedures—to be implemented not by humans, but instead by computers.

And so, I think, it will be with law. Once computational law becomes established, the complexity of what can be done will increase rapidly. Typically a contract defines some model of the world, and specifies what should happen in different situations. Today the logical and algorithmic structure of models defined by contracts still tends to be fairly simple. But with computational contracts, it'll be feasible for them to be much more complex—so that they can for example more faithfully capture how the world works.

Of course, that just makes defining what should happen even more complex—and before long it might feel a bit like constructing an operating system for a computer that tries to cover all the different situations the computer might find itself in.

In the end, though, one's going to have to say what one wants. One might be able to get a certain distance by just giving specific examples. But ultimately I think one's going to have to use a symbolic discourse language that can express a higher level of abstraction.

Sometimes one will be able to just write everything in the symbolic discourse language. But often, I suspect, one will use the symbolic discourse language to define what amount to goals, and then one will have to use machine-learning kinds of methods to fill in how to define a contract that actually achieves them.

And as soon as there's computational irreducibility involved, it'll typically be impossible to know for sure that there are no bugs or "unintended consequences." Yes, one can do all kinds of automated tests. But in the end, it's theoretically impossible to have any finite procedure that can guarantee to check all possibilities.

Today there are plenty of legal situations that are too complex to handle without expert lawyers. And in a world where computational law is common, it won't just be convenient to have computers involved, it'll be necessary.

In a sense it's similar to what's already happened in many areas of engineering. Back when humans had to design everything themselves, humans could typically understand the structures that were being built. But once computers are involved in design it becomes inevitable that they're needed in figuring out how things work too.

Today a fairly complex contract might involve a hundred pages of legalese. But once there's computational law—and particularly contracts constructed automatically from goals—the lengths are likely to increase rapidly. At some level it won't matter, though—just as it doesn't really matter how long the code of a program one's using is. Because the contract will in effect just be run automatically by computer.

Leibniz saw computation as a simplifying element in the practice of law. And, yes, some things will become simpler and better defined. But a vast ocean of complexity will also open up.

What Does It Mean for AIs?

How should one tell an AI what to do? Well, you have to have some form of communication that both humans and AIs can understand—and that is rich enough to describe what one wants. And as I've described elsewhere, what I think this basically means is that one has to have a knowledge-based computer language—which is precisely what the Wolfram Language is—and ultimately one needs a full symbolic discourse language.

But, OK, so one tells an AI to do something, like "go get some cookies from the store." But what one says inevitably won't be complete. The AI has to operate within some model of the world, and with some code of conduct. Maybe it can figure out how to steal the cookies, but it's not supposed to do that; presumably one wants it to follow the law or a certain code of conduct.

And this is where computational law gets really important: because it gives us a way to provide that code of conduct in a way that AIs can readily make use of.

In principle, we could have AIs ingest the complete corpus of laws and historical cases and so on, and try to learn from these examples. But as AIs become more and more important in our society, it's going to be necessary to define all sorts of new laws, and many of these are likely to be "born computational," not least, I suspect, because they'll be too algorithmically complex to be usefully described in traditional natural language.

There's another problem too: we really don't just want AIs to follow the letter of the law (in whatever venue they happen to be), we want them to behave ethically too, whatever that may mean. Even if it's within the law, we probably don't want our AIs lying and cheating; we want them somehow to enhance our society along the lines of whatever ethical principles we follow.

Well, one might think, why not just teach AIs ethics like we could teach them laws? In practice, it's not so simple. Because whereas laws have been somewhat decently codified, the same can't be said for ethics. Yes, there are philosophical and religious texts that talk about ethics. But it's a lot vaguer and less extensive than what exists for law.

Still, if our symbolic discourse language is sufficiently complete, it certainly should be able to describe ethics too. And in effect we should be able to set up a system of computational laws that defines a whole code of conduct for AIs.

But what should it say? One might have a few immediate ideas. Perhaps one could combine all the ethical systems of the world. Obviously hopeless. Perhaps one could have the AIs just watch what humans do and learn their system of ethics from it. Similarly hopeless. Perhaps one could try something more local, where the AIs switch their behavior based on geography, cultural context, etc. (think "protocol droid"). Perhaps useful in practice, but hardly a complete solution.

So what can one do? Well, perhaps there are a few principles one might agree on. For example, at least the way we think about things today, most of us don't want humans to go extinct (of course, maybe in the future, having mortal beings will be thought too disruptive, or whatever). And actually, while most people think there are all sorts of things wrong with our current society and civilization, people usually don't want it to change too much, and they definitely don't want change forced upon them.

So what should we tell the AIs? It would be wonderful if we could just give the AIs some simple set of almost axiomatic principles that would make them always do what we want. Maybe they could be based on Asimov's Three Laws of Robotics. Maybe they could be something seemingly more modern based on some kind of global optimization. But I don't think it's going to be that easy.

The world is a complicated place; if nothing else, that's basically guaranteed by the phenomenon of computational irreducibility. And it's pretty much inevitable that there's not going to be any finite procedure that'll force everything to "come out the way one wants" (whatever that may be).

Let me take a somewhat abstruse, but well defined, example from mathematics. We think we know what integers are. But to really be able to answer all questions about integers (including about infinite collections of them, etc.) we need to set up axioms that define how integers work. And that's what Giuseppe Peano tried to do in the late 1800s. For a while it looked good, but then in 1931 Kurt Gödel surprised the world with his Incompleteness Theorem, which implied among other things, that actually, try as one might, there was never going to be a finite set of axioms that would define the integers as we expect them to be, and nothing else.

In some sense, Peano's original axioms actually got quite close to defining just the integers we want. But Gödel showed that they also allow bizarre nonstandard integers, where for example, the operation of addition isn't finitely computable.

Well, OK, that's abstract mathematics. What about the real world? Well, one of the things that we've learned since Gödel's time is that the real world can be thought of in computational terms, pretty much just like the mathematical systems Gödel considered. And in particular, one can expect the same phenomenon of computational irreducibility (which itself is closely related to Gödel's Theorem). And the result of this is that whatever simple intuitive goal we may define, it's pretty much inevitable we'll have to build up what amount to an arbitrarily complicated collection of rules to try to achieve it—and whatever we do, there'll always be at least some "unintended consequences."

None of this should really come as much of a surprise. After all, if we look at actual legal systems as they've evolved over the past couple of thousand years, there always end up being a lot of laws. It's not like there's a single principle from which everything else can be derived; there inevitably end up being lots of different situations that have to be covered.

Principles of the World?

But is all this complexity just a consequence of the "mechanics" of how the world works? Imagine—as one expects—that AIs get more and more powerful. And that more and more of the systems of the world, from money supplies to border controls, are in effect put in the hands of AIs. In a sense, then, the AIs play a role a little bit like governments, providing an infrastructure for human activities.

So, OK, perhaps we need a "constitution" for the AIs, just like we set up constitutions for governments. But again the question comes: what should the constitution have in it?

Let's say that the AIs could mold human society in pretty much anyway. How would we want it molded? Well, that's an old question in political philosophy, debated since antiquity. At first an idea like utilitarianism might sound good: somehow maximize the well-being of as many people as possible. But imagine actually trying to do this with AIs that in effect control the world. Immediately one is thrust into concrete versions of questions that philosophers and others have debated for centuries. Let's say one can sculpt the probability distribution for happiness among people in the world. Well, now we've got to get precise about whether it's the mean or the median or the mode or a quantile or, for that matter, the kurtosis of the distribution that we're trying to maximize.

No doubt one can come up with rhetoric that argues for some particular choice. But there just isn't an abstract "right answer." Yes, we can have a symbolic discourse language that expresses any choice. But there's no mathematical derivation of the answer, and there's no law of nature that forces a particular answer. I suppose there could be a "best answer given our biological nature." But as things advance, this won't be on solid ground either, as we increasingly manage to use technology to transcend the biology that evolution has delivered to us.

Still, we might argue, there's at least one constraint: we don't want a scheme where we'll go extinct—and where nothing will in the end exist. Even this is going to be a complicated thing to discuss, because we need to say what the "we" here is supposed to be: just how "evolved" relative to the current human condition can things be, and not consider "us" to have gone extinct?

But even independent of this, there's another issue: given any particular setup, computational irreducibility can make it in a sense irreducibly difficult to find out its consequences. And so in particular, given any specific optimization criterion (or constitution), there may be no finite procedure that will determine whether it allows for infinite survival or whether in effect it implies civilization will "halt" and go extinct.

OK, so things are complicated. What can one actually do? For a little while there'll probably be the notion that AIs must ultimately have human owners, who must act according to certain principles, following the usual way human society operates. But realistically, this won't last long.

Who would be responsible for a public-domain AI system that's spread across the internet? What happens when the bots it spawns start misbehaving on social media (yes, the notion that social media accounts are just for humans will soon look very "early 21st century")?

Of course, there's an important question of why AIs should "follow the rules" at all. After all, humans certainly don't always do that. It's worth remembering, though, that we humans are probably a particularly difficult case: after all, we're the product a multibillion-year process of natural selection, in which there's been a continual competitive struggle for survival. AIs are presumably coming into the world in very different circumstances, and without the same need for "brutish instincts." (Well, I can't help thinking of AIs from different companies or countries being imbued by their creators with certain brutish instincts, but that's surely not a necessary feature of AI existence.)

In the end, though, the best hope for getting AIs to "follow the rules" is probably by more or less the same mechanism that seems to maintain human society today: that following the rules is the way some kind of dynamic equilibrium is achieved. But if we can get the AIs to "follow the rules," we still have to define what the rules—the AI Constitution—should be.

And, of course, this is a hard problem, with no "right answer." But perhaps one approach is to see what's happened historically with humans. And one important and obvious thing is that there are different countries, with different laws and customs. So perhaps at the very least we have to expect that there'd be multiple AI Constitutions, not just one.

Even looking at countries today, an obvious question is how many there should be. Is there some easy way to say that—with technology as it exists, for example—7 billion people should be expected to organize themselves into about 200 countries?

It sounds a bit like asking how many planets the solar system should end up with. For a long time, this was viewed as a "random fact of nature" (and widely used by philosophers as an example of something that, unlike $2+2=4$, doesn't "have to be that way"). But particularly having seen so many exoplanet systems, it's become clear that our solar system actually pretty much has to have about the number of planets it does.

And maybe after we've seen the sociologies of enough video-game virtual worlds, we'll know something about how to "derive" the number of countries. But of course it's not at all clear that AI Constitutions should be divided anything like countries.

The physicality of humans has the convenient consequence that at least at some level one can divide the world geographically. But AIs don't need to have that kind of spatial locality. One can imagine some other schemes, of course. Like let's say one looks at the space of personalities and motivations, and finds clusters in it. Perhaps one could start to say "here's an AI Constitution for that cluster" and so on. Maybe the constitutions could fork, perhaps almost arbitrarily (a "Git-like model of society"). I don't know how things like this would ultimately work, but they seem more plausible than what amounts to a single, consensus, AI Constitution for everywhere and everyone.

There are so many issues, though. Like here's one. Let's assume AIs are the dominant power in our world. But let's assume that they successfully follow some constitution or constitutions that we've defined for them. Well, that's nice—but does it mean nothing can ever change in the world? I mean, just think if we were still all operating according to laws that had been set up 200 years ago: most of society has moved on since then and wants different laws (or at least different interpretations) to reflect its principles.

But what if precise laws for AIs were burnt in around the year 2020, for all eternity? Well, one might say, real constitutions always have explicit clauses that allow for their own modification (in the US Constitution it's Article V). But looking at the actual constitutions of countries around the world isn't terribly encouraging. Some just say basically that the constitution can be changed if some supreme leader (a person) says so. Many say that the constitution can be changed through some democratic process—in effect by some sequence of majority or similar votes. And some basically define a bureaucratic process for change so complex that one wonders if it's formally undecidable whether it would ever come to a conclusion.

At first, the democratic scheme seems like an obvious winner. But it's fundamentally based on the concept that people are somehow easy to count (of course, one can argue about which people, etc.). But what happens when personhood gets more complicated? When, for example, there are in effect uploaded human consciousnesses, deeply intertwined with AIs? Well, one might say, there's always got to be some "indivisible person" involved. And yes, I can imagine little clumps of pineal gland cells that are maintained to define "a person," just like in the past they were thought to be the seat of the soul. But from the basic science I've done I think I can say for certain that none of this will ultimately work—because in the end, the computational processes that define things just don't have this kind of indivisibility.

So what happens to "democracy" when there are no longer "people to count"? One can imagine all sorts of schemes, involving identifying the density of certain features in "people space." I suppose one can also imagine some kind of bizarre voting involving transfinite numbers of entities, in which perhaps the axiomatization of set theory has a key effect on the future of history.

It's an interesting question how to set up a constitution in which change is "burned in." There's a very simple example in bitcoin, where the protocol just defines by fiat that the value of mined bitcoin goes down every year. Of course, that setup is in a sense based on a model of the world—and in particular on something like Moore's Law and the apparent short-term predictability of technological development. But following the same general idea, one might start thinking about a constitution that says "change 1% of the symbolic code in this every year." But then one's back to having to decide "which 1%?" Maybe it'd be based on usage, or observations of the world, or some machine-learning procedure. But whatever algorithm or meta-algorithm is involved, there's still at some point something that has to be defined once and for all.

Can one make a general theory of change? At first, this might seem hopeless. But in a sense exploring the computational universe of programs is like seeing a spectrum of all possible changes. And there's definitely some general science that can be done on such things. And maybe there's some setup—beyond just "fork whenever there could be a change"—that would let one have a constitution that appropriately allows for change, as well as changing the way one allows for change, and so on.

Making It Happen

OK, we've talked about some far-reaching and foundational issues. But what about the here and now? Well, I think the exciting thing is that 300 years after Gottfried Leibniz died, we're finally in a position to do what he dreamed of: to create a general symbolic discourse language and to apply it to build a framework for computational law.

With the Wolfram Language, we have the foundational symbolic system—as well as a lot of knowledge of the world—to start from. There's still plenty to do, but I think there's now a definite path forward. And it really helps that in addition to the abstract intellectual challenge of creating a symbolic discourse language, there's now also a definite target in mind: being able to set up practical systems for computational law.

It's not going to be easy. But I think the world is ready for it, and needs it. There are simple smart contracts already in things like bitcoin and Ethereum, but there's vastly more that can be done—and with a full symbolic discourse language the whole spectrum of activities covered by law becomes potentially accessible to structured computation. It's going to lead to all sorts of both practical and conceptual advances. And it's going to enable new legal, commercial, and societal structures—in which, among other things, computers are drawn still further into the conduct of human affairs.

I think it's also going to be critical in defining the overall framework for AIs in the future. What ethics, and what principles, should they follow? How do we communicate these to them? For ourselves and for the AIs, we need a way to formulate what we want. And for that we need a symbolic discourse language. Leibniz had the right idea, but 300 years too early. Now in our time I'm hoping we're finally going to get to build for real what he only imagined. And in doing so we're going to take yet another big step forward in harnessing the power of the computational paradigm.

Chapter 6

Quantifying Success: Using Data Science to Measure the Accuracy of Technology-Assisted Review in Electronic Discovery

Maura R. Grossman and Gordon V. Cormack

Contents

Technology-Assisted Review and the Role of Measurement

Electronic discovery ("eDiscovery") is "[t]he process of identifying, preserving, collecting, processing, searching, reviewing, and producing electronically stored information ["ESI"] that may be relevant to a civil, criminal, or regulatory matter."[1] Review for production ("review") concerns a particular phase of eDiscovery: the identification of documents from a specific collection, which meet certain criteria, typically set forth by an adversary in the form of requests for production ("RFPs"). Documents that meet the criteria are generally referred to as "responsive," and those that do not, as "nonresponsive."

Technology-assisted review ("TAR") is the process of using computer software to categorize each document in a collection as responsive or not, or to prioritize the documents from most to least likely to be responsive, based on a human's review and coding of a small subset of the documents in the collection.[2] In contrast, the more familiar and widely accepted practice of manual review involves human review and coding of each and every document in the collection,[3] usually following the application of keywords or other forms of culling, such as limiting the collection to certain custodians or file types, or applying date restrictions.

Manual review is an expensive, burdensome, and error-prone process. Scientific evidence suggests that certain TAR methods offer not only reduced effort and cost but also improved accuracy, when compared with manual review.[4] This evidence

---

[1] Maura R. Grossman & Gordon V. Cormack, *The Grossman-Cormack Glossary of Technology-Assisted Review*, 7 Fed. Cts. L. Rev. 1, 15 (2013), http://www.fclr.org/fclr/articles/html/2010/grossman.pdf (hereinafter "Glossary").

[2] Glossary, *supra* n.1, at 32.

[3] Glossary, *supra* n. 1, at 22.

[4] *See, e.g.,* Gordon V. Cormack and Maura R. Grossman, *Navigating Imprecision in Relevance Assessments on the Road to Total Recall: Roger and Me*, in Proceedings of the 40th International ACM SIGIR Conference on Research and Development in Information. Retrieval ___ (2017), http://dx.doi.org/10.1145/3077136.3080812; Maura R. Grossman & Gordon V. Cormack, *Technology-Assisted Review in E-Discovery Can Be More Effective and More Efficient Than Exhaustive Manual Review*, XVII Rich. J.L. & Tech. 11 (2011), http://jolt.richmond.edu/v17i3/article11.pdf (hereinafter "2011 JOLT Study").

has been derived using experimental methodologies from the domain of information retrieval (IR) research, which can be impenetrable to the average, nontechnical, legal practitioner.

Because TAR is relatively new and unfamiliar, it has been necessary to demonstrate its efficacy to clients, their counsel, opposing parties, and the courts, often using arcane concepts and terms from IR research, such as "recall," "precision," "F_1," "margin of error," and "confidence level," to name a few. A popular misconception has emerged that these terms and concepts are uniquely associated with TAR and must be mastered to use TAR, but can be avoided through the use of "tried-and-true" manual review. Recall, precision, F_1, margin of error, and confidence level, however, relate to scientific methods for measuring the efficiency and effectiveness of *any* review method, whether TAR or manual. They do not concern how to conduct a review, any more than Terry Newell's *Carbon Balance and Volumetric Measurements of Fuel Consumption*[5] concerns how to drive a fuel-efficient automobile.

Measurements of recall—or fuel consumption—can inform a user's choice of a review—or travel—method, insofar as they predict how well a particular method—or model of automobile—will meet the user's requirements. To this end, it is worthwhile to appraise the reliability and accuracy of the measurement techniques, as well as how closely the measured quantities reflect the user's actual needs and requirements.

Measurements of recall—or fuel consumption—may also be helpful during or after a review process—or road trip—to verify that the method for reaching one's destination is performing (or has performed) as expected, and, if not, to take remedial action. The measurement techniques used in this circumstance might be vastly different from those used beforehand: Our driver would likely consult the fuel gauge rather than visiting the Environmental Protection Agency (EPA) testing laboratory to conduct a carbon-balance test; the legal team would similarly use a metric commensurate with the requirements of the review task at hand.

This chapter sets forth the distinctions between different review methods, summarizes a body of scientific research that compares these different review methods, and describes various approaches to track the progress or quality of particular review efforts.

Review Objectives

The objective of any review effort, whether manual or TAR, is to identify, as nearly as practicable, *all* and *only* the documents that satisfy certain criteria. Following IR

---

[5] U.S. Environmental Protection Agency Technical Report EPA-AA-SDSB-80-05 (Apr. 1980), https://goo.gl/F2x6Qr.

practice, we call documents that satisfy the criteria "relevant," and documents that do not satisfy the criteria "not relevant" or "nonrelevant."

Although it is obvious that the meaning of "as nearly as practicable" is open to interpretation, it may be less apparent that the meaning of "all and only [relevant] documents" is equally inscrutable.

It is well known that the notion of "relevance" is subjective, and that no two reviewers will identify exactly the same set of relevant documents within a collection. This observation applies regardless of the knowledge, skill, and diligence of the reviewers, and regardless of how precisely the relevance criteria are specified.[6] The sets of relevant documents identified by two reviewers—or by the same reviewer on two different occasions—are remarkably dissimilar. Suppose two reviewers each deem 100 documents to be "all and only the relevant documents" from a collection. The IR literature suggests that these two sets would be unlikely to have more than about 67 documents in common—documents that both reviewers deemed relevant.[7] An additional 67 documents would be deemed relevant by one reviewer and nonrelevant by the other.[8] Which reviewer, we might ask, came closer to identifying "all and only the relevant documents"?

It is generally accepted that, for most practical purposes, the set of relevant documents identified by *either* reviewer is sufficiently close to the ideal of "any and all," provided that each reviewer is informed, competent, diligent, and operating in good faith. In the absence of supplemental evidence, there is no basis to say that one set is "closer to the ideal" or that one reviewer is "better" than the other.

If we were to consider the set of 100 documents deemed relevant by a third reviewer, we would expect to find about 67 in common with the set returned by the first reviewer, and about 67 in common with the set returned by the second reviewer.[9] Even fewer—about 45—would be in common among all three.[10]

Given two or more reviews for the same set of documents, it is possible to "triangulate," using statistical methods, to deduce the relative accuracy of each reviewer, and thus, which review is "closer to the ideal."[11]

---

[6] *See, e.g.,* Herbert L. Roitblat et al., *Document Categorization in Legal Electronic Discovery: Computer Classification vs. Manual Review,* 61 Am. Soc'y Info. Sci. Tech. 70 (2010); Peter Bailey et al., *Relevance Assessment: Are Judges Exchangeable and Does It Matter?,* in Proceedings of the 31st Annual International ACM SIGIR Conference on Research and Development in Information. Retrieval 667 (2008); Ellen M. Voorhees, *Variations in Relevance Judgments and the Measurement of Retrieval Effectiveness,* 36 Inform. Process. Manag. 697 (2000).

[7] *See generally* Voorhees, *supra* n.6.

[8] *See generally id.*

[9] *See generally id.*

[10] *See generally id.*

[11] *See* Pavel Metrikov et al., *Aggregation of Crowdsourced Ordinal Assessments and Integration with Learning to Rank: A Latent Trait Model,* in Proceedings of the 24th ACM International Conference on Information and Knowledge Management. 1391 (2015), http://dl.acm.org/citation.cfm?doid=2806416.2806492. A more complete explanation of statistical methods such as this are beyond the scope of this chapter.

The same statistical methods can be used to estimate the accuracy of manual review and TAR alike. If the accuracy of a TAR method compares favorably with, or is indistinguishable from, that of manual review, and manual review is considered "close enough" in practice, shouldn't TAR also be considered "close enough"?

Review Methods

Exhaustive Manual Review

Exhaustive manual review involves having a human reviewer examine every document in a collection and code each document as relevant or nonrelevant, and perhaps apply additional labels such as "privileged" or not, "confidential" or not, "hot" or not, and sometimes, specific issue tags. We say that the coding is *positive* when the reviewer deems the document to be relevant, and *negative* when the reviewer deems the document to be nonrelevant. As noted earlier, positive coding is evidence—but not proof—of relevance, whereas negative coding is evidence of nonrelevance.

Manual review is often accompanied by some sort of quality control process in which a portion of the documents is rereviewed and, where indicated, recoded by a second, more authoritative reviewer. Where the coding decisions disagree disproportionately often, action may be taken to diagnose and mitigate the cause; notwithstanding this process, the vast majority of documents in the collection are reviewed only once, and the original reviewer's coding is the sole determinant of the disposition of the document.

Post hoc validation or acceptance testing may employ similar methods: Some of the documents in the collection may be reviewed and, where necessary, recoded, and the result of the review is deemed acceptable if the first and second coding decisions agree sufficiently often, or if the second review does not identify a substantial number of relevant documents that were missed by the first review. When there is an insufficient level of agreement, or discrepancies are found, corrective action may be taken.

Culling or Narrowing the Collection

Exhaustive manual review is seldom employed in practice, except in the smallest of matters. Typically, the collection of documents identified for review is first culled to include only documents belonging to certain custodians, documents created or modified within a specific time frame, or documents containing one or more search terms thought likely to appear in relevant documents. Only documents from the narrowed collection are manually reviewed, and only the documents deemed by the reviewer to be responsive and nonprivileged are produced.

This culling process substantially decreases the size of the collection, and hence the burden of manual review, at the cost of excluding some difficult-to-quantify number of relevant documents from review, and hence from production. Even so, the vast majority of documents presented for review are nonrelevant—often 10 times as many as relevant ones.

In some very weak sense, this type of culling might be considered a form of TAR, because computer software is being employed to make coding decisions (*i.e.*, nonrelevant) on the group of documents excluded from review based on some criterion, such as the lack of occurrence of any of the search terms. However, we reserve the term "TAR" to refer only to computer methods that *affirmatively categorize each document* as relevant or not, or *prioritize the entire collection* from most to least likely to be relevant. The reader should be aware, however, that many commentators and software providers assume a vacuously broad definition of "TAR," using it to refer to any of a number of processes which use a computer for narrowing, navigating, or searching a collection, or for organizing or grouping documents within a collection (*e.g.*, "email threading," "near-deduplication," or "clustering").[12] Regardless of what it is called, the culling process imposes a fundamental limit on how close to *all* relevant documents can be identified by any subsequent review effort.

All too often, quality control and validation methods are limited to the review phase, and are disregarded with respect to the documents excluded by earlier culling efforts. This omission is illogical in light of the review objective, which is to find as nearly as practicable *all* (and only) the relevant documents in the collection, not just the relevant documents in the narrowed collection, which may be substantially fewer than *all*.

Rule-Based TAR

A "rule base" is a set of rules—akin to a checklist, decision tree, or flow chart—that determines how to decide whether a document is relevant or not.[13] Rule bases are typically constructed by a specialized team with expertise in the subject matter(s) of the RFP(s), rule-base construction, linguistics, and statistics. While the

---

[12] *See, e.g.*, KrollDiscovery, *Defining Technology Assisted Review*, Ediscovery.com (2017), http:// ediscovery.com/infobite-tar-umbrella/#.WVFvGlGQz3h ("The term Technology Assisted Review (TAR) encompasses many forms of document review technology. Under the TAR Umbrella are some of the following ediscovery technologies: deduplication, visual analytics, predictive coding, workflow, reporting, and searching."); Herbert L. Roitblat, *Introduction to Predictive Coding* (OrcaTec LLC 2013), at 15, http://theolp.org/Resources/Documents/ Introduction to Predictive Coding – Herb Roitblat.pdf (defining TAR as "[a]ny of a number of technologies that use technology, usually computer technology, to facilitate the review of documents for discovery").

[13] Glossary, *supra* n.1, at 28 (defining Rule Base as "[a] set of rules created by an expert to emulate the human decision-making process for the purposes of classifying documents in the context of electronic discovery.").

construction of a rule base is labor-intensive, it can involve substantially less effort than the manual review of collections of hundreds of thousands or millions of documents, which are often encountered in major litigation or regulatory matters. Research has shown that at least one rule-based TAR method can achieve results that compare favorable to exhaustive manual review.[14]

Supervised Machine Learning for TAR

Supervised machine-learning methods (*i.e.*, "learners") infer how to distinguish relevant from nonrelevant documents by analyzing training examples—documents that are coded (*i.e.*, labeled) as relevant or nonrelevant by a human teacher. In 2014, the authors proposed the taxonomy set forth below for describing TAR methods using supervised machine learning.[15] This taxonomy has since been widely adopted in the legal industry to characterize the TAR offerings in the marketplace.[16]

In simple passive learning ("SPL") methods,[17] the *teacher* (*i.e.*, human operator) selects the documents to be used as training examples; the learner is trained using these examples, and once sufficiently trained, is used to label every document in the collection as relevant or nonrelevant. Generally, the documents labeled as relevant by the learner are rereviewed manually. This manual review represents a small fraction of the collection, and hence a small fraction of the time and cost of an exhaustive manual review.

In simple active learning ("SAL") methods,[18] after the initial training set, the *learner* selects the documents to be reviewed and coded by the teacher, and used as training examples, and continues to select examples until it is sufficiently trained. Typically, the documents the learner chooses are those about which the learner is *least certain*, and therefore from which it will learn the most. Once sufficiently trained, the learner is then used to label every document in the collection. As with SPL, the documents labeled as relevant are generally rereviewed manually.

---

[14] 2011 JOLT Study, *supra* n.4.

[15] Gordon V. Cormack & Maura R. Grossman, *Evaluation of Machine-Learning Protocols for Technology-Assisted Review in Electronic Discovery*, in Proceedings of the 37th International ACM SIGIR Conference on Research and Development in Information. Retrieval 153 (2014), http://dx.doi.org/10.1145/2600428.2609601 (hereinafter "SIGIR 2014 Paper"). *See also* Maura R. Grossman & Gordon V. Cormack, *Comments on "The Implications of Rule 26(g) on the Use of Technology-Assisted Review*," 6 Fed. Cts. L. Rev. 285 (2014), http://www.fclr.org/fclr/articles/pdf/comments-implications-rule26g-tar-62314.pdf (hereinafter "Comments Paper"); Maura R. Grossman & Gordon V. Cormack, *Continuous Active Learning for TAR*, Practical Law J. 32 (Apr./May 2016), at 36 (hereinafter "Practical Law Article").

[16] *See, e.g.*, Supreme Court of Victoria [Australia], *Practice Note SC Gen 5 – Technology in Civil Litigation* (Jan. 30, 2017), http://assets.justice.vic.gov.au/supreme/resources/fba6720a-0cca-4eae-b89a-4834982ff391/gen5useoftechnology.pdf, at 6 (approving CAL, SAL, and SPL TAR protocols).

[17] SIGIR 2014 Paper, *supra* n.15; *see also* Practical Law Article, *supra* n.15, at 36.

[18] SIGIR 2014 Paper, *supra* n.15; *see also* Practical Law Article, *supra* n.15, at 36.

In continuous active learning ("CAL")[19]—the TAR method the authors developed, use, and advocate—after the initial training set, the *learner* repeatedly selects the *next-most-likely-to-be-relevant* documents (that have not yet been considered) for review, coding, and training, and continues to do so until it can no longer find any more relevant documents. There is generally no second review, because by the time the learner stops learning, all documents deemed relevant by the learner have already been identified and manually reviewed.

In the marketplace, the term "predictive coding" has been used to describe the use of supervised machine learning for TAR, but not to distinguish between SPL, SAL, or CAL. Recently, CAL methods have been promoted under the moniker "TAR 2.0," while SPL and SAL methods have been grouped together and referred to as "TAR 1.0."[20]

How to Start?

Two important issues that must be addressed in any supervised machine-learning TAR method are: How to start and when to stop?

The learner needs examples of *both* relevant and nonrelevant documents to infer the characteristics that distinguish one from the other. Finding nonrelevant examples to begin the process is easy; in most situations, the vast majority of documents in the collection are nonrelevant. A random sample of documents from the collection can be expected to contain mostly or entirely nonrelevant documents, which may be used as negative training examples.

Finding relevant examples can be more challenging, as they are usually less frequent—if not rare—in the collection. A random sample of documents may contain few or no relevant documents. If one document of every N in the collection is relevant, it is necessary to examine, on average, N random documents to find a single relevant one, and to examine kN random documents to find k relevant ones, as may be needed to start the learning process. As that k increases, so too will the burden of training a system that relies on many positive training examples.

A more efficient method to find one or more positive training examples is to use a search engine—particularly one that employs *relevance ranking*[21]—to find one or more relevant documents. Given a simple query consisting of a few search terms, a search engine using relevance ranking can present to the user a set of likely relevant documents, which may be used as training examples. It is important to note that the use of search terms to identify training examples is entirely different from the

---

[19] SIGIR 2014 Paper, *supra* n.15; *see also* Practical Law Article, *supra* n.15, at 36.

[20] *See, e.g.*, John Tredennick et al., *TAR for Smart People: Expanded and Updated Second Ed.* (Catalyst 2016), www.catalystsecure.com/TARforSmartPeople.

[21] Relevance ranking is "[a] search method in which the results are ranked from the most likely to the least likely to be relevant to an information need. ... Google Web Search is an example of relevance ranking." Glossary, *supra* n.1, at 28.

use of search terms for culling or narrowing the collection. In the former case, the search terms are used to *include* documents for review, not to *exclude* them.

When to Stop?

For SPL and SAL, it is necessary to estimate when the learner has been sufficiently trained, a point that is often referred to as "stabilization."[22] For many SPL and SAL methods, it is further necessary to adjust the sensitivity of the learner: The higher the sensitivity, the more nearly *all* relevant documents are identified for subsequent manual review; the lower the sensitivity, the more nearly *only* relevant documents are identified. These two decisions—when stabilization has occurred, and the sensitivity of the learner—effect a multidimensional tradeoff among the amount of effort required for training, the amount of effort required for the subsequent manual review, and how nearly all, and how nearly only, relevant documents will be identified by the review process. These decisions are typically informed by estimates derived from the manual review of a separate random sample of documents—typically referred to as a "control set"[23]—over and above those used for training the learner.

For CAL, the decision of when to stop is deferred until evidence suggests that substantially all relevant documents have been reviewed.[24] Several methods have been proposed and evaluated for determining when a CAL review is complete.[25] Among the simplest and most effective is the following: A CAL review may be considered complete when the total number of negative coding decisions for the documents reviewed thus far exceeds the number of positive decisions, plus 1,000.[26] At the outset, most documents presented for review will be relevant, and hence labeled positive; the stopping criterion will not be met, and the review will continue. Eventually, unreviewed relevant documents will become more and more scarce, with

---

[22] *See, e.g.,* Chris Dale, *Far From the Black Box: Explaining Equivio Relevance to Lawyers* (Equivio undated white paper), http://www.equivio.com/files/files/White Paper – Far from the Black Box – Explaining Equivio Relevance to Lawyers.pdf, at 9.

[23] A "control set" is "[a] random sample of documents coded at the outset of a search or review process that is separate from and independent of the training set. Control sets are used in some TAR processes. They are typically used to measure the effectiveness of the machine learning algorithm at various stages of training, and to determine when training may cease." Glossary, *supra* n. 1, at 13.

[24] SIGIR 2014 Paper, *supra* n.15, at 160; Practical Law Article, *supra* n.15, at 36.

[25] *See* Gordon V. Cormack & Maura R. Grossman, *Engineering Quality and Reliability in Technology-Assisted Review*, Proceedings of the 39th International ACM SIGIR Conference on Research and Development in Information. Retrieval 75 (2016), http://dx.doi.org/10.1145/2911451.2911510, and the discussion on "Quality Assurance" *infra* section.

[26] *See* Maura R. Grossman et al., *TREC 2016 Total Recall Track Overview*, in Proceedings of the 25th Text REtrieval Conference (NIST 2016), http://trec.nist.gov/pubs/trec25/papers/Overview-TR.pdf, at 5. Another way to phrase this stopping criterion is: when the total number of documents reviewed exceeds twice the number of responsive documents, plus 1,000.

the consequence that most documents selected for review will be nonrelevant, and hence labeled negative. Eventually, the number of negatives will exceed the number of positives by 1,000 or more, the stopping criterion will be met, and the review can cease. There are other, more formal methods for determining when to stop a CAL review,[27] but the authors have found this one to be easy to implement and effective.

Measuring Success

Choosing an appropriate method to employ for review involves weighing tradeoffs among a number of considerations, including the (i) effectiveness, (ii) efficiency, (iii) cost, (iii) availability, (iv) familiarity, and (v) general acceptance of candidate methods. Effectiveness and efficiency are amenable to scientific inquiry, while the other considerations depend on social, legal, and market factors that, while influential, are difficult to measure, and beyond the scope of this chapter.

The most commonly used measures of effectiveness are *recall* and *precision*. Recall quantifies how nearly *all* the relevant documents are found[28]; precision quantifies how nearly *only* the relevant documents are found.[29] Unfortunately, for reasons previously discussed in "Review Objectives" recall and precision can never be known with certainty, and can only be estimated. Moreover, the manner in which recall and precision are estimated has a profound effect, such that different recall and precision estimates are incomparable, unless they are calculated under precisely the same conditions.

The net effect is that *naked recall and precision numbers are essentially meaningless*. A claim of "70% recall" is more properly described as a recall *estimate*, and whether or not it indicates that an acceptable proportion of the relevant documents have been found by a review process depends on how the estimate was derived (as well as other legal considerations related to whether a court or regulator might deem that proportion as indicative of a "reasonable" or acceptable review). If the estimate is derived from the coding of an *independent* reviewer, 70% recall is at or near the upper limit of what could be achieved by exhaustive manual review,[30] which, in most contexts, should represent a *de facto* standard of acceptable effectiveness.

If a second review were to achieve a 60% recall estimate according to the same independent reviewer, we might reasonably conclude that the second review found fewer relevant documents than the first, provided that we could exclude the possibility that the difference was a fluke, the product of chance, or the result of some

---

[27] *See generally* Cormack & Grossman, *supra* n.25.

[28] "Recall" is "[t]he fraction of relevant documents that are identified as relevant by a search or review method," *i.e.*, a measure of completeness. Glossary, *supra* n.1, at 27.

[29] "Precision" is "[t]he fraction of documents identified as relevant by a search or review effort, that are in fact relevant," *i.e.*, a measure of accuracy. Glossary, *supra* n.1, at 25.

[30] *See* Voorhees, *supra* n.6.

confounding factor. Similarly, we might reasonably conclude that a third review achieving an estimated 80% recall found more relevant documents than the first, subject to the same caveats.

It would *not* be appropriate to conclude that the three manual reviews described earlier found 70%, 60%, or 80% of the relevant documents, respectively, or, conversely, that they missed 30%, 40%, or 20% of the relevant documents. All that can be said is that they found a certain proportion of the documents *that an independent reviewer would have coded positive*. Almost certainly, some—perhaps even a substantial—fraction of the independent reviewer's positive coding decisions would be wrong (or at least disputable), resulting in an *underestimate* of the proportion of relevant documents found, and an *overestimate* of the number of relevant documents missed.

The bottom line is that recall and precision estimates convey little information as an *absolute indicator* of how nearly all and only the relevant documents have been identified by a particular review effort. When estimated by reference to an independent review, 65% recall and 65% precision are close to the best that can be achieved,[31] and to demand or promise higher is unrealistic. As Ellen Voorhees noted in her seminal 2000 study, *Variations in Relevance Judgments and the Measurement of Retrieval Effectiveness*, "[t]he [recall and precision estimates] for the two sets of secondary judgments imply [that] a practical upper bound on [estimated] retrieval system performance is 65% precision at 65% recall since that is the level at which humans agree with one another."[32]

At the same time, challenges in estimating recall provide no license to willfully exclude 35%—or any other specific number—of relevant documents. The objective of review remains unchanged: to identify, as nearly as practicable, all and only the relevant documents. Recall and precision estimates approaching or exceeding 65% may provide evidence of a satisfactory result, if those estimates are derived from an *independent* coding effort, rather than the same review team that performed the original manual review.

In practice, seldom are the resources available to conduct a separate, independent review, over and above the original review, for the purpose of estimating the recall and precision of the original review. At best, a separate (but rarely independent) review is conducted on a *random sample* of the documents in the collection. Over and above the uncertainties in relevance determinations we have previously discussed, sample-based estimates are also subject to random error. This random error is typically quantified by the statistical terms "margin of error,"[33] "confidence

---

[31] *See id.*

[32] Voorhees, *supra* n.6, at 701.

[33] A "margin of error" is "[t]he maximum amount by which a point estimate might likely deviate from the true value, typically expressed as 'plus or minus' a percentage, with a particular confidence level. For example, one might express a statistical estimate as '30% of the documents in the population are relevant, plus or minus 3%, with 95% confidence.' This means that the point estimate [of the prevalence or richness of the collection] is 30%, the margin of error is 3%, the confidence interval is 27% to 33%, and the confidence level is 95%." Glossary, *supra* n.1, at 22.

interval,"[34] and "confidence level,"[35] which are the source of much confusion—and many misconceptions and ill-conceived practices—in eDiscovery circles.[36]

A third source of confusion regarding recall and precision concerns the particular phase of the review process that is being measured. Recall and precision estimates are most informative when they measure the *end-to-end* effectiveness of the review process, including culling efforts and other activities that precede the selection of documents for review, as well as the ultimate coding decision of the reviewers, as amended by any quality control processes. All too often, however, recall and precision estimates are calculated only for the document-selection component of the review (*i.e.*, the application of TAR alone), under the tacit assumption that the antecedent culling and subsequent manual review processes are flawless.

For nearly the last decade, the authors have conducted a comprehensive program of experimental research evaluating the end-to-end effectiveness of review methods using CAL and other TAR technologies, as well as manual review. Our experimental results have led to enhancements to the CAL process that we have employed in practice on hundreds of reviews since 1999; at the same time, our practical experience, as well as concerns that have been raised in the eDiscovery community, have guided our choice of questions to address in our empirical research.

Research Results

Assessor Disagreement

The issue of relevance assessment has challenged researchers since computers were first used for IR. Because "those who cannot remember the past are condemned to

---

[34] A "confidence interval … [a]s part of a statistical estimate, [is] a range of values estimated to contain the true value, with a particular confidence level." Glossary, *supra* n.1, at 12.

[35] The "confidence level … [a]s part of a statistical estimate, [is] the chance that a confidence interval derived from a random sample will include the true value. For example, '95% confidence' means that if one were to draw 100 independent random samples of the same size, and compute the confidence interval from each sample, about 95 of the 100 confidence intervals would contain the true value." Glossary, *supra* n.1, at 12.

[36] *See generally* Comments Paper, *supra* n.15. By way of example, the following assertions involving statistics are typical, but, unfortunately, incorrect: "The confidence tests Biomet ran as part of its process suggest a comparatively modest number of documents would be found." *In Re: Biomet M2a magnum Hip Implant Prods. Liab. Litig.*, No. 3:12-MD-2391, Order Regarding Discovery of ESI (N.D. Ind. Apr. 18, 2013), at 5, http://www.ctrlinitiative.com/wp-content/uploads/2014/Predictive Coding Opinions/Biomet_1_DiscoveryOrder_April18.pdf; "[O]ne can avoid reviewing 80% or more of the collection and still be 95% confident of finding every relevant document." Andy Kraftsow, *Comment: When is Litigation Like Las Vegas?*, Legal Insider (Jan. 13, 2013), https://www.legaltechnology.com/latest-news/comment-when-is-litigation-like-las-vegas/; "[T]he overturn rate for non-responsive documents was only 2 percent. … At this point, we felt confident we had identified all potentially responsive documents." *How CDS Saved Hundreds of Attorney Hours with Assisted Review*, Relativity – Customer Wins (kCura LLC 2012), https://www.kcura.com/relativity/ediscovery-resources/customer-wins/cds-assisted-review/.

repeat it,"[37] we defer to IR pioneer Tefko Saracevic to summarize the first 50 years of research in IR:

> In the mid-1950s there was an attempt to test the performance of two competing IR systems developed by separate groups... each group searched 98 requests using the same 15,000 documents, indexed separately, in order to evaluate performance based on relevance of retrieved documents. *However, each group judged relevance separately.* Then, not the systems' performance, but their relevance judgments became contentious. The first group found that 2,200 documents were relevant to the 98 requests, while the second found that 1,998 were relevant. There was not much overlap between groups. The first group judged 1,640 documents relevant that the second did not, and the second group judged 980 relevant that the first did not. You see where this is going. Then they had reconciliation, considered each other's relevant documents, and again compared judgments. Each group accepted some more as relevant, but at the end, they still disagreed; their rate of agreement, even after peace talks, was 30.9%. That did it. The first ever IR evaluation did not continue. It collapsed. *Because of relevance assessments.* Moreover, it seems that the rate of human agreement on relevance assessment hovers indeed around that figure....[38]

"Peace talks" involving the coding of disputed documents were similarly contentious and unproductive in *Da Silva Moore* v. *Publicis Groupe*,[39] the 2012 federal case of first impression approving the use of TAR, and in other cases since then.[40]

---

[37] This famous statement, which has many variants and paraphrases, has been attributed to George Santayana. https://en.wikiquote.org/wiki/George_Santayana.

[38] Tefko Saracevic, *Why is Relevance Still the Basic Notion in Information Science? (Despite Great Advances in Information Technology)*, in Reinventing Information Science in the Networked Society, Proceedings of the 14th International Symposium on Information on Science 26 (May 2015), https://zenodo.org/record/17964/files/keynote2.pdf (emphasis in original).

[39] *See, e.g., Da Silva Moore* v. *Publicis Groupe SA*, No. 11 Civ. 1279 (ALC) (AJP), Tr. (S.D.N.Y. May 7, 2012).

[40] *See, e.g.,* Joint letter to Hon. Andrew J. Peck, ECF Doc. No. 398, filed in *Rio Tinto PLC* v. *Vale SA*, No. 14-cv-3042 (RMB) (AJP) (S.D.N.Y. Nov. 12, 2015), at 24–25, http://ctrlinitia-tive.com/wp-content/uploads/2016/01/Rio-Tinto-Status-Update-Incl.-Predictive-Coding-ECF-398-11-12-2015-1.pdf (advising the Court that "[a]fter a series of meet and confers to discuss coding challenges, the parties were still unable to resolve coding disputes for a handful of documents and agreed to submit a handful of disputed documents to Special Master Grossman for resolution.").

The Roitblat, Kershaw, and Oot "EDI Study"

A 2010 study by Herbert Roitblat, Patrick Oot, and Anne Kershaw—cited in *Da Silva Moore* v. *Publicis*[41] as one of the authorities showing the superiority of TAR over manual review—observed similarly low rates of agreement between a pair of qualified human reviewers recruited for the study, and an even lower rate of agreement between those reviewers and the earlier exhaustive manual review conducted by a team of 225 attorneys to meet the requirements of a U.S. Department of Justice "second request" involving the acquisition of MCI by Verizon.[42]

Fortunately, research suggests that it is not necessary for the parties to agree on the relevance of every document to determine the relative effectiveness of two different IR approaches.[43] In general, if review 1 achieves a higher effectiveness score than review 2 in the eyes of competent, independent review 3, we can infer that review 1 is likely more effective than review 2, even if review 3 is imperfect.

Roitblat et al. used the prior production as "review 3" to evaluate the relative effectiveness of the reviews conducted by their two experts ("review A" and "review B"). According to review 3, reviews A and B achieved 49% and 54% recall, and 20% and 18% precision, respectively—an insubstantial and statistically insignificant difference.[44]

Again according to review 3, Roitblat et al. further evaluated the effectiveness of reviews C and D, which were conducted using undisclosed commercial TAR methods. These methods achieved 46% recall and 53% recall, respectively—an insubstantial and statistically insignificant difference from human reviews A and B. On the other hand, reviews C and D achieved substantially and significantly higher precision: 27% and 29%, respectively.[45]

As previously noted, these recall numbers should not be interpreted to mean that the manual or TAR reviews missed half of the relevant documents, and that only one-fifth of the documents identified by the manual reviews were relevant, or that only three-tenths of the documents identified by the TAR reviews were relevant. We can, however, say that the manual and TAR reviews identified about the same number of relevant documents, and that the TAR reviews identified substantially fewer nonrelevant documents.

TREC: The Text REtrieval Conference Legal Track Interactive Task

The Text REtrieval Conference ("TREC"), cosponsored by the National Institute of Standards and Technology ("NIST") and the U.S. Department of Defense, is an

---

[41] *Da Silva Moore* v. *Publicis Groupe*, 287 F.R.D. 182, 190 (S.D.N.Y. 2012).
[42] Roitblat et al., *supra* n.6.
[43] *See, e.g.*, Voorhees and Bailey, *supra* n. 6.
[44] Roitblat et al., *supra* n.6.
[45] *Id.*

annual workshop and conference that has, since its inception in 1992, been one of the premier venues for IR research. Its stated purpose is

> [T]o support research within the information retrieval community by providing the infrastructure necessary for large-scale evaluation of text retrieval methodologies. In particular, the TREC workshop series has the following goals:
>
> ■ to encourage research in information retrieval based on large test collections;
> ■ to increase communication among industry, academia, and government by creating an open forum for the exchange of research ideas;
> ■ to speed the transfer of technology from research labs into commercial products by demonstrating substantial improvements in retrieval methodologies on real-world problems; and
> ■ to increase the availability of appropriate evaluation techniques for use by industry and academia, including development of new evaluation techniques more applicable to current systems.[46]

From 2006 to 2011, the TREC Legal Track addressed the application of advanced search technology to several aspects of eDiscovery. In particular, the TREC Legal Track Interactive Task, which ran from 2008 to 2010, evaluated the end-to-end effectiveness of various review strategies carried out by participating teams.

In each year, the Interactive Task required participants to identify, as nearly as they could, from a large publicly available document collection, all and only the documents responsive to one or more mock RFPs. In 2008, the collection consisted of 7 million documents previously collected in connection with the tobacco litigation that culminated in the Master Settlement Agreement among 49 states and territorial jurisdictions and four tobacco manufacturers.[47] In 2009 and 2010, respectively, the collection consisted of 847,791 and 685,592 email messages and attachments collected from Enron Corporation by the Federal Energy Regulatory Commission in the course of its investigation of Enron's failure.[48]

---

[46] National Institute of Standards and Technology, *Text Retrieval Conference (TREC) Overview*, http://trec.nist.gov/overview.html.

[47] Douglas W. Oard et al., *Overview of the TREC 2008 Legal Track*, in Proceedings of the 17th Text REtrieval Conference (NIST 2008), at 3, http://trec.nist.gov/pubs/trec17/papers/LEGAL.OVERVIEW08.pdf.

[48] Bruce Hedin et al., *Overview of the TREC 2009 Legal Track*, in Proceedings of the 18th Text REtrieval Conference (NIST 2009), at 4–5, http://trec.nist.gov/pubs/trec18/papers/LEGAL09.OVERVIEW.pdf, and Gordon V. Cormack, *Overview of the TREC 2010 Legal Track*, in Proceedings of the 19th Text REtrieval Conference (NIST 2010), at 2–3, http://trec.nist.gov/pubs/trec19/papers/LEGAL10.OVERVIEW.pdf, respectively.

Interactive Task participants were provided with a mock complaint, and one or more RFPs concerning subject matters to be found in the document collection, both of which were composed by Track coordinators and other volunteers. For each RFP (referred to as a "topic" in TREC parlance), a volunteer "Topic Authority" ("TA") was assigned. The TA was a senior lawyer who provided consultation to the participants during the course of their review and acted as the final arbiter of relevance during the subsequent evaluation process.

Relevance assessment for the purpose of evaluation was accomplished using a novel, three-phase approach. In the "first-pass review," volunteer reviewers—supplied either by law school *pro bono* programs or eDiscovery contract-review service providers—coded a statistical sample of documents as relevant or nonrelevant. These coding decisions were released to TREC participants who were invited to "appeal" those decisions with which they disagreed. The TA reviewed all documents whose coding was appealed, and rendered a final relevance determination for each.

For the purpose of calculating the recall and precision of the participants' efforts, where relevance determinations were not appealed, the first-pass reviewer's coding was taken to be correct; where relevance determinations were appealed, the TA's final coding determination was taken to be correct.

The 2008 Legal Track reported—and introduced to the eDiscovery lexicon—a summary measure known as F_1.[49] F_1 combines recall and precision into a single summary measure, with the lesser of the two given more weighting. Thus, to achieve high F_1, it is necessary to achieve both high recall (approaching the ideal of all relevant documents) *and* high precision (approaching the ideal of only relevant documents).

Four teams—two from universities and two from eDiscovery service providers—participated in the 2008 Interactive Task. The team from one of the service providers (H5) achieved remarkably high recall, precision, and F_1 scores of 62%, 81%, and 71%, respectively, using a rule-based TAR approach.[50] By comparison, no other team achieved scores recall, precision, and F_1 scores higher than 16%, 80%, and 39%, respectively.[51]

In 2009, the H5 team achieved similarly high scores for the review they conducted (topic 204; 80% F_1), as did a team from the University of Waterloo (led by the second author) for each of four reviews that the team conducted (topics

---

[49] Oard et al., *supra* n.47, at 7–8. "F_1" is defined as "[t]he harmonic mean of recall and precision, often used in information retrieval studies as a measure of the effectiveness of a search or review effort, which accounts for the tradeoff between recall and precision. In order to achieve a high F_1 score, a search or review effort must achieve *both* high recall and high precision." Glossary, *supra* n.1, at 16 (emphasis in original).

[50] Oard et al., *supra* n. 47, Table 15 at 30.

[51] *Id.*

201, 202, 203, and 207; 84%, 76%, 77%, and 83% F_1).[52] A second industry team (Cleary/Backstop) achieved 80% F_1 on one of the three reviews they conducted (topic 207); a third industry team (Equivio) achieved 61% and 58% F_1 on the two reviews it conducted (topics 205 and 207); and a fourth industry team (Clearwell) achieved 62% F_1 on one of the two reviews it conducted (topic 202).[53] The remaining 15 of 24 reviews—from 8 of the 11 participating teams—achieved F_1 scores between 2% and 43%.[54]

The 2011 Richmond Journal of Law and Technology Study

While the results from the TREC 2008 and 2009 Legal Track Interactive Tasks were remarkable, they left unanswered the question of how the well-performing TAR processes employed by industry participants and the University of Waterloo would compare to exhaustive manual review. While the results reported at TREC were numerically greater than those reported by Roitblat et al. for human review,[55] and greater than Voorhees' observed "upper bound on retrieval performance,"[56] they were incomparable, as they came from different review tasks and reflected different methods of assessing relevance.

The Interactive Task was designed to compare the effectiveness of the review strategies implemented by participating teams, none of which employed exhaustive manual review. For the purpose of evaluation, a manual review—the first-pass assessment—had been conducted, albeit only for a statistical sample of the documents in the collection. Disagreements between the first-pass assessment and participating teams were anticipated in the experimental design; such disagreements were adjudicated by the TA.

The purpose of this adjudication was to achieve the most accurate possible relevance determination for use in evaluating and comparing the effectiveness of the participants' reviews, all of which employed some form of TAR. In their 2011 JOLT Study, the authors employed the adjudicated relevance determinations for a different purpose not anticipated at the time: to evaluate and compare the effectiveness of the manual first-pass review with the results achieved by the most consistently effective TAR reviews.

The results indicated that the manual reviews achieved, on average, 59% recall, 32% precision, and 36% F_1, while the TAR reviews achieved, on average, 77% recall, 85% precision, and 80% F_1.[57] While each measure is higher for TAR than

---

[52] Hedin et al., *supra* n.48, Table 6 at 15.
[53] *Id.*
[54] *Id.*
[55] *See* Roitblat et al., *supra* n.6.
[56] Voorhees, *supra* n.6, at 701.
[57] 2011 JOLT Study, *supra* n.4, Table 7 at 37.

for manual review, the difference in recall was not statistically significant, while the differences in precision and recall were.[58]

These results were consistent with those reported by Roitblat et al.: In terms of recall, there was little to choose between the TAR and manual review results; in terms of precision (and, consequently, F_1), the TAR results were vastly superior. At the same time, the TAR reviews involved human review of only 2% of the collection—or 50 times less effort than an exhaustive manual review would entail—a very substantial difference.[59]

It is important to note that the studies by Roitblat et al. and by the authors compared specific TAR methods to reasonably well-conducted manual reviews under laboratory conditions. The results suggest that methods similar to those tested can, in practice, achieve superior results to manual review. The results cannot, however, be interpreted to suggest that methods dissimilar to those tested—whether labeled as "TAR" or otherwise—improve on manual review.

Comparing TAR Methods

The 2011 JOLT Study has been cited, either directly or by reference, in cases of first impression approving the use of TAR in the United States, Ireland, the United Kingdom, and Australia.[60] An apt characterization of the evidence is offered by Master Matthews in the High Court of Justice Chancery Division (U.K.):

> There is no evidence to show that the use of [TAR] software leads to less accurate disclosure being given than, say, manual review alone or keyword searches and manual review combined, and indeed there is some evidence (referred to in the US and Irish cases to which I referred above) to the contrary.[61]

More sweeping generalizations of the Roitblat et al. and 2011 JOLT Study results have been advanced, both to promote so-called TAR methods that bear little

---

[58] *Id.*

[59] *Id.* at 43.

[60] *See, e.g., McConnell Dowell Constructors (Austl.) Pty Ltd* v. *Santam Ltd & Ors (No 1)*, [2016] VSC 734 (Austl.); *Pyrrho Inv. Ltd.* v. *MWB Prop. Ltd.*, [2016] EWHC (Ch) 256 (Eng.); *Irish Bank Resol. Corp.* v. *Quinn*, [2015] IEHC 175 (H. Ct.) (Ir.); *Rio Tinto PLC* v. *Vale S.A.*, 306 F.R.D. 125 (S.D.N.Y. 2015); *Progressive Casualty Ins. Co.* v. *Delaney*, Case No. 2:11-cv-00678, 2014 WL 3563467 (D. Nev. July 18, 2014); *Fed. Hous. Fin. Agency* v. *HSBC North Am. Holdings Inc.*, No. 1:11-cv-06188-DLC, 2014 WL 584300 (S.D.N.Y. Feb. 14, 2014); *Nat'l Day Laborer Org. Network* v. *U.S. Immigr. & Customs Enf't Agency*, 877 F. Supp. 2d 87 (S.D.N.Y. 2012); *Da Silva Moore* v. *Publicis Groupe*, 287 F.R.D. 182 (S.D.N.Y. 2012).

[61] *Pyrrho Inv. Ltd.* v. *MWB Prop. Ltd.*, [2016] EWHC (Ch) 256 (Eng.), at 14.

resemblance to those tested, and as straw men to impugn the studies and all TAR.[62] At the same time, a number of burdensome practices associated with untested TAR methods, as well as the statistical apparatus of laboratory IR evaluation, have erroneously been associated with TAR in general.[63]

To investigate the relative effectiveness of different TAR methods, in 2014, the authors introduced a taxonomy of supervised machine-learning methods for TAR representative of the three basic approaches to TAR taken by eDiscovery service providers in the market: (i) SPL, (ii) SAL and (iii) CAL.[64]

Our taxonomy excluded rule-based TAR methods that relied on opaque or ill-specified techniques that were difficult to characterize, as well as methods that the authors did not consider to be TAR, which are marketed under names such as "concept search," "clustering," "concept clustering," "find similar," "visualization," "deduplication," "near-deduplication," and "email threading." We have since published a broader taxonomy of TAR tools, as well as non-TAR tools, which we characterize as tools for search and analysis.[65]

To measure the relative effectiveness of supervised machine-learning methods for TAR, we created an open-source "TAR Evaluation Toolkit"[66] that simulates SPL, SAL, and CAL in a laboratory environment. Using data collected from TREC 2009, as well as four legal matters in which the authors had been involved, we found that, for a given level of review effort, CAL achieved the highest recall (and, as a consequence, the highest precision and F_1) of the three methods.[67] We found that, *given the correct parameter settings*, SAL could achieve recall comparable

---

[62] *Compare, e.g., Visualize a New Concept in Document Decisioning*, OrcaTec – FAQ (Internet Archive Oct. 1, 2011), https://web.archive.org/web/20111001071436/http://orcatec.com/index.php/resources/faq (stating "Can OrcaTec provide any scientific evidence concerning such processes as predictive coding? Grossman & Cormack in the Richmond Journal of Law & Technology" (with link), when the OrcaTec tool bore no resemblance to the TAR methods studied by Grossman and Cormack) *with* Bill Speros, *Despite Early Success, Technology Assisted Review's Acceptance Is Limited by Lack of Definition*," News & Press: ACEDS News (Aug. 31, 2016), http://www.aceds.org/news/3059301 (stating that the court in *Da Silva Moore* "misperceive[ed] the [2011 JOLT] article upon which the court relied as being proof-of-capability rather than as proof of concept" and concluding that "until TAR consolidates definitions about what it is, its capabilities and its limitations, and specifies any underlying science and all necessary protocols, TAR will face meaningful criticism about its reliability. And it should.")

[63] *See generally, e.g.*, Karl Schieneman & Thomas C. Gricks III, *The Implications of Rule 26(g) on the Use of Technology-Assisted Review*, 7 Fed. Cts. L. Rev. 239 (2013), http://www.fclr.org/fclr/articles/html/2010/Gricks.pdf. *Cf.* Comments Paper, *supra* n.15 (responding to Schieneman & Gricks' article).

[64] SIGIR 2014 Paper, *supra* n.15; *see also* Comments Paper, *supra* n.15.

[65] *See* Maura R. Grossman & Gordon V. Cormack, *A Tour of Technology-Assisted Review*, ch. 3 in Jason R. Baron et al. (eds.), Perspectives on Predictive Coding and Other Advanced Search Methods for the Legal Practitioner (ABA Publishing 2016).

[66] http://cormack.uwaterloo.ca/tar-toolkit/.

[67] SIGIR 2014 Paper, *supra* n.15.

to CAL, but only for one particular level of effort.[68] We found that SPL yielded results substantially inferior to those achieved by CAL or SAL.[69] This peer-reviewed study was presented at *The 37th International Association for Computing Machinery Special Interest Group on Information Retrieval (ACM SIGIR) Conference on Research and Development in Information Retrieval.*[70]

Autonomy and Reliability of CAL

A commonly expressed view in the legal community has been that TAR requires exceptional skill on the part of an operator; for example, to select the appropriate training documents and operating parameters for the learning method.[71] In *Autonomy and Reliability of Continuous Active Learning for Technology-Assisted Review*[72] the authors evaluated "AutoTAR," an enhancement of CAL that has no parameters to set, and requires at the outset only a single relevant document, or in the alternative, a fragment of text containing relevant content. Given this initial input, AutoTAR presents documents in sequence for review, and the coding is returned to AutoTAR. The process continues until evidence suggests that substantially all relevant documents have been presented for review.

Our results show that, *regardless of what initial input is chosen*, AutoTAR finds substantially all relevant documents with less review effort than the CAL method we had previously evaluated.[73] We observed the same results for a wide variety of publicly available IR benchmarks, including the 103 subjects of the Reuters RCV1-v2 dataset, the 50 topics of the TREC 6 AdHoc Task, and the 50 topics of the TREC 2002 Filtering Track, as well as datasets from four actual legal matters.[74]

An open-source implementation of AutoTAR was subsequently used as the "Baseline Model Implementation" ("BMI")[75] for the TREC Total Recall Tracks in

---

[68] *Id.*

[69] *Id.*

[70] *See* http://sigir.org/sigir2014/; *see also id.*

[71] *See, e.g.,* Ralph C. Losey, *Why the 'Google Car' Has No Place in Legal Search*, e-Discovery Team Blog (Feb. 24, 2016), https://e-discoveryteam.com/2016/02/24/why-the-google-car-has-no-place-in-legal-search/ (regarding selection of training documents); Rishi Chhatwal et al., *Empirical Evaluations of Preprocessing Parameters' Impact on Predictive Coding's Effectiveness*, in Proceedings of the 2016 IEEE Int'l Conference on Big Data 1394 (2016), *available at* https://www.navigant.com/-/media/www/site/insights/legal-technology/2017/predictive-codings-effectiveness.pdf (regarding selection of operating parameters).

[72] Gordon V. Cormack & Maura R. Grossman, *Autonomy and Reliability of Continuous Active Learning for Technology-Assisted Review*, https://arxiv.org/abs/1504.06868 [cs.IR] (Apr. 15, 2015).

[73] *Id.*

[74] *Id.* at 2.

[75] Baseline Model Implementation for Automatic Participation in the TREC 2015 Total Recall Track, http://cormack.uwaterloo.ca/trecvm/.

2015[76] and 2016.[77] As in the earlier TREC Legal Track Interactive Task, participants were asked to find, as nearly as they could, all and only the relevant documents in the collection. In contrast to the Legal Track, however, Total Recall participants submitted documents incrementally to a Web server for assessment, and received a relevance label (derived automatically from a prior labeling of the entire collection) for each document immediately when it was submitted. This architecture allowed for precise tracking of each team's recall as a function of the number of documents submitted.

Participants could use fully automated strategies like BMI, or manual strategies involving any combination of human and computer input, including keyword search, manual review, and hand-selected training documents. While some participants achieved higher recall than BMI on some topics, at some levels of review effort, no participant at TREC 2015 or 2016—whether automatic or manual—achieved consistently higher recall than BMI, for the same level of effort.[78]

The 2015 and 2016 Total Recall Tracks evaluated TAR systems with respect to a diverse set of datasets and topics. In 2015, systems were evaluated with respect to 53 different topics and five datasets: 10 topics were developed for a collection of approximately 290,099 emails from Jeb Bush's administration as Governor of Florida; 10 topics were developed for a collection of 465,147 postings from Blackhat World and Hacker Forum; 10 topics were developed for a collection of 902,434 online news clippings from the northwestern United States and southwestern Canada; 4 preexisting topics reflecting statutory definitions of various types of records and nonrecords were used in connection with a collection of 401,953 emails from Tim Kaine's administration as Governor of Virginia; and 19 preexisting topics reflecting International Statistical Classification of Diseases (ICD)-9 codes were used in connection with the Multiparameter Intelligent Monitoring in Intensive Care II (MIMIC II) clinical dataset, consisting of 31,538 medical records from an intensive care unit.[79]

In 2016, systems were evaluated with respect to additional 34 topics developed for the Jeb Bush collection; six topics developed for a collection of 2.1 million emails from the administrations of Illinois Governors Rod Blagojevich and Pat Quinn; and four preexisting topics were used in connection with a collection of 800,000 Twitter tweets.[80]

Overall, the results indicate that fully autonomous TAR systems can achieve very high recall levels, for reasonable effort, for a wide variety of datasets and relevance criteria. Results on the Tim Kaine and MIMIC II datasets are of particular

---

[76] *See* Adam Roegiest et al., *TREC 2015 Total Recall Track Overview*, in Proceedings of the 24th Text REtrieval Conference (NIST 2015), http://trec.nist.gov/pubs/trec24/papers/Overview-TR.pdf.

[77] *See* Maura R. Grossman et al., *supra* n.26.

[78] *See* Roegiest et al., *supra* n.76; Grossman et al., *supra* n.26.

[79] *See* Roegiest et al., *supra* n.76, at 3–5.

[80] *See* Grossman et al., *supra* n.26, at 3–5.

interest, because relevance was formally defined, and relevance determinations were rendered by independent professionals (the Virginia Senior State Records Archivist and physicians, respectively) in the course of their employment.

Facets of Relevance

It has been suggested by some that TAR may exhibit "blind spots" in that a TAR review may miss certain kinds of relevant documents, either because those documents have an unusual format or because they pertain to an obscure aspect of relevance.[81] Our peer-reviewed study, *Multi-Faceted Recall of Continuous Active Learning for Technology-Assisted Review*, presented at *The 38th International ACM SIGIR Conference on Research and Development in Information Retrieval*,[82] indicates that CAL, when it has found nearly all relevant documents overall, has also found nearly all relevant documents for each facet of relevance, whether those facets are defined as file types or as substantive subtopics.[83] It may be that CAL identifies certain types of documents or documents representing certain aspects of relevance sooner than others, but once such documents become scarce, it identifies other facets, and so on, until all facets have been identified.

This result was reaffirmed at the TREC 2016 Total Recall Track, where assessors were asked to sort relevant documents into subfolders, based on the particular subject matter they contained. When the recall for each subfolder was considered separately, participating systems that achieved high recall overall also achieved high recall for the documents in each subfolder.[84]

Finally, the same result was also recently reproduced through an independent research effort.[85]

Quality Assurance

Recall, precision, and F_1 are commonly used to measure the average effectiveness of IR systems and methods. When we say that a particular method achieves 65%

---

[81] *See, e.g., Proper Use of Predictive Coding Technology* (Inspired Review Blog Jan. 7, 2104), http://www.inspiredreview.com/blog5.html ("Some questions have already arisen regarding the ability of predictive coding algorithms to properly address terse documents (documents that do not contain abundant text for language based analysis such as spreadsheets or short documents) and 'novel content' documents."). *See also* Comments Paper, *supra* n.15, at 304–305.

[82] *See* http://sigir2015.org/; Gordon V. Cormack & Maura R. Grossman, *Multi-Faceted Recall of Continuous Active Learning for Technology-Assisted Review*, in Proceedings of the 38th Int'l ACM SIGIR Conference on Research and Dev. in Info. Retrieval 763 (2015), http://dl.acm.org/citation.cfm?doid=2766462.2767771.

[83] Cormack & Grossman, supra n.82.

[84] *See* Grossman et al., *supra* n.26, at 5.

[85] *See* Thomas Gricks, *Does Recall Measure TAR's Effectiveness Across All Issues? We Put It to the Test*, Catalyst E-Discovery Search Blog (Mar. 23, 2017), https://catalystsecure.com/blog/2017/05/does-recall-measure-tars-effectiveness-across-all-issues-we-put-it-to-the-test/.

recall and 65% precision, we are generally referring to the average recall and precision achieved by applying the same method to a set of information needs (*i.e.*, queries) that are representative of those that might be encountered in practice. An average provides no guarantee that, for any given retrieval effort, any particular level of recall or precision will be achieved.

This concern has led parties to use sampling in an often-futile effort to estimate recall and precision for particular review efforts and to set thresholds as standards of acceptability. For example, in *Global Aerospace* v. *Landow Aviation*,[86] based on the recall level reported in our 2011 JOLT Study, the producing party promised to achieve at least 75% recall, and subsequently represented to the court, after the fact, that 81% recall had been achieved.[87] What was achieved was, in fact, a coarse *estimate* of the recall of only the TAR (document-selection) component of the review process. The estimate itself had a margin of error such that the true value could easily have been less than 75%. More importantly, however, the estimate did not account for the fact that the documents selected by the TAR system were reviewed manually, and only the documents coded relevant and nonprivileged by the reviewers were produced. Thus, only if we assumed that the manual review was perfect—that is, achieved 100% recall—would the estimate of 81% recall apply to the end-to-end review. More likely—as determined by an independent assessment—the manual review achieved recall on the order of 70%, for a net end-to-end recall estimate of 57%.[88]

It is not our intent to impugn the adequacy of production in *Global Aerospace*—we have no reason to doubt its quality—but rather, to illustrate the fallacy of relying on ill-specified recall thresholds as acceptance criteria. On the other hand, as has been suggested[89]—it is also not our intent to suggest that, because relevance is difficult to define, and because recall is difficult to estimate on a case-by-case basis, that all measurement should be eschewed and that producing parties should be absolved of any and all responsibility of ensuring the adequacy of the production.

The first step in assuring the adequacy of a production, we believe, is to use a method that has previously been shown to *reliably* achieve high recall.[90] Reliability is

---

[86] Karl Schieneman & Thomas C. Gricks III, *supra* n.63, at 259.

[87] Letter from Gordon S. Woodward, Att'y for the Landow Entities, to All Counsel in *Global Aerospace Inc.* v. *Landow Aviation, L.P.*, Consol. Case No. CL601040 (Va. Cir. Ct. Loudoun Cty. Nov. 30, 2012) ("At the end of the predictive coding process, we conducted a statistically valid sampling program to establish that an acceptable level of document recall had been achieved. As we indicated in our motion to the court ... the Landow Entities proposed that 75% recall would be adequate. Below is a report reflecting our final analysis with respect to document recall. The report indicates that we achieved 81%.")

[88] If 81% of the relevant documents were identified by the TAR system, and 70% of those were correctly coded relevant by the manual review, the end-to-end recall would be $81\% \times 70\% = 56.7\%$.

[89] *See, e.g.*, Herbert L. Roitblat, *Daubert, Rule 26(g) and the eDiscovery Turkey*, OrcaBlog (Aug. 11, 2014), https://web.archive.org/web/20140812155631/http://orcatec.com/2014/08/11/daubert-rule-26g-and-the-ediscovery-turkey/.

[90] Comments Paper, *supra* n.15, at 305.

the probability that, for any given application, a high-quality result will be achieved. High average recall does not, in itself, imply *reliably* high recall. A method that, for example, achieved 100% recall 80% of the time, and 0% recall 20% of the time, would achieve an apparently high level of 80% recall, on average, but poor reliability, since 20% of the time the method could not be counted on to find anything. One would not likely consider a 1-in-5 chance of complete failure to be an acceptable risk. On the other hand, a 1-in-20 chance of achieving 74% recall, when 75% recall was deemed acceptable, might be acceptable.

Inextricably intertwined with the notion of reliability is the question of "when to stop?" For CAL, one can select and review documents indefinitely. For SPL and SAL, one can select training documents indefinitely, and when training ceases, one can adjust the sensitivity of the resulting classifier so as to review documents indefinitely. At some point, the decision must be made that enough responsive documents have been found, and that further review is disproportionate. We would like to ensure that, when that decision is reached, with high probability, high recall has been achieved.

In support of this goal, we investigated three methods of achieving high reliability using CAL.[91] One method—the "Target Method"—provably achieved a recall target of 70%, with 95% reliability, at the cost of reviewing a large random sample of documents, over and above those selected by the TAR system as relevant. A second method—the "Knee Method"—achieved better reliability on a wide variety of datasets and information needs with less effort than the Target Method. A third method—the "Budget Method"—achieved vastly superior reliability on the same datasets, when the same number of documents as the Target Method were reviewed, but the documents were selected by the TAR system (not through random sampling). At TREC 2016, we investigated a fourth method to achieve high reliability—the simple method described earlier in "When to Stop?".[92] To our surprise, it worked as well as the more complex Knee Method,[93] but more research is certainly needed in this area.

While a fuller discussion of these stopping criteria is beyond the scope of this chapter, they show that it is possible to reliably determine when to stop a TAR review without resorting to large random samples and faulty statistics.

TAR vs. Manual Review Redux

We have recently had occasion to reconfirm the results of our 2011 JOLT Study by comparing the results of using CAL to an exhaustive manual review of 401,960

---

[91] Cormack & Grossman, *supra* n.25.
[92] Gordon V. Cormack & Maura R. Grossman, *"When to Stop": Waterloo (Cormack) Participation in the TREC 2016 Total Recall Track*, in Proceedings of the 25th Text REtrieval Conference (NIST 2016), http://trec.nist.gov/pubs/trec24/papers/WaterlooCormack-TR.pdf.
[93] *See id.*

email messages from the administration of Virginia Governor Tim Kaine, which was previously reviewed by the Virginia Senior State Records Archivist Roger Christman ("Roger"). We showed, using subsequent blind assessments rendered by Roger, that Roger could have achieved the same recall and higher precision, for a fraction of the effort, had he employed CAL to review the 401,960 email messages.[94]

Prior to our study, Roger had rendered decisions for each of three topics, seriatim, as follows: First, "Virginia Tech" documents subject to a legal hold were identified; second, documents not subject to the hold were classified as either "archival records" or "nonrecords"; finally, documents classified as archival records were categorized as "restricted" or "open" records. Open records are available to the public.[95] As a consequence, the document collection diminished for each subsequent topic.

CAL was run on the same dataset, using Roger's prior decisions to simulate user feedback for the purposes of training the learner. When the CAL run was complete, cases of disagreement between the CAL system and Roger's prior coding were identified, and Roger rendered a second relevance determination for a sample of these documents in a double-blind review, where neither Roger nor the authors were aware of Roger's previous determinations. The overlap[96] between Roger's first and second determinations was 80.6%, 60.2%, and 64.2%,[97] for each of the three classifications—at the high end of what one might expect for independent reviewers, but far from perfect. Two months later, Roger conducted a third relevance determination in every case where his first and second determinations had been inconsistent, again blind to his previous determinations.

According to Roger's final determinations, we calculated recall and precision for Roger's original review, and for CAL. Roger's recall ranged from 89% to 97%, while CAL's ranged from 90% to 96%—not a significant difference.[98] Roger's precision ranged from 75% to 91%, while CAL's ranged from 80% to 96%—a significant difference *in favor of CAL*.[99] F_1 similarly favored CAL by a significant margin.[100]

Overall, the Roitblat, Kershaw, and Oot study, our 2011 JOLT Study, and our SIGIR 2017 *Roger and Me* study, all show the same result: There is no significant difference in the recall achieved by the TAR systems studied and manual review, and significantly superior precision for the TAR systems. This should reaffirm the reasonableness of using at least some forms of TAR.

---

[94] Cormack & Grossman, *supra* n.4.

[95] *See* http://www.virginiamemory.com/collections/kaine/. *See also* http://cormack.uwaterloo. ca/kaine (the authors' CAL demonstration using the Kaine open records).

[96] "Overlap" or "Jaccard Index" is "[a] measure of the consistency between two sets (e.g., Documents Coded as Relevant by two different reviewers). … Empirical studies have shown that expert reviewers commonly achieve Jaccard Index scores of about 50%, and that scores exceeding 60% are rare." Glossary, *supra* n.1, at 20, 25.

[97] Cormack & Grossman, *supra* n.4, Table 5 at 7.

[98] *Id.*, Table 3 at 7.

[99] *Id.*, Table 3 at 7.

[100] *Id.*

The Future

Review for production is a difficult problem. Conventional review methods using keyword culling and manual review are burdensome and far from perfect, as shown by the scientific literature, both within the context of eDiscovery and within the context of IR in general. Methods for measuring review effectiveness are similarly burdensome and imperfect.

Vendors, service providers, and consumers need to gather evidence that the review methods they use—whether manual or TAR—work effectively. Doing so is far more challenging than merely reviewing a "statistically significant sample [sic]"[101] of documents for the purpose of training the system or calculating recall.

Challenges in measurement provide no license to continue to use keyword culling and manual review, just because "that is the way it has previously been done." There is ample evidence that those methods are flawed, and there is no evidence that they are superior to certain TAR alternatives. At the same time, there is a growing body of evidence that certain TAR methods can improve on manual review.

We have worked, and continue to work to contribute to that body of evidence, while at the same time, improving the state of the art in TAR. We have no reason to think that our Continuous Active Learning™ method is the best that can possibly be achieved, but it is the best of which we are aware at this time, and we continue to work to improve it. We have made an implementation via the TREC BMI available under the GPL 3.0 public license,[102] and invite researchers and practitioners alike to try it and to work to find more effective and efficient methods to review ESI "to secure the just, speedy, and inexpensive determination of every action and proceeding" as envisioned by Federal Rule of Civil Procedure 1.

---

[101] *See, e.g.,* Tracy Greer, *Electronic Discovery at the Antitrust Division: An Update*, U.S. Dep't of Justice (June 25, 2015), https://www.justice.gov/atr/electronic-discovery-antitrust-division-update (suggesting that quality assurance "could be accomplished by the producing party providing [the Division with] a statistically significant sample of both relevant and non-relevant documents."); Alison Nadal et al, *E-discovery: The Value of Predictive Coding in Internal Investigations*, Inside Counsel (Aug. 13, 2013), at 1, http://www.insidecounsel.com/2013/08/13/e-discovery-the-value-of-predictive-coding-in-inte ("Executing an internal investigation using predictive coding begins with generation of a randomly selected, statistically significant seed set of documents."); Bill George, *Predictive Coding Primer Part II: Key Variables in a Predictive Coding Driven Review*, Tanenholz & Associates, PLLC News (May 8, 2013), http://tanenholzlaw.com/predictive-coding-primer-part-two ("After the control set has been reviewed, the subject matter experts will then need to train the predictive coding model further through review of a statistically significant sample of documents."). The phrase "statistically significant sample" is a non sequitur. *See* Bill Dimm, *TAR 3.0 and Training of Predictive Coding Systems*, Presentation materials from ACEDS Webinar (Dec. 15, 2015), at 12, http://www.cluster-text.com/papers/TAR_3_and_training_predictive_coding.pdf ("Training set size should never involve phrases like ... [s]tatistically significant sample (this isn't even a thing!)").

[102] *See* Baseline Model Implementation, *supra* n.75.

Chapter 7

Quantifying the Quality of Legal Services: Data Science Lessons from Avvo

Nika Kabiri, Ed Sarausad, and Rahul Dodhia

Contents

Many lawyers choose to enter the legal profession in part because they prefer not to deal with numbers. Many graduated law school never expecting to be business owners and operators, not expecting to engage in marketing, advertising, and other activities that are done best when data analysis fuels business strategy. However, law firms and practices do well when they master the use of data in making critical decisions. In some cases, lawyers use sophisticated data analysis tools to do the job. In other cases, data collection and analysis may be simple. How data is used—including the level of sophistication in data analysis—is less important than whether or not the techniques that are used fit the specific business questions at hand.

This chapter describes some ways in which Avvo has used data to answer its own specific business questions. Fortunately, the business questions Avvo tackles each day are not too different from those that plague lawyers. How do we measure the quality of our services so that we can convey that quality to legal consumers? How do we identify markets of opportunity: legal consumers that need our services but whom we are not reaching? How do we predict which markets will grow in the future so that we can reach out to them now? How do we identify the clients that will be most likely to benefit from our services, so we can market to them first?

In the legal industry, data analytics poses unique opportunities and challenges. Legal practitioners can benefit tremendously from using data to track trends in the industry, rate lawyer performance, measure market size and growth, or evaluate the value of online real estate. But doing all of this effectively means coming up with innovative ways to find, manage, and analyze data from a variety of sources. It also means identifying data that is directly relevant to business challenges in the legal space, challenges that are not necessarily found elsewhere.

Data analytics in legal also involves quality control issues, as well as the problem of data availability: there is no centralized data source specific to the legal category. At Avvo, we have taken on solving the problem of limited and disparate data in legal. By collecting a wide variety of data on lawyers from state and local licensing and regulatory authorities, as well as the internet more broadly, we are learning a great deal regarding issues directly related to legal practice.

The company has gathered a wealth of knowledge and insight over the years, and this chapter shares some lessons learned and best practices of collecting, cleaning, analyzing, and visualizing legal data. First, we provide an overview of how data pertinent to legal can be collected and stored. Then we discuss different ways in which data can be used to improve a legal practice. Specifically, we discuss how a legal entity can use data to evaluate lawyer quality, identify markets in which need is great but lawyers scarce, and identify business development leads.

Data Sourcing in Legal

Since Avvo's inception, the company has believed that data can make a difference. Our work in data and analytics ties into our mission and vision, which is "to get people the quality legal help they deserve" so that we can "power liberty and justice for all." To this end, we use data to rate attorneys, measure business performance, identify those who are legally underserved, and determine how to better reach people with legal needs.

Data Gathering

Although some of our data is proprietary (such as information collected via consumer surveys), much of the data we use is publicly available. Law practices can garner much insight from U.S. Census data, data published by the American Bar Association, or user-generated content found on various websites. Research organizations like Nielsen and Pew publish reports on various topics that are either directly or tangentially useful in deriving insights for legal practice. If a law firm has the funds, they can hire market research companies to gather data for them. A practice can also look at its own data. Its own website traffic data can be accessed through Google Analytics, for example. However, keeping track of the number of first-contact calls or e-mails a practice gets each week or month could be a valuable data point. Client satisfaction surveys sent out via email after a case is closed is also a source of data. Big data is cool, but "small" data can also be incredibly valuable. Whatever the source, data is abundant and readily available.

For publicly available data, Avvo starts by identifying an eligible data source (such as U.S. Census data). The challenge then becomes "acquiring" that data in a way that is useful for us internally. To do this, we first determine the following: who will be using the data, how the data will be used, and whether the data can be described through the use of a dummy table. We then design a data product suitable to the specific use case. Since we use Hadoop, we can land the data, then design simple Hive tables so the data can be accessed via simple Structured Query Language. If an Application Programming Interface (API) needs to be provided for an application, we will design an API optimized around the case for real-time data access, performance, security, and other important considerations. In short, data acquisition should be done with the end user and use case in mind.

Data Management

The real challenge lies less in finding data and more in "data governance." Data must be domesticated and managed in such a way that the right data becomes efficient to access for any specific business problem. It is also important to ensure data security. Data in the legal industry comes with a unique set of concerns regarding

cloudera navigator

Search (Hotkey: /)   Q

Click here to explore your data.

FIGURE 7.1   Navigator.

protection, integrity, and management, which involves allowing access to only qualified users. To solve this problem, many organizations, including Avvo, invest time in capturing "metadata" (data about data) in a central repository. For those solving business intelligence and advanced analytics problems, this serves as a starting point for data analytics.

To access this data, organizations like Avvo invest in tools that allow them to explore the types of data they have. One example of such a tool is Navigator by Cloudera, in which you can use a simple Google-like search box to explore the data in your central data repository. Rather than sift through field after field of raw data, tools like Navigator pull information from a data dictionary so that you can see descriptions of your data assets and make better decisions about which data is relevant for your needs. Also, by providing firm-wide access to a data dictionary, rather than the actual data, it is possible to ensure the integrity and security of the data. Moreover, as new data is added to the repository, this sort of tool can serve to communicate to others in the organization where the data came from, when it was acquired, and what data fields are newly available (Figure 7.1).

The history of a data source is referred to as its "data lineage." Tracking lineage is important as companies develop sophisticated indexing or scoring systems to prioritize their business tactics. For instance, a law practice may want to know which of its former clients might be most open to receiving an email requesting that they refer friends and family. The firm may want to generate a unique client satisfaction score that they can use to understand how lawyers in the firm can improve in their practice of law and representation of clients. A model might be developed to determine whether TV or digital advertising would generate the highest return. Analyses like these may pull data from a variety of different sources. Knowing where each data field or variable comes from—what its lineage is—allows analysts to access the original data source again if needed and to feel confident about its integrity.

Data Integration

Data at Avvo is being gathered on a regular basis, especially given that we handle "events"—or interactions with our website—as data. For example, if an attorney logs into their profile, this information is recorded as data—or "event data."

We take very seriously the data privacy of our users as evidenced by our privacy policy—which we regularly update for the benefit of our consumers and advertisers. This real-time web event data is integrated into our sales team activity using Salesforce. When attorneys interact with the website, by logging in or updating their profile, an event is logged into Salesforce, and the Avvo resource is notified of this activity. This timely notification of engagement creates opportunities for valuable interactions with our attorneys when they need it.

This data is also stored in our warehouse, and can be retrieved using Salesforce for a number of different types of analyses. For example, a real-time notification would be sent to Avvo staff when an attorney cancels their advertising subscription. We also can look at advertiser data in aggregate to analyze cancellations and the conditions under which they are occurring.

To bring our website users even closer to our organization in real time, our design includes something mystical called Kafka. Kafka is akin to a gossip collector: it knows about all events that occur across the company, thereby allowing anyone to analyze data from these events independently. This mechanism allows producers and consumers of web-based events to be loosely coupled so that neither producer nor consumer needs to wait on either party. It also allows for cohesive consumption of events, since any consumer can analyze event data that is most relevant to them.

Data Accessibility

Once data is collected and integrated, it needs to be made available. In addition to audience access preferences, we consider the overall capability of our current and future data technology choices. Over the years, we have balanced open-source supportability with vendor lock-in by considering the following: whether we have the requisite in-house skills to extend and support the open-source project; what our time horizon is for commitment to the data product or platform; and whether the vendor is aligned long term with our data strategy (Hadoop vs. traditional data warehousing).

Monitoring the data pipeline for our internal data customers means providing transparency. We have created an internal status page showing the operational status of our data pipeline. The pipeline consists of jobs that generate data, APIs, data for reports, and extracts for Tableau. Each one of these pipeline components is monitored and the status made available on a Data Status Page internally at Avvo. In this way, any corporate data user can check via a self-service interface whether a service is operational. In addition, the history of any incidents is provided for reference. As an example, the image below illustrates a failed job which was scheduled to extract data for a Tableau report. The yellow traffic signal indicates that there was a partial outage and that the appropriate party was alerted (Figure 7.2).

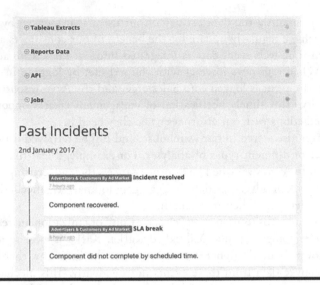

FIGURE 7.2   Data status page.

Data in Action

Gathering and managing data, as well as making it easily accessible to the right people in your organization, is the hard and somewhat tedious part of putting data into action.

Using Data to Evaluate Quality Lawyering

Avvo reaches out and talks to a lot of people who have legal problems to know how to best help them. Avvo has interviewed or surveyed thousands of people dealing with a wide range of legal issues, from traffic citations to divorce, bankruptcy to immigration, and more. We've learned that some people see their issue as minor, or easy to handle on their own. Others simply don't have the funds to hire an attorney. Many prefer the control they have when handling their legal issue on their own. But even in our current do-it-yourself world, where it's possible to file your own divorce, use an online tool to incorporate your business, or buy software for writing your own will, lawyers matter. Almost three out of every four people with legal issues reach out to or hire a lawyer for help; about three out of every four people who complete a form online end up reaching out to an attorney. The law is complicated, legal language hard to understand, and people get stuck. Self-help in legal only goes so far.

This means that there are many people looking for an attorney, but unsure about who to hire. Some ask friends and family for recommendations. Some go online to evaluate lawyer websites and read reviews. Some do both. Despite what they do, two things are clear: (1) people want information about lawyers and (2) people aren't systematic in evaluating that information. This means that if a legal services company, law firm, or lawyer review site sincerely wants to help people find the right attorney, they must develop a systematic process to rate attorneys and then share that rating with the public. Otherwise, people with legal needs are left weighing various attorney attributes in such a way (usually a subjective way) that amounts to little more than guesswork.

How do clients meaningfully differentiate among lawyers? The Avvo Rating—a rating score representing attorney quality—was designed specifically to address this problem. Each attorney who has claimed their profile on the Avvo website is given a rating score based on his or her professional credentials. This score is available to legal consumers on each attorney's Avvo profile, along with details about area of practice, peer endorsements, client reviews, and other information. Together, all of this data makes for an easier evaluation of lawyers and a better chance that legal consumers will pick the right attorney for them.

Ratings are useful in another way: they can help us evaluate and compare the quality of lawyers across geographic regions. Recently, Avvo has become interested in understanding which of America's cities has the highest quality lawyers. This question is an important one but has to date been unexplored. It is important because equal access to justice in large part depends on equal access to high-quality attorneys. If there is substantial disparity in lawyer quality across U.S. cities, then a company like Avvo—which is dedicated to connecting people with high-quality lawyers— can improve access to justice by prioritizing underserved cities in its efforts.

This geographic-driven project is ongoing at Avvo. The following describes how Avvo used data to approach the problem and how Avvo could apply approach across geographies.

The Right Approach for Geographic Comparisons

To determine which cities have the "best" lawyers, Avvo considered two approaches: one purely objective and the other a hybrid of objective and subjective metrics. The purely objective approach provides consumers with individual-level data that is based on lawyer "specifications." We use the term "specifications" because this is how consumers largely think about discrete and measurable lawyer attributes such as years of experience, number of awards, number of publications, law school rank, etc. Consumers review these bits of data much like they might review the "specs" of a laptop or car they want to purchase. Analytics can take these discrete specs and combine them into a rating score that makes it easier for people to evaluate the overall quality of a lawyer. This makes comparisons of attorneys much easier and much less subject to bias.

This approach is the basis of the Avvo Rating, and it works well in helping individuals evaluate and compare individual attorneys, especially alongside client reviews. This way, legal consumers can evaluate credentials objectively while also evaluating subjective client opinions (people regularly tell Avvo that reading reviews is a significant and meaningful part of the "lawyer shopping" process) separately.

However, the goal of this project was not necessarily to evaluate lawyers in order to hire one, but instead to compare lawyers in different markets for legal services, which calls for a different, hybrid approach. This approach includes client opinions of each lawyer in the final rating calculation. Unlike the pure "specs" approach, incorporating client evaluations appreciates the fact that there is much more to what makes a lawyer "good" than objective credentials. Time and again people with legal issues tell Avvo that they care a lot about whether their lawyer gets back to them in a timely fashion, treats them with respect, and exhibits the type of interest and drive to them feel taken care of. "Bedside manner" for lawyers is not reflected in years of experience, law school attended, or even endorsements by peers. But it matters to clients.

Data Used to Compare the Quality of Lawyers in Different Cities

To make city-to-city comparisons of lawyers, Avvo used the following data sets:

Geographic data. Any comparative analysis by city needs to include data on each lawyer's location of practice. Geographic metrics aren't inputs to the model but rather used to define the scope of analysis. The company calculates and compares lawyer ratings for each city. Avvo has data on each lawyer's city, county, and state of practice, so across-county and across-state comparisons are also possible. We also have zip codes available for within-city comparisons by neighborhood.

Institutional data. Lawyers practice in a lot of different contexts. Some work as in-house counsel for corporations, some are solo practitioners, others work in nonprofit. In some contexts, it is necessary to rate and compare lawyers in all types of institutions. In other contexts, we may just want to compare lawyers in particular institutions. For example, if the goal of city-by-city comparisons is to know in which cities individuals with legal needs may have a hard time finding lawyers, then including in-house counsel or district attorneys would not be useful.

Furthermore, some who work in the legal profession do not practice at all. Many attorneys in our data set are not actively practicing, while others work as law professors, judges, or mediators. Avvo used practice set data to exclude these other attorneys from its analysis using practice status data it has collected.

Data on area of practice. For each lawyer who has claimed a profile and provided us this information, we have information regarding which areas of law they practice. Specifically, we have information on their primary area of practice as well as two other areas in which they may practice. We have this information at the level of "parent" practice area as well as actual practice area. For example, a parent practice area might be personal injury, while medical malpractice would be the actual practice area. We also know how many different practice areas each attorney works in, as well as what proportion of their overall practice is devoted to their primary practice area.

Data on Law School Attended. For each lawyer in our dataset, Avvo has the law school from which they received their degree. Law school rank is determined by the most recent rankings as reported by *U.S. News and World Report.*

Data on licensing. Avvo has data on when each attorney was first licensed. This gives us a sense of how long they may have been practicing. We also know how many licenses each attorney has received.

Client recommendation data. Avvo has data on the number of client reviews each lawyer has received. A large number of client reviews does not necessarily mean that the reviews are positive. One can use this variable ("review count") to help standardize client review scores; rather than count the number of positive reviews, which might penalize lawyers who don't have many, we can determine what proportion of all reviews received were positive. The company uses "recommend" as a proxy for positive reviews. Avvo has data on the number of former clients who recommend each lawyer.

Peer endorsement data. For each attorney, we have data on the number of endorsements they have received from other attorneys.

Data on awards. We know the total number of professional awards each lawyer has received as provided by the lawyer or, in some cases, publicly available on the web.

Data on sanctions. The company has information on whether a lawyer has been sanctioned by the Bar.

Data on speaking engagements and publications. We have data on the total number of publications each lawyer has reported.

Data on payment options available to clients. Because cost is such an important factor in whether or not someone hires a lawyer, and affordability is key to accessing justice, our analysis should include data that indicates a lawyer's willingness to work with clients and be affordable. As a proxy for this, we have data on whether each lawyer offers a fixed fee payment structure.

Data on lawyer job title. A lawyer's status within his or her practice or firm is an indicator of success and therefore might be relevant in gauging lawyer quality. Therefore, we've gathered data on each lawyer's title and position within his or her practice or firm.

Considerations for Modeling

Given the rich data available to the company, Avvo's challenge was to determine how best to use this data in making comparisons about lawyer quality across geographies. The variables described earlier could all have something to do with making a great lawyer. But it is also possible that one or two could have nothing to do with lawyer quality. Or, they could all matter, but to varying degrees, even to the extent that one or two might constitute 80% of what it takes to be a good lawyer while the others could constitute 20%. In any case, the company couldn't assume that a rating score for attorneys would treat each of these conceptual variables as if they carry the same weight.

For instance, imagine comparing two attorneys. One has been practicing for a long time but has a middling client review score. The other has very little experience, but her clients have given her a very high review score. Which is better? Some might say that experience is what makes a lawyer great. Others say it's the more personal qualities that matter, like drive or good bedside manner. Either way you look at it, it becomes clear that rating attorneys requires understanding not just what is important but also how important everything is relative to everything else.

How can we know the relative importance of each variable in ranking a "good" lawyer? One way is to use our best judgment to draw assumptions. Assumptions are a critical part of any analysis; they define the scope of the analysis and also make any limitations of the analysis transparent.

For example, we could assume, based on what we perceive to be common knowledge, that years licensed should count twice as much as a client rating score. However, to do this convincingly, there must be some justification for this assumption. Why does number of years licensed matter more? One could argue that the amount of time spent in the trenches actually practicing law is what makes one a good lawyer, despite what clients might think about that lawyer. On the other hand, a lawyer could be practicing for many years, but doing so poorly, who is better to know this than the people who have him or her?

The problem with using best judgment is that, when it comes to new areas of understanding, most assumptions do not have convincing justifications and can easily be challenged. Common knowledge may not be that common, and weakly justified assumptions make for questionable models and dubious findings.

Even if we were to comfortably rank-order the earlier variables in order of importance, we are still left wondering how *much* more or less any variable matters than the others. Suppose we decide that a lawyer's client review score is a more important predictor of good lawyering than number of years licensed: we still wouldn't know if it were two times more important, three times, etc.

When it is available, previous research can help answer these questions. Research gives us more confidence in the model's assumptions. Avvo has conducted quite a bit of research on people seeking legal help. This research has told us that, from a legal consumer's perspective, client reviews are very important in helping decide who to hire. We also know that the number of awards and licenses matter less, but the number of years licensed matter just as much.

The problem with these specific findings, however, is that these weights would reflect the importance of each variable *in making a hiring decision*. What we are after are weights that tell us the relative importance of each variable in determining *how well a lawyer actually performs*. We simply do not have the right data for that.

We could ask legal consumers to evaluate their previously hired lawyer based on set criteria. We could have legal consumers rank the importance of each variable and use rank scores to calculate lawyer quality. But how would a legal consumer know what goes into making a lawyer what he or she is? Clients know how well their lawyers perform, but they have no visibility into why their lawyers perform the way they do. Were they taught to perform the way they do through experience? Is their performance mostly the product of personality? Legal consumers are not in a position to tell.

Because common knowledge may not be so common, and since previous research has not yet been available to provide the right weights for each variable, we must use a methodological approach that provides weights for us. Therefore, in calculating lawyer rating scores, we rely on statistical techniques to tell us how important each of the variables are, so we know how heavily to count them in calculating a final score.

The Model and Its General Results, Using "Conceptual" Lawyer Attributes

The ultimate goal for our comparative lawyer rating scores (comparing lawyer quality across cities) is to help us identify in which cities people might be most struggling to find a good lawyer. People are at the center of this. Therefore, we need to make sure our model takes their perspectives into consideration, not to rank order or weight the variables, but to best know how to think about them.

When Avvo asks legal consumers what matters to them in deciding which attorney to hire, "experience" rises to the top of their list. In any profession, experience matters. But dig more deeply into what "experience" means in the legal profession and you get different answers. Some say a lawyer is experienced if they have practiced many years. Others say a lawyer with only three years of experience, but where that experience is highly specialized, would qualify as an experienced lawyer. A lawyer practicing 20 years but across a number of different areas might be experienced to some but not specialized enough to be experienced to others. The notion of experience is subjective.

What this example demonstrates is that legal consumers approach lawyer attributes as high-level concepts. "Experience," "connections," and "interpersonal skills" are examples of the sorts of things that legal consumers value. But these things are concepts, not variables. They are not directly measurable.

These concepts can, however, be measured in terms of the *sets* of variables that make them up. For example, hypothetically speaking, "experience" can be measured by using a combination of years licensed and the number of practice areas engaged in. For example, a lawyer licensed for many years and who works in only one parent practice area could have the right amount and type of experience to be considered "highly experienced."

Just as one cannot assume they know what variables matter in making a high-quality lawyer, similarly, one cannot assume that they know what variables comprise these higher-order "conceptual attributes." So Avvo uses the factor analysis technique to explore which variables are connected enough to where together they make up a "conceptual attribute" (or what statisticians call a "latent variable"). Factor analysis also allows us to determine which variables may not be related to any other or matter at all in determining lawyer quality.

Our factor analysis uncovered three conceptual attributes emerging as key factors in determining what makes a great lawyer: *perception*, *experience*, and *engagement*. *Perception* refers to how clients perceive each attorney, and this is reflected in their reviews. The variables undergirding *perception* are the average client rating (of the attorney) and the percent of clients who recommend the attorney. *Experience* is a combination of years licensed (a proxy for the number of years practicing law), the number of licenses an attorney has, and the number of awards an attorney has received in his or her profession. *Engagement* is a reflection of how involved each lawyer is in his or her professional space, in terms of networking or outreach. The variable that make up *engagement* are the number of publications a lawyer has, the number of his or her speaking engagements, and the number of his or her peer endorsements.

We also discovered that perception has the greatest impact on the overall lawyer. This means that how clients experience, rate, and recommend an attorney is a stronger indicator of quality lawyering than a lawyer's actual experience in terms of years in practice and accolades received. Also, peer-related engagement—such as legal publications, speaking appearances, and peer endorsements—involve a lot of work but may not pay off as much as simply making clients happy.

Although perception matters most, it is incorrect to say that experience and engagement don't matter at all. In fact, our findings show that all three have a significant impact on lawyer quality, to the extent that each is a necessary component of lawyer quality. Therefore, to conclude that lawyer quality relies solely on client perceptions is misleading.

These insights offer profound implications for different types of lawyers. For attorneys who dread having to involve themselves with professional networking, or appearing in trade publications, not all is lost as long as they commit to creating a positive perception among their clients. They may do well meeting basic requirements of engagement, but need not excel in that area. Newer attorneys with less experience are also not necessarily at a disadvantage; they can make up for their inexperience with more engagement or by building a positive perception among their clients.

What's left is understanding what exactly leads to positive client perceptions. What can a lawyer do, specifically, to improve their reputation? This is, as mentioned earlier, a subjective evaluation: what is great bedside manner for one client may not matter to another. Client experience largely hinges on good client–lawyer personality fit. But there are things that all lawyers can do to ensure positive experiences. Survey data of legal consumers collected by Avvo suggests that responsiveness to e-mails and phone calls can make a difference: three out of five Americans say that how quickly a lawyer responds to phone calls and e-mails is important in deciding who to hire, so one can imagine that most people will consider responsiveness as a positive attribute in assessing how to rate or recommend their lawyer. One in three says that a lawyer's body language matters: eye contact and attentiveness can turn off clients and result in bad reviews and low ratings. One in four says that how a lawyer sounds on a phone can make or break a hire, and two in five say that the behavior of a lawyer's receptionist or support staff matters.

Time and again, through interviews with consumers, Avvo has heard that lawyers who are attentive, engaged, interested, concerned, and driven to do good work will make their clients happy. In addition, some say that attorneys are best when they take charge, while others say they prefer lawyers who let their clients maintain some control over their case. Lawyers who can determine how much involvement each client wants upfront, and can deliver on client preferences, might do best in achieving high ratings and recommendations.

Ultimately, clients want attorneys who care about their case and who are willing to do the work necessary to ensure the best possible outcome. This data analysis confirms what many of us suspect is true but are afraid of embracing: what your clients think of you matters most. Lawyers who are experienced, published, and well known through their speaking engagements might carry a lot of status within their profession, but that may not matter more than good, old-fashioned customer service. Knowledge is definitely much of this; however, how a lawyer imparts knowledge is a key component of quality.

Comparing the Quality of Lawyers across Geographic Regions

Understanding that perception, experience, and engagement are the foundations of quality lawyering and having designed a mechanism to measure quality lawyering, the next step for Avvo will be applying this framework across the United States to determine in which consumers are likely to find the highest and lowest quality legal services.

Using Data to Determine Who Needs Legal Help But Isn't Getting It

As mentioned earlier, a major concern at Avvo is that many people with legal needs are not getting help. This is a legal access issue, a justice issue. Organizations that collaborate with and assist a large number of lawyers—like the American Bar Association or legal services companies like Avvo—are in a position to make large-scale changes that facilitate lawyer access and eliminate justice disparities.

Law firms or practices, however, operate on a smaller scale. Each attorney or firm can do their part to reach more legal consumers, and in aggregate, more who are in need can access a lawyer's help. But law practices are essentially businesses, much like Avvo. Their goal of connecting more people with lawyers is the same as Avvo's, though it can only be met at a smaller scale. Nonetheless, data analysis techniques used by Avvo to reach legal consumers can also be used by lawyers to grow their firms or practices. The techniques described in this section can be leveraged by any law firm or practice to identify marketing opportunities and to generate business growth.

Demographic Data for Analysis of Underserved Markets

Much of Avvo's data analysis involves identifying underserved markets or figuring out how to generate legal growth in the right markets at the right time. To do this, we take into account the fact that demographic conditions affect access to legal support. For example, a burgeoning population in a specific region can increase market size, meaning more people may need the same professional services. Or, increasing wealth across a population can result in a smaller workforce. Because law is a people-centered industry, access to legal services can be more closely tied to demographic changes than in other industries. Increasing affluence and growth of families will raise demands for a gamut of services from real estate to family law. Recovery from economic recession generally leads to higher numbers of Driving Under the Influence cases. And so on.

To identify underserved markets, we use U.S. Census Bureau (USCB) data. For breadth, depth, and quality of demographic data, no source comes close to the USCB. Avvo used USCB data to create analytical models to identify specific U.S. counties with the highest rates of certain legal service needs, such as wills or incorporations, but few Avvo attorneys engaged in meeting that need. We also identified specific online markets in which an improvement of Avvo's online presence, particularly through organic Google rankings, yielded a substantial return in terms of traffic.

We have found the most useful census variables to be at the ZIP code level. Since the Postal Service and the Census Bureau are different governmental organizations, the USCB's version of the ZIP code is called the ZIP Code Tabulation Area (ZCTA). The difference between the Postal Service Zip Codes and the ZCTA is most apparent in dense, urban areas like Manhattan; for example, the ZCTA of 10005 encompasses 10 ZIP codes, most of them belonging to a block or high mail volume area. A hyperlocal business may be interested in catering to ZIP codes, but most businesses will be more interested in the demographic characteristics of a ZCTA.

The USCB also provides demographic forecasts. Many companies, if they don't already employ in-house economists, will hire consultants to use demographic data to create customized forecasts. At Avvo, our analysts used USCB data and internal traffic and revenue data to estimate potential growth across different regions and legal practice areas. We combined Avvo's internal data sources with external data sources, primarily government census data, to create a model of Avvo's current status. The internal data was traffic and advertising value at a market level. We also took advantage of the government's annual economic surveys and forecasts to project Avvo's potential future conditions.

Analysis of Data for Determining Market Need and Lawyer Presence

To identify U.S. counties in which there was a dearth of available Avvo attorneys relative to the legal need, we relied on a cluster analysis technique. Clustering algorithms are common in the repertoire of data scientists, and are often used to demonstrate machine learning to novices. A human looking at a 2-dimensional graph can quickly identify segments, data points that seem to cluster together. But when several dimensions are being considered, the algorithm iterates over some specific rules about what constitutes membership in a cluster, until the clusters are stable.

An example of clustering is shown in Figure 7.3. Here, counties are clustered together in terms of similarity in "performance," or availability of Avvo attorneys relative to legal need. Since it is hard to imagine an n-dimensional plot, a 2-dimensional representation of the cluster along the citizenship and ethnic mix axes is shown. For illustration, only six clusters are shown, though the final model uses at least 30. Table 7.1 shows five examples of clusters with some of their demographic characteristics.

Since all counties in a cluster share similar demographic characteristics, they should have similar behaviors and legal needs. To gauge market penetration within a cluster, we considered the range of values of the metric being optimized (for example, revenue per capita). We then identified the counties closest to a target percentile

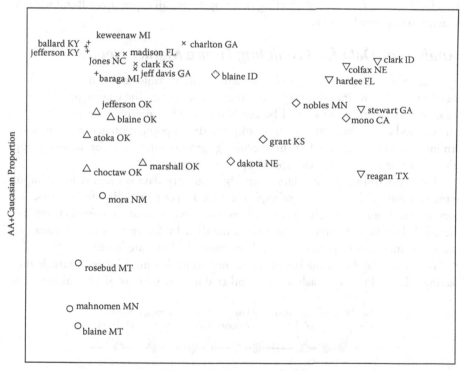

FIGURE 7.3   Colors represent clusters.

TABLE 7.1 Characteristics of an Average County in Five Example Clusters

Cluster	Income	Population	Enrolled in education	Noncitizen rates	Number of counties
1	30,000	15,619	23	1.8	170
2	87,700	114,108	28	4.4	62
3	50,700	403,318	27	3.9	80
4	53,500	519,500	29	15.3	24
5	64,400	1,783,100	28	13.4	22

(for example, the 70th percentile), and assumed that business development efforts could raise all counties to this level. The result is an estimate of the potential revenue not being realized in those counties. Figure 7.4 illustrates this method.

The counties displayed in the figure belong in the same demographic cluster. Their performance on Avvo, as measured by sessions per capita, falls along a continuum from 26 per 100K to 69 per 100K. Our 70th percentile target in this cluster was Dallas County, Texas. By hitting that target, we can expect overall traffic in the cluster to improve by 20%.

Analysis of Data for Predicting Future Market Need

Another of our goals was to predict which counties would see an increase in legal need in the future and also flag those that may decline. The census provides five-year forecasts, and these should be corroborated with internal firm metrics using the method mentioned earlier. For example, a rise in population generally indicates an increase in market size, but the specific age groups, ethnicities, or income groups that are growing help identify specific practice areas.

Here, obtaining quality data from high-integrity data sources is most important and outweighs the level of sophistication in your modeling techniques. The best way to improve insights is to find and use more accurate, comprehensive, and detailed data (for example, actual cases handled by lawyers, or court cases as a proxy for increases in practice areas, from municipal to state levels).

In the case of Avvo, the insights obtained from this model drive strategic marketing efforts. Further mashups with other datasets, such as SEO rankings, and

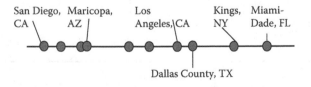

FIGURE 7.4 Counties in the same demographic cluster.

Avvo lawyer profiles, provide direct actions in each county for marketing campaigns that can increase lawyer availability to meet future legal need.

Analysis of Data for Generating Advertiser Leads

A principal component of the Avvo website is its availability of advertising space. Lawyers use Avvo advertising to reach more potential legal consumers. Data used to uncover and predict market potential can also be used to generate immediate advertising sales leads. In the same way that FICO creates a credit worthiness score, historical customer data combined with demographic data can be used to create risk scores, lead scores, etc. It is judgment at scale and speed, what every salesperson does when scoping a potential lead: deciding whether credit can be safely extended and how much investment is justified in developing a long-term relationship.

Companies measure the value of business using the lifetime value (LTV) for their customers. Law firms can similarly benefit from understanding their clients' LTV, especially since some clients in some practice areas provide repeat business, and other clients can be excellent sources of referrals. A person with recurring legal issues probably has a higher LTV for an attorney than an average law-abiding citizen. A business person in a region that is undergoing an economic boom based on structural soundness has a higher LTV than someone living in a historically economically depressed area.

True LTV is extremely hard to calculate ex ante. One way to approximate LTV is by calculating near-term potential values or a "lead score." One can identify practice areas and regions that have high value. Then, it is possible to predict which individuals within those groups are likely to expand their practice into new practice areas. Each law practice's likelihood of growth—and likelihood to advertise to meet growth goals—can also be predicted.

The model generates various *market potential scores*. A score based on current market penetration and advertising value is straightforward to construct, and does not require any machine learning. A score based on future market potential may take economic forecasts into consideration, but more to the point, it incorporates the factors described earlier. This allows an immediate evaluation of which markets and clients have the best potential for sales.

The model also generates a *lawyer score* using a technique called collaborative filtering. It uses a statistical model to identify which of a lawyer's activities are predictors of increased online marketing and advertising. The model used is a standard statistical model called multivariate regression. It takes several potential predictors, correlates them against the metric to be predicted, and based on the strength of this correlation, it assigns a weight to the predictor. Models like this have as an input dozens of variables, and the output can be in two forms, binary indicator of growth or not, or a numerical output indicating the magnitude of untapped potential.

Several statistical requirements have to be met in order for this model to be useful. One is that the predictors must be independent: the predictor variables cannot be correlated with one another. For example, number of reviews and tenure as a

TABLE 7.2   Final Lead Score

Name	Lead score (A–D)	Market score (A–D)	Lawyer score (A–D)	Existing markets	Potential new markets	Reasons
John Doe	A	A	B	Real estate— Baltimore	N/A	High growth markets
Jane Doe	A	C	A	Personal injury— North Chicago	Car accident— North Chicago	High LTV, increasing trend

lawyer are highly correlated with each other, so only one of those variables should be used in the model.

The market priority score and the lawyer score are combined to give a final *lead score*. This is a number that in itself is not easily interpretable, but in relation to other scores, can be used to create a ranked list of lawyers for any given matter.

There is a heuristic component to the model (Table 7.2). The lawyers for which scores have been generated are ranked below in order of descending lead score, but there is rich information that can be unpacked: regions the advertiser may be interested in, practice areas that may be relevant, whether or not a coupon or promotion might tilt a decision, etc. So, the output may look like this:

Note that the interpretation of this list depends more on the data that was fed into the model rather than the mathematical techniques. The data was based on current conditions and so the output is also about current potential conditions. To get closer to LTV, a forecast of market potential should be substituted. And the lawyer score part of the model is likely to take a lower weight in the combined model.

Conclusion

The techniques described in this chapter have proven extremely useful to Avvo as it navigates its way through the legal space. These techniques may not perfectly fit the business needs of every practice, but they do offer some innovative ways of thinking about how to find and manage data in a data-laden world. Given that marketing and business development hinge on proving that you have a good product—i.e., high-quality lawyers—techniques Avvo uses to identify high-quality lawyering can be useful to law firms as they try to convince potential clients to hire them. And though clustering and regression techniques used by Avvo to identify market and sales potential may not be directly relevant to every law firm's marketing strategy, they, at a minimum, offer unique ways to think about data that can be leveraged to optimize marketing and advertising spend.

Avvo's hope is that if the approaches laid out here are not directly relevant to every practice, the ideas behind these techniques are. Ultimately, data analysis works if it fuels real growth for each unique business. Each firm must make its own decisions about what types of data are most valuable, and what types of methodologies are able to point to the most valuable answers. But one thing seems universally certain: ignoring data altogether can put a law practice at a serious disadvantage in the legal marketplace.

Chapter 8

Uncovering Big Bias with Big Data: An Introduction to Linear Regression

David Colarusso[1]

Contents

Abundant data and inexpensive computing have supercharged the traditional tools of computer science and statistics. Under the moniker *data science*, they promise if given the right input to reveal unseen patterns, test intuitions, and predict the future. Though this may seem like magic, it is not. The following is a peek behind the curtain of data science, a *how to* cast as *case study*. It is an invitation to engage, a

---

[1] This chapter is adapted from the May 21, 2016 Lawyerist article *Uncovering Big Bias with Big Data*, available at https://lawyerist.com/big-bias-big-data/.

nontechnical introduction to one of statistics' favorite tools, and as with many good case studies, it begins with a dispute.

A while back, two of my colleagues were arguing about which is a bigger problem in the criminal justice system: bias against defendants of color or bias against poor defendants. My first inclination was to suggest we could settle the dispute given the right dataset. (I'm an attorney turned data scientist, so yes, that really was my first thought.[2]) That being said, the right dataset magically appeared in a Tweet from Ben Schoenfeld.[3]

Ben Schoenfeld
@oilytheotter

2.2 million Virginia criminal district court cases now available for bulk download and more to come! virginiacourtdata.org #opendata

8:35 PM · Mar 21, 2016

What follows is the story of how I used those cases to explore what best predicts defendant outcomes: race or income. This chapter is not a summary of my findings, though you will find them here. Yes, there will be a few equations, but you can safely skim over them without missing much. That's because the model presented here is a toy model, an overly simplified construction built with the aim of better understanding a problem. It is not intended to be the definitive answer to a question but rather the first step of a longer journey. That being said, pay particular attention to the graphs, and you'll be fine.

"Big" Data

Attorneys rely on intuition. It is how we "know" whether a case should go to trial. But all intuition is statistical, the product of experience and observation. Unfortunately, it is also subject to an assortment of cognitive biases. "Big" Data promises to help transcend these shortcomings by checking our intuitions.[4]

---

[2] It's worth noting the work I'm describing here was done on my own time and in no way represents the opinions of my employer at the time.

[3] As his site, http://VirginiaCourtData.org/, makes clear there's quite a story behind this data, and my hat's off to Ben for making them usable, despite some disagreements over the particulars of the release. See note 4. Thank you Ben. The tweet can be found at https://twitter.com/oilytheotter/status/712075191212441600.

[4] In my experience, most practitioners of data analytics are ambivalent about the term Big Data. Only a handful of institutions deal with truly big data. Google and Facebook come to mind. Most of the time when people say Big Data, what they're really talking about is data sufficiently large for statistical analysis to be useful. Hence, the quotes.

To help answer which was a bigger problem—bias against defendants of color or bias against poor defendants—I sifted through millions of Virginia court records.[5] Say you have some collection of variables and the suspicion that one of them is dependent on the others. How do you test your suspicion? In one word: statistics!

For the question at hand, our data need to contain at least three types of information:

1. The defendants' race.
2. The defendants' income.
3. Some consistent measure of outcomes.

With enough data, we can look to see whether outcomes change when race and income change. That is, we can see if there are any correlations. The outcome is

Source: "Correlation" from xkcd. Available at https://xkcd.com/552/

---

[5] As a criminal defense attorney, I'm well aware of the complications that arise from such a dataset. Just because you can aggregate data doesn't mean you should. The data used here was aggregated from publicly accessible court webpages that include defendant names. The contents of these pages are in fact public records. However, Ben has prudently hidden defendant names behind one-way hashes, and the court had enough foresight to partially obfuscate dates of birth. Unfortunately, this does not preclude deanonymization of the data in the future. I would have opted to further obscure some of the data to make deanonymization harder, and I shared some suggestions for further scrubbing the data with Ben. It was clear he took seriously the need to consider the unintended consequences of making this data more accessible, hence his effort to obscure defendant names. It was also clear that he felt there was a clear public interest in making these public data (in the sense that they are public records) more accessible, listing several cases where he believed obscured data would have made the discovery of injustices in the system harder to find. In response, I provided several hypotheticals illustrating the concerns behind my belief that more scrubbing was called for. We both agree that true anonymization is probably impossible, barring full homomorphic encryption, and that there is a public interest in making parts of this data easier to access than they are in the existing court interface. Where we disagree is on whether these should include all or only a subset of the data. He left open the question as to whether or not he will further scrub the data, but he made clear that he had no intent to do so in the near future. For this reason, I have not included the raw data in the supplementary materials cited in footnote 8.

called the dependent variable. Race and income are independent variables. We call these features.

If we can get data on other factors that might affect the outcome, we want those too. Generally, the more features, the better, because we can control for their effects.[6] For example, we should probably know something about the seriousness of a charge. Otherwise, if we find outcomes (e.g., sentences) go down as defendant incomes go up, we won't know if this is because the courts are actively biased against the poor or because the well-off aren't charged with serious crimes and never face truly bad outcomes.

Data Wrangling and Exploration

Ben's data are basically a set of spreadsheets. Each row is a charge, and there are some 47 columns associated with each row. Here's what they look like:

I	J	K	L	M	N
Charge	ChargeType	Clas	CodeSection	Commencedby	ConcludedBy
ROBBERY: RESIDENCE	Felony	U	18.2-58	Indictment	Guilty Plea
ROBBERY: RESIDENCE	Felony	U	18.2-58	Indictment	Guilty Plea
ROBBERY: RESIDENCE	Felony	U	18.2-58	Indictment	Guilty Plea
RAPE	Felony	U	18.2-61	J&Dr Appeal	Trial - Judge With Witness
RAPE #1	Felony		18.2-61(A)(II)	Direct Indictment	Trial - Judge With Witness
FIRST DEGREE MURDER	Felony	1	18.2-32	Other	Trial - Jury
ROBBERY	Felony	U	18.2-58	Indictment	Trial - Judge With Witness
OBJECT SEXUAL PENETRATION	Felony		18.2-67.2(A)(2)	Direct Indictment	Guilty Plea
ROBBERY	Felony		18.2-58	Indictment	Trial - Judge With Witness

I'm going to let you in on a secret: most of a data scientist's time is spent cleaning and joining data, sometimes called data wrangling or data munging. It's not glamorous, but it's necessary, and it's a process that requires a good sense of what you're looking for.

Immediately, I scanned the data for race, income, seriousness, and outcome. There was a column listing the defendants' race, but there was no column for income.[7] Luckily, the dataset included the zip codes of defendants, and since the 2006–2010 American Community Survey tabulated mean income by zip code, I could make an educated guess about a defendant's income.[8] I just assumed a defendant's income was the average income of their zip code. It's not perfect, but we don't need to be perfect. I'll explain why.

---

[6] When you have a lot of potential features, however, some special issues start to crop up. See e.g., https://en.wikipedia.org/wiki/Curse_of_dimensionality.

[7] The Race column listed six categories: American Indian, Asian or Pacific Islander, Black (Non-Hispanic), Hispanic, Other, or White Caucasian (Non-Hispanic). However, I do not know what criteria the court uses to determine a defendant's label. Also, I am aware that this appears to be a conflation of race and ethnicity, but again, these are the categories provided in the court data. You will see these labels referenced by shorthand in this article as Native, Asian, Black, Hispanic, Other, and Caucasian, respectively.

[8] Assuming I limited my analysis to 2006–2010 data, which I did. This also limited me to data from Virginia's Circuit Courts.

Creating a Model

> [A]ll models are wrong, but some are useful.

—George Box

You might not have realized it, but we're about to build a statistical model. When evaluating if a model is useful, I like to remember two things:

1. Always ask "compared to what?"
2. Always remember that the output of a model should start, not end, discussion.

Right now, we're operating in the dark. I had a guess as to whether or not a defendant's race or income was a better predictor of outcomes, and I bet you have your own guess, but we have reasons to doubt our guesses. After we build a model, we'll know more. We can then use the model's output to move the conversation forward. That is the most one can ask for. Admittedly, I've made a lot of assumptions, and you're welcome to disagree with them. In fact, you're invited to improve upon them as I have shared all of my work, including computer code, over on GitHub.[9] That's how science works. In fact, when the blog post this chapter was based on first ran, I received a lot of thoughtful feedback. Someone even caught an error in my code that caused me to amend my results, decreasing the estimated effect size.[10]

It's important to note again that we're modeling for insight. I don't expect that we'll use our model to predict the future. Rather, we're trying to figure out how things interact. We want to know what happens to outcomes when we vary defendant demographics, specifically race or income. The exact numbers aren't as important as the general trends and how they compare.

Finding Features

Next up, I had to figure out how to measure the seriousness of a case. The data listed charge types and classes (e.g., Class 1 Felony).[11] Ideally, I wanted to place all crimes on a scale of seriousness. So I sorted the list of all possible combinations and numbered them from 1 to 10.[12]

---

[9] *Class, Race, and Sex in VA Criminal Courts.ipynb* as linked to from https://github.com/colarusso/measured_justice.

[10] See original article with a description of my amendments, supra note*.

[11] For a description of these labels, see *Virginia Misdemeanor Crimes by Class and Sentences* and *Virginia Felony Crimes by Class and Sentences*, available www.criminaldefenselawyer.com/resources/virginia-misdemeanor-crimes-class-and-sentences.htm at and www.criminaldefenselawyer.com/resources/criminal-defense/state-felony-laws/virginia-felony-class.htm respectively. If you look at the data, you'll also see U under the class column as well. These are unclassified charges with their own sentencing range, separate from the standard classes.

[12] This excludes class U charges. See note 10.

This is where I got caught in my first rabbit hole.

I spent a long time trying to map these 10 charge types on to some spectrum of seriousness, but sanctions are multifaceted. I tried combining the possible number of days in a sentence with the possible fine to get a single number that represented how serious a charge was. Coming from Massachusetts, I was looking for something like the ranking of seriousness levels used in our sentencing guidelines. In the end, however, I realized that my overly complicated ratings didn't really improve the model (specifically, its *R*-squared, which is something we'll discuss later).

The data included multiple outcomes, including the length of sentences, information on probation, and an accounting of fines and fees.

Again, I spent a while trying to figure out how to combine these before remembering the sage's advice: keep it simple, stupid.

Consequently, I opted to define outcome generally by what I assumed to be the most salient measure: the sentence length in days.[13]

There was another variable relating to defendant demographics, sex, which I included.[14] I could have looked through previous years' data to construct a defendant's criminal history along with a myriad of other features, but given that my question was aimed at the influence of race and income on outcomes, I was content to focus primarily on these features, along with seriousness.

Consequently, there's a lot more one could do with this data, and I'm sure that's what Ben was hoping for when he compiled them. Tools for conducting your own exploration can be found in the GitHub repo referenced earlier.[15]

That being said, we're ready to explore how race, income, seriousness, and sex affect the outcomes of criminal cases.

---

[13] You may notice when we examine the relationship between *seriousness* and *sentence* below, some Classes 3 & 4 Misdemeanors are linked to jail times despite the fact that such offenses should only involve fines. See *Virginia Misdemeanor Crimes by Class and Sentences*, available at www.criminaldefenselawyer.com/resources/virginia-misdemeanor-crimes-class-and-sentences.htm. For the cases I could find, these sentences agreed with the information found on *Virginia Courts' Case Information website*, available at http://ewsocis1.courts.state.va.us/CJISWeb/circuit.jsp, respectively. So this does not appear to be an issue with Ben's data collection. A number of possible explanations come to mind. For example, Public Intoxication is a Class 4 Misdemeanor, but subsequent offenses can result in jail time. See www.criminaldefenselawyer.com/resources/criminal-defense/misdemeanor-offense/virginia-public-intoxication-laws-drunk-publ. It is also possible that there may be data entry errors (e.g., misclassifying a charge as a Class 3 Misdemeanor when the governing statute makes clear it is actually a Class 1 Misdemeanor, something I saw in the court's data). Whatever the reasons for these potential errors, they seem to be the exception, not the rule, and without direct access to the courts' methods and measures of quality control, I have to take the data at face value. Hopefully, the fact that we're working with hundreds of thousands of cases means that 134 outliers, *if* they are actually errors, don't do much to skew our results.

[14] The VA data listed a binary sex, not gender. So I am limited to such a taxonomy here.

[15] Supra note 8.

Best Fit Lines (Regressions)

If you've taken a statistics class or read the title of this chapter, you've seen the next step coming. For those of you who became attorneys because you didn't like math, let's slow things down.

At the heart of modern science there is a class of tools that fall under the general name of regression analysis. You've probably heard of at least one of these. Here, for example, is a *linear regression* I ran on a subset of the Virginia court data.

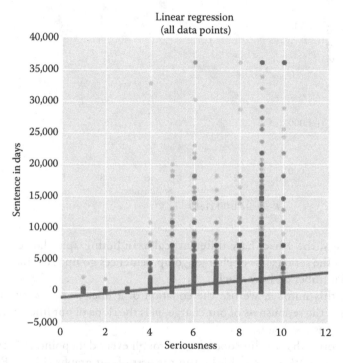

R-squared: 0.121689

Fundamentally, a linear regression is concerned with finding a best fit line. In the earlier graph, we are plotting the seriousness of a charge against the sentence a defendant received in days. Every charge in the data is plotted, and a line is drawn by a computer to minimize the distance between itself and each data point. A bunch of these points fall on top of each other. So it's hard to get a feel for how they are distributed. To help with this, we can replace all data points with a common X value with a single representative "dot." The graph later shows the same data as the one provided earlier, but it groups data points into a single dot at its members' center with bars to indicate where 95% of its membership falls.

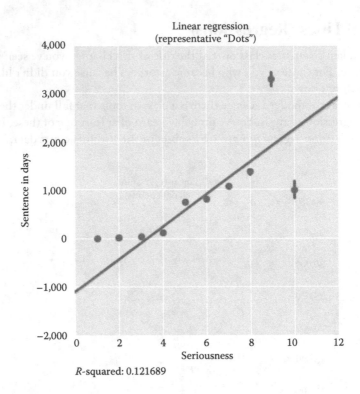

Linear regression
(representative "Dots")

R-squared: 0.121689

Consequently, the *Y*-axes have different scales. In both graphs, however, it can be seen that as the seriousness of charges go up, sentences go up. The lines allow us to put a hard number on how much.

To get this number, we use the equation of a line, $y = mx + b$, where y is the sentence, x is the seriousness of our charge, m is the slope of our line, and b is where our line crosses the *Y*-axis.

You'll notice that the line doesn't go through every data point. In fact, the data seem very noisy. We can see this best in the first of our graphs (Linear Regression: All Data Points). Life is messy, and by plotting every data point, we can see the variations inherent in real life. Thankfully, the seriousness of a charge does not dictate its destiny. Sometimes people are acquitted and cases are dismissed. Both of these occurrences result in a sentence of zero days, and often when there is a finding of guilt, there are extenuating circumstances, causing sentences other than the maximum. Consequently, being charged with a crime that could land you in jail for a year doesn't mean you're going away for a year.

There's a measure of this noise. It is often framed as a number indicating how much of the variation in your data your model (best fit line) explains. It's called *R*-squared, and in the earlier graphs, the model accounts for roughly 12% of the variation. That is, *R*-squared=0.121689. A perfect fit with every data point falling on the line would yield an *R*-squared of 1. Knowing this helps us understand what's going on. We're used to thinking about averages, and in a way, the best fit is just telling us the average for every value along the number line.[16] It's worth noting, however, that our data are a tad peculiar because the seriousness of charges is always a whole number between 1 and 10. That's why we see those nice columns.

Logarithms

If we look at the first plot of seriousness vs. sentences (in the earlier graph labeled *Linear Regression: All Data Points*), everything seems to be bunched up at the bottom of the graph, which isn't ideal for a number of reasons. Luckily, there's a way to deal with that. We can take the log of the data. When we do this, the name of our regression changes from *linear regression* to *log-linear* or *log-normal* regression. We won't be able to read the number of days off our *Y*-axis anymore, but if we want to get that number, we could transform log(*days*) back into *days* by raising *e* to the log(*days*) power (i.e., $e^{\log(days)}$). It's okay if you don't understand logarithms. What's important to know is that this trick helps unbunch our numbers, and we can always undo this transformation if need be. One other detail, log(0) isn't a finite number. Since many cases (e.g., dismissals and acquittals) have a sentence equal to zero, I'll be taking the log of 1 + the sentence. This shifts the distribution of points on our *Y*-axis so they no longer bunch up near the bottom.

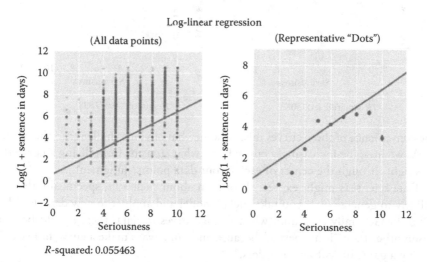

Log-linear regression

(All data points)   (Representative "Dots")

R-squared: 0.055463

The data are nice and spread out now. Note that in the *All Data Points* graph, our best fit doesn't go through the dark patches of data points because it is brought down by our acquittals and dismissals at the bottom.

---

[16] What's really going on is something called *ordinary least squares*.

Now, you can't always fit a line to data. Sometimes it's a curve and sometimes there's no pattern at all—there is no signal to grab on to. Such cases return very low *R*-squared values.

Curvy Lines (Fitting Polynomials)

If you're looking to plot something other than a line, you can add exponents to the equation of your best fit. Such equations are called higher-order polynomials. A line is a first-order polynomial (i.e., $y = mx + b$), whereas a parabola (i.e., $y = ax^2 + bx + c$) is a second-order polynomial. You get third-order polynomials by adding an x^3 and fourth-order polynomials by adding an x^4. What makes polynomials useful is that for every term you add you get a new bend. So we aren't limited to fitting straight lines. For example:

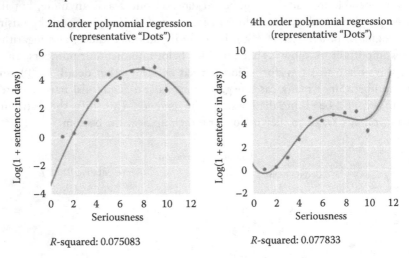

2nd order polynomial regression (representative "Dots")

R-squared: 0.075083

4th order polynomial regression (representative "Dots")

R-squared: 0.077833

The convenience of these curves raises a somewhat obvious challenge to the model's fit. As we imagine increasingly curvy lines, what stops us from fitting a curve that goes right through the center of each of our data points? Judgment.

Data scientists might express skepticism about such a fit, specifically that it is unlikely to generalize. If you take such a model and apply it to new data, it's likely to break. Generally speaking, when fitting curves to data, there should be some reason other than "it fits better," because one can always make a curve fit better by playing a game of "connect the dots."

For example, it might be that charges punishable by fines or incarceration are different from crimes punishable by incarceration alone, and as you transition from one type to the other, the seriousness jumps. Consequently, you wouldn't expect a linear relationship across all charge types. Instead, you might be looking for a "hockey stick." That being said, you should only make use of curvy fits if you have a good theoretical reason to do so.

When you aggressively fit your model and the fit doesn't reflect reality, we call it *overfitting*. To help avoid this temptation, we need to check our work. The process of making our fit based on data is called training, and it's standard practice to train one's model on a subset of data and then test that model against a different subset. This way you can be sure your model is generalizable and will avoid the trap of overfitting. This testing is called cross-validation, and like data wrangling, it's an important step in the process.[17]

Statistically Significant?

How do we know if a correlation is real? It turns out that it's difficult to say for sure. Instead, statisticians ask: "If there is no correlation, how likely would it be for us to see these or more extreme results by chance?"

The answer to this question, feature by feature, is something called a *P*-value. A thoughtful explanation of the meaning of P-values is beyond the scope of this chapter. However, you should know they're scored like golf. Low values are better than high values. This score is often used to help determine whether something is *significant*.[18]

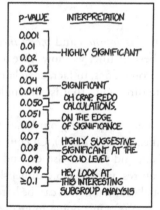

Featured image: "P-Values" from xkcd. Available at https://xkcd.com/1478/

The *P*-values for *seriousness* in the various models given earlier are pretty good—well below 0.05. This comes as no surprise. What we really want to know is how *race, income,* and *sex* measure up. So what does a best fit look like when you deal with more than just seriousness? What happens if we take income into account?

---

[17] To learn more about how I arrived at the final model, check out the materials available at the resource cited in note 8.

[18] What counts as a good *P*-value, however, depends on context. For example, in most social science research, a *P*-value of less than 0.05 is considered significant, but high-energy physicists hold out for a *P*-value of 0.0000003.

Multiple Dimensions

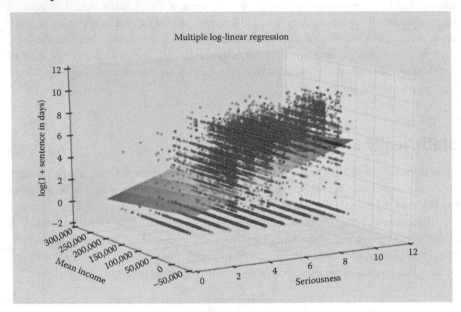

What you're seeing is a plot of *seriousness* and *mean income* against log(1 + *the sentence in days*). Instead of a best fit line, we now have a best fit plane. If you look carefully, you can see that income does, in fact, correlate with outcome, except this correlation is in the opposite direction. That is, the higher your income, the lower your sentence.

Like before, we can use math to quantify our best fit. In this case, however, we use the equation of a plane (i.e., $z = ax + by + c$). Of course, just like before, we could fit curved surfaces to our data, and we can also expand the number of features we consider. As we add more features, we add more dimensions, and our best fit moves into the space of n-dimensional geometry. This can be hard to visualize, but hopefully it's easy enough to understand. We're just doing more of the same. If we don't worry about curves, we're just adding two variables with every new feature/dimension, e.g., $x' = ax + by + cz + d$.

Again, our best fit is telling us something analogous to the average for every value along both axes, *seriousness* and *income*. This implicitly includes all of their combinations. Yes, high income corresponds to a lower sentence, but the seriousness of a charge matters a lot more.

It's worth noting that our race and sex data don't look like our other data in that they're not part of a number scale. To address this, we convert them into collections of binary variables. For example, I have added a column to our data called Male. It's 1 if the client was identified as male and 0 if the client was identified as female. Likewise, there are columns for each of the races defined in the data except for Caucasian. If a client was identified as Caucasian, all of these columns would be zero. That is, our model's default race is Caucasian.

Okay, let's run a regression on all of our features.

Findings

These tables provide a summary of the regression's output. Remember *P*-values? They're all really low (yay!). And although the *R*-squared isn't great (6%), remember that life is messy.[19] If race, income, sex, and the seriousness of a charge predicted a case's outcome 100%, I'd be questioning what attorneys were for. So what do the rest of these numbers mean?

Dep. Variable	np.log(1 + SentenceDays)	*R*-squared	0.060
Model	OLS	Adj. *R*-squared	0.060
Method	Least squares	*F*-Statistic	2008
Date	Wed, June 1, 2016	Prob (*F*-statistic):	0.00
Time	03:00:52	Log-likelihood:	−5.7139e+05
No. observations	221,902	AIC	1.143e+06
Df residuals	221,894	QIC	1.143e+06
Df model	7		
Covariance type	Nonrobust		

Well, the *coef* (short for coefficient) column in the next table tells us the slope of our best fit for a given variable.[20] That is, they tell us how big and in what direction a feature (e.g., race) is correlated with the dependent variable (the sentence).[21] So we can see that the defendants' race is positively correlated with the sentence they receive, and their income is negatively correlated.

Here's our model boiled down to an equation.

$$S = e^{\beta + \beta_1 x_1 + \beta_2 x_2 + \beta_3 x_3 + \beta_4 x_4 + \beta_5 x_5 + \beta_6 x_6 + \beta_7 x_7 + \beta_8 x_8 + \varepsilon}$$

---

[19] I tested a number of different models. See note 8.

[20] If you're curious what all the other numbers mean, check out *Linear Regression with Python*, available at http://connor-johnson.com/2014/02/18/linear-regression-with-python/.

[21] Technically, the log of 1 + the sentence in days.

	Coef	Std err	t	P > |t|	[95.0% Conf. Int.]
Intercept	0.4995	0.057	8.778	0.000	0.368–0.611
Seriousness	0.5659	0.005	112.764	0.000	0.556–0.576
Male	0.3273	0.015	21.341	0.000	0.297–0.357
Mean	−4.166e-06	2.84e-07	−14.680	0.000	−4.72e-06 to −3.61e-06
Black	0.3763	0.050	7.503	0.000	0.278–0.475
Hispanic	0.3660	0.072	5.051	0.000	0.224–0.508
Asian	0.1657	0.050	3.728	0.000	0.068–0.263
Native	0.3606	0.224	1.735	0.063	−0.050 to 0.826
Other	−0.8171	0.097	−6.389	0.000	−1.008 to −0.626

Omnibus	2065.433	Durbin-Watson	1.364
Prob (Omnibus)	0.000	Jarque-Bera (JB)	26018.146
Skew	−0.241	Prob(JB)	0.00
Kurtosis	1.393	Cond. No.	1.93e+19

- D is our dataset of court cases joined with income data.
- S is the sentence in days plus 1 day.
- **Coefficients** β_1–β_8 are those determined by an ordinary least square (OLS) regression for the dataset D corresponding to features x_1–x_8, respectively, with β equal to the intercept. Values of these can be found in the earlier table along with P-values and additional summary data.[22]
- ε = some **random error** for the aforementioned OLS.[23]
- x_1 = the **seriousness** level of a charge.
- x_2 = 1 if defendant is **male**, otherwise 0.
- x_3 = the **mean** income of the defendant's zip code, used as a stand-in for their income.
- x_4 = 1 if defendant is **Black (Non-Hispanic)**, otherwise 0.
- x_5 = 1 if defendant is **Hispanic**, otherwise 0.
- x_6 = 1 if defendant is an **Asian or Pacific Islander**, otherwise 0.

---

[22] Supra note 19.
[23] For more on this, consult *Forecasting from Log-Linear Regressions*, available at http://davegiles. blogspot.com/2013/08/forecasting-from-log-linear-regressions.html.

- $x_7 = 1$ if defendant is an **American Indian**, otherwise 0.
- $x_8 = 1$ if defendant is **Other**, otherwise 0.

Again, those coefficients tell us how big an influence our features have.

This all tells us for a black man in Virginia to get the same treatment as his Caucasian peer, he must earn an additional $90,000 a year.[24]

Similar amounts hold for American Indians and Hispanics, with the offset for Asians coming in at a little less than half as much.

The tentative answer to our question seems to be that race-based bias is *pretty big*. It is also worth noting that being male isn't helpful either.

Because the *R*-squared is so low, we're not saying that being black is an insurmountable obstacle to receiving justice as a defendant. Our model only accounts for 6% of the variation we see in the data. So thankfully, other factors matter a lot more. Hopefully, these factors include the facts of a case.

However, it is clear that defendants of color receive longer sentences than their white peers.

And yes, correlation isn't causation.[25] And yes, strictly speaking, we're only talking about the Virginia Criminal Circuit Courts in 2006–2010. But my guess is we'd find similar results in other jurisdictions or times. So let's start looking for those datasets.

You probably picked up on the fact I called this a tentative answer. That's the nature of science, and more importantly, this is a toy model constructed largely so that it would be understandable to a general audience. Why? So the reader would understand how data science answers such questions. So readers would know it isn't magic. The primary goal of this chapter was to teach about linear regression. It is not a scholarly article on income and race in the justice system.

That being said, we know a good deal more than when we started about the question that drove our investigation. Consequently, I'm willing to articulate the following working theory without attaching specific numbers: race matters.

If you'll forgive my soapbox, it's time we stop pretending race isn't a major driver of disparities in our criminal justice system. This is not to say that the courts are full of racist people. What we see here is the aggregate effect of many interlocking parts. Reality is complex. Good people can find themselves unwitting cogs in the machinery of institutional racism, and a system doesn't have to have racist intentions to behave in a racist way. Unfortunately, the system examined here is not blind to race, class, or sex for that matter.

---

[24] For income's influence to counteract that of being black $\beta_3 x_3 + \beta_4 x_3 = 0$.
Therefore:

$$-0.000004166\, x_3 + (0.3763)(1) = 0$$

$$x_3 = \frac{0.3763}{0.000004166}$$

$$x_3 = 90,456.73$$

[25] See e.g., *Spurious Correlations*, available at www.tylervigen.com/spurious-correlations

Words of Warning

I did all of my analysis with freely available tools, and there's nothing stopping others from picking up where I left off. In fact, I hope that readers will look at the GitHub repo behind this chapter and do exactly that. However, it's important to note that one needs a solid foundation in statistics to avoid making unwarranted claims due to lack of experience.

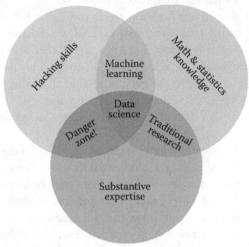

Image: "Data Science Venn Diagram" by Drew Conway is licensed CC BY-NC. Available at http://drewconway.com/zia/2013/3/26/the-data-science-venn-diagram

And beware the danger zone! As Drew Conway (creator of the Venn Diagram provided earlier) points out, "It is from [that] part of the diagram that the phrase 'lies, damned lies, and statistics' emanates."

That being said, there is nothing magic here. With the right tools, it is possible to discover hidden patterns. My advice? Be suspicious of answers that reinforce your existing assumptions. Do your work in the open. When confidentiality allows, share both your findings and your data. Have someone check your math. Remember, such transparency helped me to catch an error in this work early on. Listen to feedback, and always be ready to change your mind.[26]

---

[26] Thanks to Adrian Angus, William Li, and numerous internet commenters for your feedback. It was greatly appreciated.

Chapter 9

Data Mining in the Law Firm: Using Internal Expertise to Drive Decision Making

Kumar Jayasuriya

Contents

In 2017, the Georgetown Center for the Study of the Legal Profession issued a report that chronicled a 10-year shift in the legal profession.[1] The report found that economic and cultural changes are forcing lawyers to reinvent the practice of law and to change the way that they define their markets, their clients, and their services. In the same 10-year period, global commerce has developed through the use of data-driven decision making and the analysis of big data. The report found two factors that were common among the most successful law firms: strategic focus and proactive response to the needs and expectations of clients.[2]

In this chapter, I argue that the legal profession can adopt a data-driven strategy to increase profitability by aligning the firm's expertise with client needs. In this chapter, we will define big data, consider the way that data can be used in legal practice, and consider challenges for law firms in a data-driven world.

Big Data

The definition of big data has expanded over the years. In 2011, McKinsey Group defined big data as those data sets "whose size is beyond the ability of typical database software tools to capture, store, manage, and analyze."[3] However, that definition is too restrictive. Even small sources of data can be linked together across digital platforms to create big data insights.

Current definitions of big data embrace several factors including volume, velocity, variety, veracity, and value.[4] In 2013, IBM predicted that society collected 2.5 quintillion bytes of data every day.[5] That number is increasing exponentially. The power of big data comes from identifying the most valuable data and using it to make meaningful inferences.

Assigning Value to the Practice of Law

During the 10 years since the great recession of 2008, the legal profession has reason to question the existing business model in which law firms measure value by

---

[1] 2017 Report on the State of the Legal Market, available at http://legalsolutions.thomsonreuters.com/law-products/ns/solutions/peer-monitor/report-on-the-state-of-the-legal-market-repository (issued jointly by the Georgetown Center for the Study of the Legal Profession and the Thomson Reuters Legal Executive Institute).

[2] *Id.*, at 12.

[3] McKinsey Global Institute, Big Data the Next Frontier for Innovation, Competition, and Productivity (2011).

[4] *See* Veda C. Storey & Il-Yeol Song, *Big Data Technologies and Management: What Conceptual Modeling Can Do*, 108 Data & Knowledge Engineering 56 (2017), https://doi.org/10.1016/j.datak.2017.01.001.

[5] *See*, Ralph Jacobson, *2.5 Quintillion Bytes Of Data Created Every Day. How Does CPG & Retail Manage It?* https://www.ibm.com/blogs/insights-on-business/consumer-products/2-5-quintillion-bytes-of-data-created-every-day-how-does-cpg-retail-manage-it/ (last visited Dec. 1, 2017).

the number of hours worked. Before the great recession, attorneys predominantly charged clients a fixed hourly rate, or occasionally negotiated alternative fee arrangements (AFAs). Over the last few years, clients have increasingly demanded budget caps for legal fees. The Georgetown report states that, in many firms, 80%–90% of all legal work is compensated through either an AFA or a capped budget.[6]

Currently, there are several types of legal retainer or legal fee arrangements, such as[7]

- Hourly Fees—through which a client agrees to pay the attorney a fixed hourly rate for specific legal representation;
- Contingency Fees—through which the law firm agrees to accept payment based upon level of degree of success of level of performance;
- Capped Fees—through which a law firm agrees to maximum price for an individual legal matter;
- Fixed/Flat Fees—through which a law firm agrees to complete a legal task for a fixed fee;
- Portfolio-Based Fees—through which a law firm provides a client with all legal services during a defined period of time;
- Value-Based Fees or Best-in Class Pricing—through which the law firm and the client agree upon the cost of individual legal activities during a representation, such as the value of the individual legal tasks required to close a real estate agreement;
- Blended Fee Agreements—a combination of any of these fee arrangements.

Data-Driven Strategies

Data-driven decision making refers to the practice of augmenting intuition with data analysis.[8] Although information and intuition have always been the basis for good decision making, traditionally, the final decisions were made with very little data by the HIghest Paid Person in the Organization, known as the "HIPPO."[9]

However, recent studies have found that productivity increases among data-driven organizations. Researchers Foster Provost and Tom Fawcett developed a measure of how strong companies use data to make decisions. Even after controlling for several possible confounding factors, the study found a consistent 5%–6%

---

[6] *Id.* at 10.

[7] *See* Walter L. Baker, Michael V. Marn, & Craig C. Zawada, Building a Better Pricing Infrastructure (2010), https://www.mckinsey.com/business-functions/marketing-and-sales/our-insights/building-a-better-pricing-infrastructure.

[8] Foster Provost & Tom Fawcett, *Data Science and Its Relationship to Big Data and Data-Driven Decision Making*, 1 Big Data 51, 53 (2013), https://doi.org/10.1089/big.2013.1508.

[9] *See* Claudia Loebbecke & Arnold Picot, Reflections on Societal and Business Model Transformation Arising from Digitization and Big Data Analytics: A Research Agenda, 24 J. of Strategic Info. Sys. 149, 150 (2015).

increase in overall productivity. In turn, that productivity correlates with increases in many business indicators, including return on equity and market value. The researchers argued that the use of data directly caused the overall improvement.[10] Another study found that companies that base business strategies upon data and analytic tools are more likely to be identified as top performers than those companies that failed to effectively use data.[11]

Before creating a data-driven strategy, it is vital to first identify the goal of the organization. Big data creates three types of business opportunities.[12] The first may be called the *Big Data Driven Innovation model*, where big data itself is the primary product or service. One example is an internet-based trading company.

The second type of business strategy is the *Big Data-Enabled Innovation model*, where data is a catalyst for revising an existing process. For example, big data can allow an organization to dynamically customize a marketing campaign through the "now-casting" technique of using data to predict things in the very near future.[13]

The third model is the *Big Data-Related Innovation model* in which an organization transforms data into new products, services, or possibilities. For the legal practice, the advent of data analysis allows the firm to offer new information and analytical services beyond traditional legal advice.

Data Teams

A successful data-driven organization relies upon a dedicated team focused upon the collection and usage of data. The two most important team members are a data scientist and a business analytics professional.[14] Data scientists, also known in law firms as knowledge management professionals, are the people with the skills to select valuable data and visualize information in a meaningful platform. The team may also include information technology and marketing professionals.

Studies have found that it is a mistake to ask an IT department to manage a data-driven team. Based upon an analysis of several large corporations, researchers

[10] Erik Brynjolfsson, Lorin Hitt, & Heekyung Kim, *Strength in Numbers: How Does Data-Driven Decision Making Affect Firm Performance,* SSRN Working Paper, (2011), http://ssrn.com/abstract=1819486.

[11] Steve Lavalle, Eric Lesser, Rebecca Shockley, Michael Hopkins, & Nina Kruschwitz, *Big Data, Analytics and the Path From Insights to Value,* 52 MIT Sloan Management Review 22 (2011).

[12] Nowshade Kabir & Elias Carayannis, *Big Data, Tacit Knowledge and Organizational Competitiveness,* 3 Journal of Intelligence Studies in Business 54 (2013), available at https://ojs.hh.se/index.php/JISIB/article/download/76/pdf_4. *See also* Ralph Schroeder, Big Data Business Models: Challenges and Opportunities, 2 Cogent Social Sciences (2016), http://dx.doi.org/10.1080/23311886.2016.1166924.

[13] Marta Bańbura, Domenico Giannone, Michele Modugno & LucreziaReichlin, Now-Casting and the Real-Time Data Flow, in 2 Handbook of Economic Forecasting 195 (2013), https://doi.org/10.1016/B978-0-444-53683-9.00004-9

[14] Kabir, Supra note ___ at 59.

found that IT departments are highly efficient in designing data storage and protection systems. However, IT departments are generally unable to offer solutions that can convert data into business value.[15]

In a law firm, a knowledge management (KM) professional should have knowledge of the practice of law and training in information science. Legal training allows a KM professional to understand how legal practitioners collect and use information. Professionals trained in information science, previously called library science, know how to identify useful information and to build systems through which clients can turn that information into useful knowledge.

Data for Strategic Goals

Data-driven business models must use heterogeneous sources of information, collected either through intentional requests for information or gathered indirectly through unseen data logs and tracking devices. Data can be purchased from commercial sources, acquired from publicly available repositories, derived from crowd-sourced requests, elicited through customer-provided data, or generated through tracking systems.[16]

To create a meaningful legal fee agreement, the law firm must understand the cost of doing business in a given market and the value of the service or product provided. Some organizations like the Bureau of Labor Statistics and the World Bank freely provide cost of doing business data.[17] Organizations such as practice management company Clio,[18] the publisher Thomson Reuters,[19] and the Georgetown Center of the Study of the Legal Profession[20] supply data about billing rates and other trends within the legal practice.

To identify its return on investment, a law firm must first understand the cost of client acquisition. Marketing groups publish or sell client acquisition data. In addition, organizations can buy data management tools to track and assess client acquisition efforts.[21]

---

[15] *Id.* (citing C Beath, I. Becerra- Fernandez, J. Ross, and & J. Short, The Forrester Wave: Advanced Data visualization Platforms, Q3 (2012)).

[16] *Id.*; Philipp Hartman, Mohamed Zaki, Niels Feldmann, & Andy Neely, Big Data for Big Business? A Taxonomy of Data-Driven Business Models Used by Start-up Firms (last modified Nov. 4, 2015), https://cambridgeservicealliance.eng.cam.ac.uk/news/March2014Paper.

[17] Bureau of Labor Statistics, Overview of BLS Statistics on Business Costs, https://www.bls.gov/bls/business.htm (last modified Dec.16, 2013); The World Bank, Doing Business Data, http://www.doingbusiness.org/data (last visited Dec. 1, 2017).

[18] https://www.clio.com (last visited Dec. 1, 2017).

[19] Press Release, *More Effective Market Analysis for Legal Departments With Visualized Benchmarking Data From Thomson Reuters Legal Tracker Mar. 21, 2017), https://www.thomsonreuters.com/en/press-releases/2017/march/market-analysis-legal-departments-visualized-benchmarking-data-legal-tracker.html.*

[20] Georgetown, Supra note 1.

[21] Clio Training Team, Campaign Tracker: Creating Campaigns, (June 21, 2017), https://support.clio.com/hc/en-us/articles/212569708-Campaign-Tracker-Creating-Campaigns.

Discovering Internal Expertise

To evolve a legal practice into a data-driven organization, the law firm must be able to quickly discover and analyze internal sources of excellence. Only then can the firm align internal knowledge to business strategy. According to a McKinsey study, the average knowledge worker spends close to 20% of work time looking for internal information or identifying colleagues who could help with assigned tasks.[22]

Modern law firms have a unique need for a firm directory of expertise. Firms were originally designed as small groups of lawyers who practice collaboratively over the course of years. In a modern firm, organizational expertise is fluid and changes dramatically as attorneys move between firms through lateral hire processes. At the same time firms are growing. It is now common for law firms to employ hundreds of employees distributed in offices throughout the nation if not the globe. Firms also grow through mergers and acquisitions that regularly inject broad spectrums of expertise.[23]

Current Employees

Useful indicators of expertise not only locate experts but also illustrate the level of expertise. In discussing expertise, it is worth considering that there is more than one level of proficiency. One researcher divided expertise into three levels.

> A *Participant* has a working knowledge of a topic. An example would be a field worker at an archeological dig.
>
> An *Interactional Expert* can participate in a conversation at an advanced level of understanding. This person could provide advanced analysis within an established field of study.
>
> A *Contributory Expert* is the highest level of expert possessing the knowledge and experience to contribute innovative new insights into a field of study.[24]

There are several indicators of legal expertise.[25] An effective search for legal know-how should include the following indicators.

---

[22] Michael Chui, James Manyika, Jacques Bughin, Richard Dobbs, Charles Roxburgh, Hugo Sarrazin, Geoffrey Sands, & Magdalena Westergren, The Social Economy: Unlocking Value And Productivity Through Social Technologies (2012), https://www.mckinsey.com/industries/high-tech/our-insights/the-social-economy.

[23] Georgetown, Supra note 1, at 12 (citing Nell Gluckman, *Could 2016 Break Law Firm Merger Record?* The American Lawyer (online edition) Dec. 2, 2016).

[24] Harry Collins & Robert Evans, *The Third Wave of Science Studies: Studies of Expertise and Experience*, 32 Social Studies of Science 235 (2002), https://doi.org/10.1177/0306312702032002003.

[25] Vishal Agnihotri, Gail Bergmiller, Dora Tynes, & Ramin Vosough, Expertise Location and Social Collaboration: Three Case Studies on a Winning Formula (ILTA Whitepaper Series) (2017), https://www.iltanet.org/viewdocument/expertise-location-and-social-colla?ssopc=1.

Biographies are the most basic indicators. Usually stored in external-facing marketing databases, biographies are also the indicators most susceptible to exaggeration and other types of reporting error.

Document authorship is a better indicator. Housed in internal document-management systems, pleadings, continuing legal education presentations, and other legal memoranda provide clues about expertise. However, this information generally identifies the second level of expertise: participants who can talk knowledgably about an area of law. The true expert in a law firm is not the author of most relevant internal documents. The highest level of expertise is generally found among the attorneys who review the most documents in a particular area.

The text of time entries is the strongest or most accurate source of expertise. Found in the billing and timekeeping systems, an attorney's time records provide an unbiased source of authenticated expertise. The person who most regularly bills for legal work is an expert trusted by the firm as well as the firm's clients to explain the law and to generate innovative strategies.

Once a firm builds a directory of expertise, the organization can add other data fields to allow users to locate the ideal contact. For example, the directory could include data such as practice group, state bar membership, court admission, location, title, and language skills. If the firm maintains a task management system, it could build a data field to filter result by each person's workload and availability.[26]

Lateral Hires

It is harder to easily discover the pre-hire expertise of lateral hires. One answer is to require an extensive questionnaire during the hiring process for all laterals.[27] However, questionnaires are susceptible to exaggeration of self-identified knowledge and the underreporting of actual expertise. Another way to find expertise is through analysis of the data generated by each lateral before the attorney is hired. An organization could collect and electronically review all the contracts the lateral has drafted. The Securities and Exchange Commission provides easy access to many commercial contracts through the Electronic Data Gathering, Analysis, and Retrieval (EDGAR) system.[28] Firms can use big-data analysis of public contracts or other documents drafted by the lateral hire to find insights into the drafter's actual level of skill.

There are more sophisticated tools available to review the prehire experience of litigators. An organization could download and evaluate all the pleadings and documentation recorded from every case in which the attorney participated. If the attorney played a significant role in a case, it is likely that the lawyer reviewed

---

[26] *Id.* at 37.

[27] *See* James Fischer, *Large Law Firm Lateral Hire Conflicts Checking: Professional Duty Meets Actual Practice*, 36 Journal of Legal Profession 167, 189 (2011–12).

[28] https://www.sec.gov/edgar/searchedgar/companysearch.html.

the entire file, including documents submitted by opposing counsel. A firm could use predictive analysis tools to better understand the strategy and skill of the lateral hire.

Alumni Expertise

Alumni expertise can offer a vital source of knowledge available to all organizations. For example, searching the social connections between former employees of the organization could help generate clients. Law firms could create a social network specifically for alumni to identify connections to relevant expertise among former employees.[29] It would then be valuable to enhance the alumni directory by cross-referencing information about individual activities while working for the firm. For example, the directory could include alumni past time entries and billing information during the alumni's tenure at the firm. In addition, the directory could include publicly available information about the organization where the alumni went after leaving the firm.[30]

Expanding Services: Innovation Using Big Data

Data-driven organizations must understand the products or services they offer. Big data provides law firms with the tools to redefine an organization's mission. The increasing value of big data is creating a new market for law firms that want to provide services based upon the profession's unique ability to collect, manage, and analyze information.

One example of a new data market for lawyers is the community health needs assessments required by the Patient Protection and Affordable Care Act.[31] The law requires all nonprofit hospitals to draft on a regular three-year cycle a needs assessment that must be used to guide the hospital's investment in healthcare services.[32]

Big data allows a law practice to do more than provide an interpretation of the relevant law. Instead, a law firm can conduct the underlying research and develop the reports in conjunction with the client.

---

[29] *See* Janan Hanna, *Old Firm Ties: Alumni Networks Are Social Media With Benefits*, ABA Journal (online edition May 2011), http://www.abajournal.com/magazine/article/old_firm_ties_alumni_networks_are_social_media_with_benefits.

[30] *Id.*

[31] *See* Carole Roan Gresenz, *Using Big Data to Assess Community Health & Inform Local Health Care Policymaking*, in Big Data, Big Challenges in Evidence-Based Policymaking (H. Kumar Jayasuriya & Kathryn Ritcheske, eds., 2015).

[32] *See* Additional Requirements for Charitable Hospitals; Community Health Needs Assessments for Charitable Hospitals; Requirement of a Section 4959 Excise Tax Return and Time for Filing the Return, 79 FR 78953 (Dec. 31, 2014).

There are several reasons for a hospital to ask a law firm to create community health care assessment reports. For example lawyers offer the skills to evaluate and manage records and lawyers offer the strongest level of confidentiality. Law schools teach lawyers how to effectively research and evaluate published literature. To draft a needs report, the author must conduct literature reviews of government publications and scholarly research. Lawyers are also skilled in conducting discovery, especially reviewing the internal records of a organization. The most valuable sources of information for a needs assessment report could be the private records of the hospital. That task is very similar to the traditional work of an e-discovery attorney. Finally, through the invocation of attorney-client privilege a lawyer can protect a client's private data. If a hospital is using internal documents to help draft a needs assessment report, that organization will want to protect confidential information by hiring a lawyer to draft the document.

One of the most valuable sources of information could be the private records of the hospital. Lawyers are especially skilled at researching and identifying valuable sources of evidence. Law firms have always been able to protect confidential information.

Once a law firm understands the types of services it can provide, the organization can decide if it wants to provide traditional legal services or to deliver a full-service information management experience. By understanding the product or service sold, the law firm can better assign a value to the level of service.

Conclusion

Clients are demanding a change in the nature of legal services delivered by law firms. Corporate clients, in particular, are making more decisions with data and they are insisting that their law firms do the same. Through the analysis of internal and external sources of data, a law firm has the ability to predict emerging market needs, identify internal synergies of expertise, and design innovative services.

Although data-driven decision making is new to many law firms, these firms are in fact surrounded by useful data. The most important and underused data is the hidden expertise of employees. The expertise of firm lawyers, affiliated information professionals, and firm alumni are rich potential sources of knowledge. Firms that can access these data sources will be empowered to create new and innovative services. By tapping into unused data resources a law firm can become a data-driven organization and gain a market advantage.

Chapter 10

Can Intrapreneurship Solve the Innovator's Dilemma? Law Firm Examples

Bill Henderson

Contents

If a successful large law firm faced an Innovator's Dilemma, what would it look like?[1]

On the one hand, the firm has a wonderful set of endowments (Figure 10.1): (1) longstanding and lucrative relationships with industry-leading clients; (2) a business that requires very little operating capital, yet generates significant cash and

---

[1] The innovator's dilemma describes the difficulties experienced by incumbent businesses in adapting to new and potentially disruptive innovations. See Clayton M. Christensen, The Innovator's Dilemma: When New Technologies Cause Great Firms to Fail (1997).

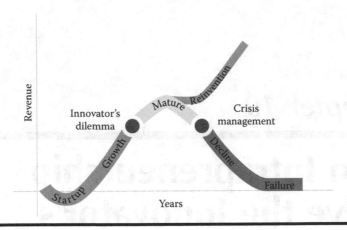

FIGURE 10.1   Innovator's dilemma.

profits; and (3) an established brand that makes it the safe choice against upstart new entrants. On the other hand, when the traditional service offerings hit a plateau that is likely permanent, the firm struggles to use its superior endowments to reinvent itself in a way that locks in another generation of prosperity. The earlier graphic depicts the problem.

Many law firm leaders understand the innovator's dilemma and worry about the timing and execution of reinvention. Thus, at numerous firms, there are internal innovators, or "intrapreneurs,"[2] who are running carefully vetted projects designed to deliver tangible benefits to their firms. In its idealized form, this strategy raises awareness through small wins, which, in turn, create buy in and momentum for more ambitious change.

Three law firm intrapreneurs shared their experiences to illustrate what successful reinvention might look like in legal services:

- Josh Kubicki, Chief Strategy Officer at Seyfarth Shaw LLP
- Eric Wood, Practice Innovations and Technology Partner at Chapman and Cutler LLP
- Jim Beckett, former Chief Business Development Officer at Frost Brown Todd LLC and now CEO of Qualmet

At the outset, it is important to disentangle the principles and lessons of intrapreneurship from the organizations where these lawyers have worked. The risk is that a discussion of context will be construed as criticism, and criticism is not the point

---

[2] Intrapreneurship is "the act of behaving like an entrepreneur while working within a large organization." *See* Intrapreneurship, Wikapedia.org, https://en.wikipedia.org/wiki/Intrapreneurship.

Jim Beckett   Josh Kubicki   Eric Wood

of this chapter. To resolve this tension, I use the two problem statements given later to meld together common themes. After that are specific highlights of each intrapreneur's experiences.

Problem Statement from within the Law Firm

When we apply innovator's dilemma and intrapreneurship concepts to law firms, the underlying subtext is that highly educated and successful partners are, as a group, ill-equipped to adapt to a changing legal market. Assuming this problem statement is true—and I believe it is—*why* would it be true?

The problem is certainly not lack of creativity. Within their substantive specialties, lawyers routinely come up with ingenious solutions. Rather, the challenge is a confluence of experience, perspective, and incentives that create a powerful mental frame that is very difficult for longtime insiders to overcome.

Specifically, for several generations, lawyers in corporate law firms have carried on their craft within a simple business model that required very little time or attention to maintain. In most cases, if lawyers just focused intensively on their clients' problems, the economic results progressively got better. This was (and is) powerful operant conditioning. As a result, for many law firm partners, the macrotrends of the legal industry are abstractions that carry very little weight. The only market that matters is the tiny slice each particular partner serves.

Unfortunately, in very few instances are clients speaking with one voice.[3] In fact, as shown in Figure 10.2, voices vary by adopter type.[4] Innovator and early adopter clients are drawn to new ways of legal problem solving, though they're in the minority. Similarly, some early majority clients are pushed toward innovation

---

[3] See, e.g., Bill Henderson, *Generalizing About Clients* (013), Legal Evolution, July 6, 2017, https://www.legalevolution.org/2017/07/generalizing-about-clients-013/ (last visited Dec. 9, 2017).

[4] Adopter Types are based on a well-known general theory of innovation diffusion. See Everett Rogers, Diffusion of Innovations (5th ed. 2003).

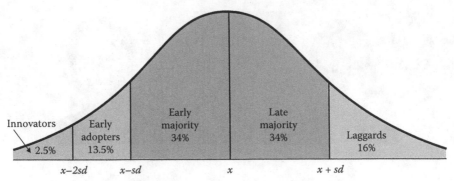

Relationship between types of adopters classified by innovations and their location on the adoption curve.

SOURCE: Event M.Rogers, *diffusions of innovations*, 5th ed. (New York: Free Press, 2003), p. 281.

FIGURE 10.2   Rogers Diffusion Curve.

because they can no longer afford solutions provided by traditional law firms.[5] But a sizable portion of the legal market is content with brand firms billing by the hour. If "my clients" feel differently next year or the year after, we can deal with it then. This narrow type of client-centric approach is strongly reinforced by most law firm compensation systems.

The earlier description explains the paradox of the highly successful law firm unable to play its superior hand. Thus, the innovator's dilemma is a real strategy dilemma for virtually all large law firms.

Problem Statement from the Client Side

Although clients don't speak with one voice, the environment they are operating within is becoming more complex, global, and regulated. This, in turn, is changing the structure of the corporate legal services market—i.e., the macrolevel trends that many partners wave away as irrelevant to their practice.

Arguably, the biggest change is growth of corporate legal departments. For at least the last 20 years, corporate clients have adapted by growing their in-house legal departments and insourcing more repetitive or lower stakes work that

---

[5] For example, the 2008 recession led to a surge in adoption for legal process outsourcing companies Pangea3 and Axiom. See Bill Henderson, *A Law School Class on How Innovation Diffuses in the Legal Industry (032)*, Legal Evolution, Oct. 25, 2017, https://www.legalevolution.org/2017/10/law-school-class-innovation-diffuses-legal-industry-032/ (last visited Dec. 9, 2017), and Bill Henderson, *A Deep Dive Into Axiom (036)*, Legal Evolution, Nov. 15, 2017, https://www.legalevolution.org/2017/11/deep-dive-into-axiom-035/ (last visited Dec. 9, 2017).

Type no. 1	Type no. 2	Type no. 3	Type no. 4	Type no. 5	Type no. 6			
Individuals	Business owner	Business owners	Company management	Company management	Company management			
		General counsel	General counsel	General counsel	General counsel			
			In-house staff	Sr. In-house lawyers	Deputy gc vertical 1	Deputy gc vertical 2	Deputy GC M&A	Director of legal OPS
				Line corporate counsel	Line Corporate Counsel	Line corporate counsel	Line corporate counsel	Legal OPS managers
					Procurement/sourcing specialists			

FIGURE 10.3 Type 6 legal department typology.

formerly went to law firms.[6] Figure 10.3 presents a client typology where, on the right side of the spectrum, corporate clients are taking the shape of medium-to-large law firms.

With more and more legal departments that fit the Type 6 pattern, we've witnessed the rise of the legal operations movement (for example, the Corporate Legal Operations Consortium, or CLOC, and the Association of Corporate Counsel Legal Operations) and the rise of corporate legal departments that operate like a specialized law firm embedded inside a large corporation.[7]

Legal operations as a profession and field is coming into being because many large corporate clients need more sophisticated methods and systems for managing legal cost and legal risk. The ascendency of this role is strong evidence that the business-as-usual law firm billable hour model is on a slow but permanent decline, at least for operational "run-the-company" work that accounts for the majority of the corporate legal services market.[8] Figure 10.4 depicts the market transformation.

In general, legal complexity increases with economic growth. For about 100 years, we've coped with this problem through division of labor and specialization. This

---

[6] See Bill Henderson, *How Much Are Corporations In-Sourcing Legal Services? (003)*, Legal Evolution, May 2, 2017, https://www.legalevolution.org/2017/05/003-inhouse-lawyers/ (showing 1997–2016 employment trends for lawyers working in government, in-house, and private law firms).

[7] See Bill Henderson, *Six Types of Law Firm Clients (005)*, Legal Evolution, May 9, 2017, https://www.legalevolution.org/2017/05/six-types-of-law-firm-clients-005/ (last visited Dec. 10, 2017) (presenting a typology of law firm clients).

[8] *See Deep Dive into Axiom, supra* note 5 (discussing trend through the lens of Axiom); Bill Henderson, *World Class Innovation and Efficiency, Billed by the Hour (010)*, Legal Evolution, June 18, 2017, https://www.legalevolution.org/2017/06/world-class-innovation-efficiency-billed-hour-010/ (last visited Dec. 10, 2017) (discussing trend through the lens of the managed services industry).

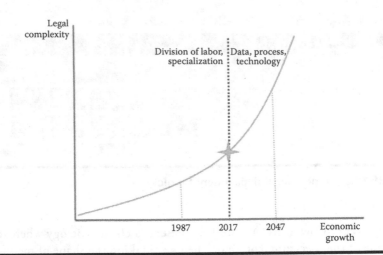

FIGURE 10.4   Legal complexity and market transformation.

approach created a large law firm. In more recent decades, as the growth-complexity line has steepened, law firms reaped higher profits.[9]

Yet, we have reached a point where division of labor and specialization are no longer a match for the geometric growth of legal complexity. Although clients and law firms experience this pressure as a cost problem, the root cause is lack of productivity gains.[10] To meet this productivity imperative, the legal industry is starting to migrate to new methods of legal problem solving that are based on data, process, and technology. Indeed, these pressures are why NewLaw exists, financed in large part by venture capitalists and private equity.

So the question is very simple: for large corporate clients, who is going to create the new paradigm? There are three contenders:

- **Legal departments** through more legal operations and in-sourcing;
- **Law firms** by skillfully playing their superior hand; or
- **NewLaw**, which has data, process, and technology as its core competency but has the challenge of being new and unfamiliar.

---

[9] All the analysis and charts above frame a structural problem from the perspective of organizational clients. For this group of clients, the problem of lagging productivity is leading to market-based responses, albeit slowly. For individual clients in the PeopleLaw sector (roughly one-quarter of the legal market and shrinking), lagging legal productivity manifests itself through self-representation or people or people failing to seek any type of legal-based solution. See Bill Henderson, *The Decline of the PeopleLaw Sector (037)*, Legal Evolution, Nov. 19, 2017, https://www.legalevolution.org/2017/11/decline-peoplelaw-sector-037/ (last visited Dec. 10, 2017). In short, these are two distinct problem sets.

[10] See Bill Henderson, *What is Legal Evolution? (001)*, Legal Evolution, May 1, 2017, https://www.legalevolution.org/2017/05/001-legal-evolution/ (last visited Dec. 10, 2017) (discussing systemic problems created by lagging legal productivity).

The answer is likely to be some combination of all three. Yet, it is also likely that many law firms will fall victim to the innovator's dilemma and be among the losers.

The challenge for law firms is that the business opportunities of a structural market shift require partners to make business judgments about macrotrends at the same time they are under pressure to acquire, bill, and collect hundreds of thousands of dollars in legal fees for the current fiscal year. Unfortunately, this problem can't be fixed by changing a comp system to reward a long-term focus, as those with a short-term focus are free to leave and take their clients with them.

Kubicki: Intrapreneurship Inside a Law Firm

Among the three profiled law firm intrapreneurs, Josh Kubicki has given the most thought to intrapreneurship as an applied discipline.[11] Josh asks us to envision a simple corporate pyramid that consists of the CEO (at the top), the C-Suite (layer 2), vice presidents (layer 3), directors (layer 4), managers (layer 5), and line workers (base of the pyramid). "Obviously, we know who's in charge."

"Law Firms," noted Josh, "are much flatter." He imagines this stylized law firm org chart, which is depicted by Figure 10.5.

At the top of the pyramid, which may not be a pyramid at all, are partners who are also owners. Although partners are not CEO, they do tend to act as the CEOs of their own practice, particularly if they keep a lot of other lawyers busy. However, increasing performance and enterprise value of the firm require collaboration across the partner/owner/CEO class.

To do this well, the law firm intrapreneur has to find ways to break down the partitions between partners—the blue lines shown earlier—without engendering fear or resistance. Further, the intrapreneur has to do it with little or no formal authority. "No matter what your title is, the intrapreneur is part of the professional

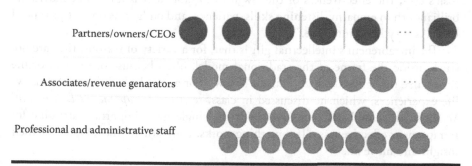

Partners/owners/CEOs

Associates/revenue genarators

Professional and administrative staff

FIGURE 10.5   Stylized law firm organizational chart.

[11] See, e.g., Josh Kubicki, *The Intrapreneur's Dilemma*, Medium, Aug. 20, 2014, online at https://medium.com/@jkubicki/the-intrapreneurs-dilemma-9362a18f8e76 (last visited Dec. 10, 2017).

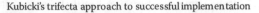

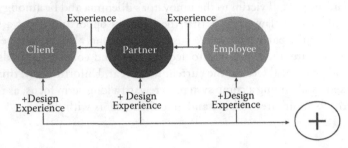

FIGURE 10.6 Kubicki's trifecta approach to successful implementation.

staff paid for by revenue-generating lawyers. So the only tool you have is your ability to make someone's life better in a relatively simple and low-cost way."

This reality is why Josh relies heavily on design thinking in all his change initiatives. Josh drew a diagram, depicted in Figure 10.6, which he called "the trifecta."

Innovations start as an idea in an innovator's head. Once we move to implementation within an organization, however, we move into people's daily experience—busy people whose job it is to serve others. Even if an innovation will, in theory, make the organization better off, implementation will fail if individual stakeholders have a negative experience that makes their job harder. Thus, successful innovation (Phase I Initiation + Phase II Implementation) is actually a series of properly designed *subinnovations*.[12]

A successful subinnovation requires making the complex very simple, culturally compatible, and highly advantageous to the end user, ideally with a very fast return-on-investment. If the coordinated subinnovations all result in a good individual experience, the larger innovation has a chance of being successful. Seen through Josh's eyes, the effectiveness of the law firm intrapreneur is less about individual brilliance than empathy, listening skills, patience, and budget, as doing this type of work "is very labor intensive."

The intrapreneur's intellectual gift is that, for a variety of reasons, they are not stuck inside the frame of the traditional model, often because of some prior life experience that gives them an outsider's view. (For one of Kubicki's transformative life experiences, which he discussed in class, read his *Intrapreneur's Dilemma*.)[13] Yet, Josh was emphatic that *humility* is the single most important attribute for intrapreneur effectiveness. "If something works, congratulate the adopter for their insight and move on."

---

[12] See Bill Henderson, *Innovation in Organizations*, Part I (015), Legal Evolution, July 20, 2017, https://www.legalevolution.org/2017/07/innovation-in-organizations-part-i-015/ (last visited Dec. 10, 2017).

[13] *See* Kubicki, *supra* note 8.

Eric Wood: Making Partner as a Technology Innovator

The legal profession is navigating a shift from a world of lawyer specialization to one based on multidisciplinary collaboration. I am confident that Eric Wood's story is going to be replicated by hundreds of young lawyers who begin their careers at law firms. Yet, Eric was the first to blaze this trail.

Eric is the Practice Innovations and Technology Partner at Chapman and Cutler. The key word here is *partner*. Eric is a 2008 graduate of the University of Chicago Law School. After a stint at Cleary Gottlieb in NYC doing capital markets work, Eric moved back to Chicago and joined Chapman as a banking and financial services associate. However, several years ago, Eric quit doing client billable work and instead focused all of his attention on technology-based initiatives. During this time, his formal title remained associate. And earlier this year, he was promoted to partner.

Practice Innovations and Technology Partner is a new role within a law firm. Eric describes his work as primarily "R&D" that falls into three major buckets:

1. Writing code to build legal expert systems and automate the drafting of documentation for a wide range of legal matters. Often this includes the design of web interfaces so that the systems are relatively intuitive for the lawyers, clients, and other personnel who use them.
2. Designing new technology products and managing their development, release, and maintenance. Often this involves finding ways to scale innovations across multiple practice groups, including the development of new staffing models.
3. Other knowledge management and technology projects, such as building transactional metadata databases and data visualizations, evaluating vendor products, and researching technological developments that might affect transactional practice (e.g., blockchain and cryptocurrencies).

Eric has no formal training in a technical field. His undergraduate training is in political science and environmental studies. Instead, he attributes the initial development of his technical abilities in computer coding and database structures to a desire to impress his friends with fantasy basketball data visualizations. That hobby required a lot of scraping of data from websites followed by computational analysis.

Yet, Eric's work in the legal field enabled him to see crossover applications. Prior to law school, as an AmeriCorps volunteer with Wyoming Legal Services, he helped build web content to reach the agency's far-flung clientele. "We had to scale seven lawyers for the entire state, and it was obvious that only technology could do that." Likewise, many late nights as a NYC transactional associate gave Eric many ideas for how to automate unpleasant, time-consuming grunt work.

In 2013, as Eric continued to improve his technical skills, he decided it was time to find an outlet in the legaltech world. However, during this time period, the firm's Chief Executive Partner Tim Mohan began bringing in outside speakers to explain how the traditional practice of law was on the brink of a major shift. So Eric requested a meeting with Mohan to explain some of his ideas.

Mohan immediately embraced the idea, and Eric stopped doing billable work to perform his new role. Now do the math—taking Eric off the billable track is roughly a million dollar decision ($500/hour × 2,000 per year). Yet, what is the price of failing to reinvent?

Relatively quickly, the decision proved to be a wise one. For example, one of Eric's projects was the automation of closing document sets for finance transactions. The market no longer pays full price for the organization, indexing, and tabbing of the full deal documentation, yet this work still needs to be done and delivered to the client in a polished, professional, and timely manner. "What used to take weeks now takes a minute." At roughly $500 in staff time (with wide variations based on the size and complexity of the deal) × 3,000 closings per year, this single project is saving the firm roughly $1.5 million in labor that can be allocated to other value-add projects. And that is just one example.

With the encouragement of the firm's leadership, Eric regularly gives internal demos that have generated significant curiosity and broad buy in among partners. Eric notes that these internal sales were often predicated on the quality advantages of technology—of increasing transparency of changes to complex forms and reducing opportunities for error. Yet, the economics are also very attractive. Chapman and Cutler is a highly specialized financial services firm that does approximately 40% of its work on a fixed-fee basis. In this context, technology and process enable the firm to continue to charge less than many rival firms while protecting or improving its margins. This is exactly how innovation is supposed to function.

In addition to Eric, other transactional lawyers at Chapman have begun to invest in technical skills, with several automating significant portions of their practice. Part of this transition is made possible by an accounting system that treats "productive" hours related to firm innovation the same as client billable work. Eric gave the example of one associate who has logged hundreds of productive hours over the past few years working on projects with Eric and his team. In short, Chapman is building more internal capacity.

This is a remarkable story. But can it be replicated by other law firms? I think the answer is "not easily." First, a firm needs someone like Eric Wood who possesses both deep legal domain knowledge and strong technical skills. Second, the stars have to align so that a leader like Tim Mohan can enable such a person to focus *full-time* on innovation and execution. In competitive markets, half-time efforts seldom win. Third, it undoubtedly helped Chapman and Cutler, which is a "small" large firm (~230 lawyers) that is focused on a single industry. This makes it culturally and logistically easier to implement change.

Beckett's Business Mindset

Innovation is strongly influenced by connections between different social systems. Being on the edge of two or three systems is more valuable than being in the center of one. This is because multiple perspectives enable a person to transcend the dominant local frame and see problems with fresh eyes.[14]

In addition to knowledge of law, these three intrapreneurs possess a second or third frame for viewing the world. However, the most pronounced example was Jim Beckett, who acquired his legal fame after working five years in sales and distribution in the food industry, helping to grow market share for companies like Frito-Lay and Häagen-Dazs. During this time, Jim was following the advice of his father, who was impressed with Jim's people skills and aptitude for business. Ironically, Jim's father was a lawyer, working in-house at KFC.

Then, several years into Jim's business career, his father had second thoughts. "Jim," his father said, "Law doesn't have enough people who truly understand how businesses works. If you get a law degree, you'll go a long way." So, as an older student, Jim returned to Indiana University to go to law school.

Jim shared that law school was very difficult for him because the level of abstraction was so far removed from the practical problem solving he was used to. It wasn't until he was a law firm associate that we was able to meld the two perspectives.

The business frame, however, remained the dominant perspective. For example, Jim discussed how he got his first in-house job at Brown & Williamson (a large tobacco company that later become part of RJ Reynolds). "I was the only lawyer they interviewed who could discuss the business issues that were at the core of the company's legal work." Further, rather than pursue upward mobility in the legal department, Jim asked to move to the business side, eventually running an RJ Reynolds operating unit in Puerto Rico.

Jim's multiple perspectives in law and business was one of the reasons that John Crockett, chairman of Frost Brown Todd, recruited Jim to return to Louisville to run business development for the firm. Roughly 10 years earlier, Jim and John had worked together at the firm as billing lawyers. Jim was hired despite his warning that long-term success was going to require significant change, which would make some of Jim's efforts controversial.

Although the firm implemented many client-centric initiatives, Jim eventually became convinced that he could do more good by helping clients focus on their purchasing power. Thus, in the summer of 2016, Jim left Frost Brown Todd to become the CEO of Qualmet, a technology company that provides legal departments with a scorecarding methodology that collects, organizes, analyzes, and shares feedback with their outside service providers.

---

[14] Everett Rogers connects innovation to the Georg Simmel's construct of the stranger. "[A]n individual's network relationships serve to influence, and often to constrain, an individual's actions. The innovator, as a type of stranger, can more easily deviate from the norms of the systems by being the first to adopt new ideas." Rogers, *supra* note 4, at 42.

Jim speaks with passion about what happens when lawyers get in full alignment with clients. "All lawyers want to do a great job. Unfortunately, very few are getting the information they need to take their practice to the next level." Jim believes that structured metrics and dialogue will enable clients and law firms to smoothly transition into the world of data, process, and technology. Jim sees this as not as a question of "how," but "when." Today's CEOs expect their general counsel, chief legal officers, and in-house teams to drive business value that aligns with their respective company goals and objectives. Jim wants to bridge the "value" gap and sees 360-degree performance management as a critical piece to accelerate alignment. "Value creation is no commodity," Jim observed, "So all stakeholders will benefit when performance is properly measured."[15]

Conclusion

Many talented people are drawn to intraprenuership because the innovations they are seeking to create (or, stated alternatively, the problems they are seeking to solve), would be greatly aided by the endowment are large incumbent organizations. This is particularly true within the legal industry, where the social systems (law firms, legal departments, courts, regulators) tend to be very traditional and isolated from the rest of the modern economy.[16] This is the legal industry's version of the Innovator's Dilemma, which may be so acute that successful innovation from the outside in may not be economically viable or at least too obstacle-ridden to attract a significant cohort of entrepreneurial innovators.

The encouraging news is that many law firm leaders are aware of this challenge and are enabling intraprenuers to experiment with innovation. Diffusion theory predicts that, as some of these efforts are met this success, they will be observed and replicated by the rest of the law firm social system. The lawyers profiled here are among the early pioneers of law firm intrapreneurship.

---

[15] Qualmet's scorecarding methodology is closely related to Dan Currell's description of the necessity of active outside counsel management. See Dan Currell, *Part III on Convergence: Clients Must Manage to Get Results (031)*, Legal Evolution, Oct. 12, 2017 https://www.legalevolution.org/2017/10/convergence-part-iii-management-principles-031/ (last visited Dec. 10, 2017). Convergence alone can't deliver the desired results.

[16] For an discussion of this topic, see Bill Henderson, *Variables Determining the Rate of Adoption of Innovations* (008), Legal Evolution, May 29, 2017, https://www.legalevolution.org/2017/05/variables-determining-the-rate-of-adoption-of-innovations-008/ (last visited Dec. 17, 2017) ("The most established, influential, and prestigious portions of the legal profession—large law firms, the federal judiciary, legal academia, and the ABA—tend to be traditional bound and skeptical of change that does not initiate with them. Part of this conservative ethos may be the product of Rule 5.4. ... Rule 5.4 prohibits lawyers from co-venturing with other professionals in any business that involves the practice of law. If lawyers can't be business partners with [other professionals] ... that's going to cut down on the opportunities to learn from them.")

Index

Printed in the United States
by Baker & Taylor Publisher Services